MASTERING THE MACHINE

MASTERING THE MACHINE

Poverty, Aid and Technology

IAN SMILLIE

We are becoming the servants in thought, as in action,
of the machine we have created to serve us.
John Kenneth Galbraith

Westview Press

BOULDER, OXFORD & SAN FRANCISCO   3-28-93

Intermediate Technology Publications,
103/105 Southampton Row, London WC1B 4HH, UK

© IT Publications 1991

Published in 1991 in the United States by:
Westview Press
5500 Central Avenue
Boulder, Colorado 80301

ISBN 0-8133-1488-7 (Hardcover)
ISBN 0-8133-1489-5 (Paperback)

CIP data available upon request

Typeset by J&L Composition Ltd, Filey, North Yorkshire
Printed by Billing & Sons Ltd, Worcester

Contents

ACRONYMS

ATDA	Appropriate Technology Development Association
ATI	Appropriate Technology International
BRAC	Bangladesh Rural Advancement Committee
BKK	Bada Kredit Kecamatan, Indonesia
CIDA	Canadian International Development Agency
EEC (EC)	European (Economic) Community
FAO	Food and Agriculture Organization
FCR	Fibre Concrete Roofing
GATT	General Agreement on Trade and Tariffs
GDP	Gross Domestic Product
GNP	Gross National Product
GRATIS	Ghana Regional Appropriate Technology Industrial Service
GSP	General System of Preferences
GTZ	German Agency for Technical Co-operation
HDI	Human Development Index
IDRC	International Development Research Centre
IFAD	International Fund for Agricultural Development
IITA	International Institute for Tropical Agriculture
IMF	International Monetary Fund
ITDG	Intermediate Technology Development Group
ITTU	Intermediate Technology Transfer Unit
KENGO	Kenya Energy NGOs' Association
MEDI	Malawi Entrepreneur Development Institute
MYRADA	Mysore Resettlement and Development Agency
NORAD	Norwegian Agency for International Development
MCP	Mini-Cement Plant
MFA	Multi-Fibre Arrangement
NGO	Non-Governmental Organization
ODA	Official Development Assistance
ODA	Overseas Development Administration (UK)
OECD	Organization for Economic Co-operation and Development
OPS	Open Pan Sulphitation
PRODEM	Fundacion Para la Promocion y Desarrollo de la Micro-empresa
SCF	Save the Children Fund
SEWA	Self-Employed Women's Association (India)
TCC	Technology Consultancy Centre (Ghana)
UNCTAD	United Nations Conference on Trade and Development
UNICEF	United Nations Children's Fund
UNIFEM	United Nations Development Fund for Women
USAID	United States Agency for International Development
VITA	Volunteers in Technical Assistance
VSK	Vertical Shaft Kiln
WWF	Working Women's Forum

Preface

For the first time we may have the technical capacity to free mankind from the scourge of hunger. Therefore today we must proclaim a bold objective: that within a decade, no child will go to bed hungry, that no family will fear for its next day's bread, and that no human being's future will be stunted by malnutrition.

Henry Kissinger, World Food
Conference, Rome, 1974

THIS BOOK is about poverty, aid and technology. It is about a search that has been going on, officially in the developing world for over thirty years, and less officially in most countries since the beginning of time. It is a search that is driven today by more hard core poverty than has ever before been known, and by a realization that the technology we have applied to solving the problem has severe limitations. We have discovered how to send people safely to the moon, but we have not discovered how to ensure that people can live safely on earth – safe from war, disease, and the crushing poverty that stifles ambition, hope and enterprise.

The book is about the quest for a form of development in the Third World that gives meaning to people's lives, a form of development that is relevant to their resources and needs, and to the hopes people have for their countries and for their children. It is about how what has become known as 'appropriate technology' fits into the larger picture of technology, aid and development, and what it has accomplished in the fight against poverty. The book covers the development of appropriate technology and traces its history through the various changes in development thinking that have characterized the past three decades. Using historical and current examples, it attempts to illustrate the interaction between economic, social and technological factors that give a particular technology a positive impact on poverty reduction. The book is about the possibilities and limitations of technology. It is about failure as well as success, because I believe too many failures in the 'development business' have been ignored or covered up, condemning poor people to suffer the re-invention of too many wheels that never worked in the first place.

It is about large as well as small, for 'appropriate' is not always synonymous with 'small'. It is about policy and people and perversity.

It is a study of determination in the face of adversity; and excellence in the face of mediocrity. It is about macro interventions as well as micro interventions, because these are not substitutes for one another, but essential complements to technological progress.

The book is divided into three parts. Part One sets the stage for the following sections by describing the way in which governments and aid agencies, both official and the non-governmental, have evolved over the past thirty years in their thinking and approach to issues relating to poverty and development. This section does not deal at length with issues of technology, and may therefore seem somewhat remote from the main theme of the book. It is not. The state of the world and the way its governments and institutions function and relate to one another has everything to do with the technologies they choose to solve their problems. As Fritz Schumacher said, 'the main content of politics is economics, and the main content of economics is technology'. Part Two deals with what has been learned about technology and development, using specific examples and case studies of projects that have succeeded and failed. And Part Three draws lessons derived from many centuries of technological development, but more particularly from the experience of the three 'development decades' that began so hopefully in 1960.

Readers seeking the familiar icons of appropriate technology – biogas digesters, handpumps, latrines and windmills – will perhaps be disappointed that they do not receive top billing in the pages that follow. It may seem as though Hamlet has been sacrificed at the expense of Rosencrantz and Guildenstern, and that important aspects of appropriate technology have been ignored. The apparent oversight is deliberate. Some 'appropriate technologies', like windmills, represent both old and new solutions to the energy problem. Where they are old, their story is well told elsewhere. Where they are new, they tend to run a risk observed by Sir Walter Raleigh 400 years ago: 'Whosoever in writing a modern history, shall follow truth too near the heels, it may haply strike out his teeth'.

As for handpumps and latrines, their success in reducing child mortality, raising life expectancy and alleviating the burden on women is well chronicled, and rightly so, by the organizations that have funded their dissemination. Although windmills, handpumps and biogas are here, I have chosen to explore less familiar technological territory in greater detail – cases which may seem less grand and less obvious in the short run, but which are in some ways much more important for the longer-term ability of people to develop and adapt their own technological capacities. To my way of thinking, the Prince of Denmark is alive and well, and lives not in aid agencies, but in the back-yard foundries and informal sectors of Asia, Africa and Latin America.

Threading one's way through a business heavily influenced by fads and ideology, it is difficult – especially in a fast moving vehicle – to avoid hitting the occasional sacred cow. In the course of the book a few of these, as well as some white elephants and red herrings may have been sacrificed. The book also deliberately attempts, perhaps ambitiously, to demystify some ideas that have become lost in a numbing fog of acronyms and jargon. Among them are complex concepts described by once perfectly understandable words: *sustainability, partnership, co-ordination, empowerment, adjustment, transfer of technology, green* and *environment*.

A note on terminology is perhaps warranted at the outset: when the word 'man' is used in this book, it means 'man', not 'men and women'. 'Bilateral donors' refers to the official aid agencies of northern governments, such as the United States Agency for International Development (USAID), or the British Overseas Development Administration (ODA). 'Multilateral organizations' are membership institutions comprised of more than one national government. Examples are the World Bank, the International Monetary Fund (IMF) and United Nations agencies such as UNICEF or UNIFEM. The term 'donor agencies' means bilateral or multilateral agencies. For ease of comparison, most values in the book are expressed in United States dollars. Where other currencies are used, such as Zimbabwe dollars, they are clearly marked Z$.

I have used the word 'billion' in the American sense, meaning one thousand million. Although I prefer 'South' to 'Third World' or 'developing countries', I have used the first two more or less interchangeably for the sake of variety. 'Developing countries' has been used more sparingly, mostly in direct quotations from other publications such as those of the World Bank. That all countries are 'developing' is an old chestnut, but one worth remembering. References used in only one chapter are fully acknowledged in the notes for that chapter. Those used in more than one chapter are given a brief reference in the chapter and a full reference in the bibliography.

In a sense, the research for the book began twenty-five years ago, when I first went off to teach in a rural school in Sierra Leone. More specifically and more recently, however, my research took me from villages in Gujarat and Bangladesh, to potters' sheds in Sri Lanka; from the rolling countryside of southern Botswana to iron foundries in Ghana and roadside workshops in Kenya. It has been a fascinating journey, which included much tea in humble dwellings, and equal amounts of coffee in a variety of fortresses: a former Portuguese slaving castle in West Africa, the World Bank in Washington, Oxford University, the University of Sussex, and the United States State Department. I visited workshops in England's Black Country, not far from where the anchor for the Titanic was cast; I talked to teachers in Zimbabwe, tinsmiths in Malawi, and women operating lathes in northern Ghana. I looked at a lot of good and bad handpumps, simple oil presses and clean latrines, and I stumbled through dozens of workshops where some of the world's most genuine entrepreneurs are doing more for their country's economies than battalions of planners and economists.

Many people helped make my work both possible and enjoyable. In Ghana, John Powell, Don Morin, Solomon Adjorlolo, Francis Acquah and Sosthenes Buatsi represent the very many individuals and old friends at TCC, GRATIS and other institutions in Accra, Kumasi, Tema, Tamale and Cape Coast, who took time to get me from place to place and to explain things to me, sometimes more than once. Lynn Wallis provided great assistance and succour with logistics and hospitality. In Zimbabwe, Ebbie Dengu, Jeremy Ascough, Langford Chitsike, David Hancock, Dave Harries, Mike Humphries, Father Brian McGarry, Gibson Mandishona, Thembia Nyoni, Mike Robson, Musa Sithole and Mercy Zinyama all gave me useful perspectives, and most of them also gave me a lot of paper. In Malawi I could not have functioned without the tremendous assistance and hospitality of Garry Whitby, the information and companionship of Keith Machell and the perspectives and photocopier of Don Henry. In Botswana, Tyrell Duncan helped with introductions and insight, and I am grateful to the Botswana Technology Centre and the Rural Industries Innovation Centre at Kanye, and others for the time that was taken to discuss and demonstrate their work for me – with special thanks to Kit Morei, Teedzani Woto, Debbie Stayers and Brian Egner. Lahiru Perera drove me up hill and down dale through Sri Lanka's tea estates, while R.M. Amerasekera told me everything I ever wanted to know about fuel-efficient stoves and then sent me on a memorable tour of the brickyards of Negombo. In Kenya, Nick Hall, Nick Evans and Solomon Mwangi took time from busy schedules to talk to me, feed me, and point out things I would not have otherwise noticed.

Without the friendly help, open files and constructive comments on draft chapters by many people at ITDG in Rugby, Nairobi, Dhaka, Colombo and Harare, the book would surely have been impossible. Among them are Simon Burne, Janice Phillips, Frank Almond, Helen Appleton, Barrie Axtell, Alex Bush, Nicky Carter, Adrian Cullis, Peter Fellows, Priyanthi Fernando, Martin Hardingham, Ray Holland, Nurul Islam Khan, David Mather, Patrick Mulvany, Brian O'Riordan, Adam Platt, David Poston, Otto Ruskulis, Theo Schilderman, Andrew Scott, Bob Spencer, Peter Watts, Peter Young and John Young.

I am grateful to Raphael Kaplinsky for an important body of work on appropriate technology, and for putting me onto the 'Third Italy'. Others who helped with time, advice and valuable material include Andrew Barnett, Martin Bell, Dennis Frost, John Howe, Tony Killick, George McRobie, John Parry and his staff in Cradley Heath, and Frances Stewart. Matt Gamser helped in Rugby and Washington, and thanks to frequently crossing paths and the occasional Tusker, David Wright was able to debate both outline and content with me in London, Dhaka, Colombo and Nairobi. He and his family also very kindly put me up (and put up with me) in London. In Washington I received advice, insight (and so much paper that an extra suitcase was necessary) from Valeria Budinich, Jean Downing, Carlos Lola and others at ATI, from Beth Rhyne at USAID and from Chris Hennin at the World Bank. Chuck Weiss gave me the benefit of twenty years in the technology business and the people at Development Alternatives Inc. probably gave me a century or two. Parts of Chapters II and XIII are based on earlier work done in collaboration with Roger Young, and parts of Chapter IV are based on research done in conjunction with the Aga Khan Foundation Canada.

I am very grateful to Sharon Capeling-Alakija, Marilyn Carr, David Catmur, Keith Machell, Bill McNeill, Brian Rowe, and Paul Zuckerman for reading various drafts and offering valuable advice. I am also grateful to the very many people in many agencies who helped with information, logistics and advice. Although none of them can take any blame for what follows, they include individuals in the Bangladesh Rural Advancement Committee, CARE, the Canadian International Development Agency, the International Development Research Centre, NOVIB, Oxfam Canada, Sarvodaya, UNDP, USAID and the World Bank. Finally, I would be remiss if I did not say that the opinions contained in the book are mine alone.

Ian Smillie,
Ottawa, July 1991

PART ONE

The failure to learn from failure

'You don't know much,' said the Duchess, 'and that's a fact.'
Lewis Carroll

CHAPTER I

A tale of two worlds

International support for development is now flagging. In some of the rich countries its feasibility, even its very purpose, is in question. The climate surrounding foreign aid programmes is heavy with disillusion and distrust... On all sides we sense a weariness and a search for new direction.[1]   The Pearson Commission, 1969

FROM THE beginning of time, technology has been a key element in the growth and development of societies. Entire eras are named for the levels of their technological sophistication – the stone age; the bronze age; the iron age; the age of sail; the age of steam; the jet age; the computer era. But technology is more than jets and computers; it is a combination of knowledge, techniques and concepts; it is tools and machines, farms and factories. It is organization, processes and people. The cultural, historical and organizational context in which technology is developed and applied is the key to its success or failure. In short, technology is the science and the art of getting things done – through the application of skills and knowledge.

This book is about a hybrid era, one caught somewhere between bronze and computers, between sail and jet engines; one in which quality has become confused with quantity, and means with ends. For the South – the 'Third World' – it is a time of immense technological opportunity and optimism. It is also a period of unimaginable poverty and hopelessness. It is a time of ferment, change and technological growth. And it is unlike any other period in history; for today, in addition to artisans and artists, farmers, machinists and dreamers, the direction of technology is influenced and fashioned by bureaucrats, economists, far-away corporate planners, aid agencies and charities. Never before in history have so many non-technical people exerted so much influence on the advancement, retardation, and movement of technology. This book is about the interaction between these people, and between poverty, aid and technology in the Third World.

Deciding where to start such a complex story is a writer's prerogative, but it can also be a nemesis. Does the story begin with Neanderthal man, inventing simple tools a hundred thousand years ago? Or does it more properly begin ten thousand years ago, when Homo sapiens began to domesticate animals and raise crops? Perhaps it begins five thousand years ago with the great civilization of

3

Mohenjodaro in what is today Pakistan. Possibly it begins independently in several places at once – China, Egypt, Mexico, Peru, Zimbabwe, India, Greece, Rome. Perhaps it begins more correctly with colonialism, an age-old two-way purveyor of aid and technology. As a colony in turn of Rome, the Norse and the Normans, Britain gained and lost. As a colonizer, it gave and took. Did 'aid' begin with the farming advances taken by the Romans to Gaul and Britain? With Ashoka's conquest of South India? Did concern about credit, debt and development begin with S.S. Thorburn's 1896 report on peasant indebtedness in India? In 1925 with Malcolm Darling's *The Punjab Peasant in Prosperity and Debt*? Perhaps the modern 'aid' era begins with Lend Lease in 1941, or the Marshall Plan in 1948, or the Colombo Plan in 1951.

Chapter Five will return to Mohenjodaro, China and Rome. The starting point for the book, however, begins more recently, far from ancient Rome, and far from the factories and backyard workshops of the Third World. It begins arbitrarily in 1968, with an unlikely collaboration between a winner of the Nobel Peace Prize and a former United States Defense Secretary noted for his escalation of the war in Vietnam. In that year, Robert McNamara, newly appointed President of the World Bank, asked former Canadian Prime Minister Lester Pearson to chair a 'grand assize': an international group of individuals with 'stature and experience' would 'meet together, study the consequences of twenty years of development assistance, assess the results, clarify the errors and propose the policies which will work better in the future'. The report of what became known as the Pearson Commission was presented to the World Bank a year later, and was subsequently published under the title *Partners in Development*.

Since then a number of seminal studies on development have captured the attention of the world and the imagination of some of its leaders. *The Limits to Growth*, the first report of the Club of Rome, appeared in 1972. E. F. Schumacher's study of 'economics as if people mattered', *Small is Beautiful*, was published a year later, and its title quickly found its way into the language and the *Oxford Dictionary of Quotations*. In 1977, Robert McNamara suggested a second international study on development issues, and Willy Brandt, former Chancellor of the Federal Republic of Germany became its Chairman. Like the Pearson Commission, the Brandt Commission was made up of individuals 'of stature and experience'; unlike the Pearson Commission, it was independent of the World Bank. Although half its funding was provided by the Dutch Government, contributions came from dozens of countries in both the North and the South. In fact it was the title of the Brandt Commission's Report, *North-South: a*

4

Programme for Survival, that gave new expression to the polarity between the industrialized world and what the Pearson Report had quaintly termed 'the emerging nations'. The Brandt Report was completed in December 1979, but the Commissioners did not disband; they continued to meet through 1980, 1981 and 1982, reviewing events and reactions to their work. In 1983 they issued a second report, a follow-up entitled *Common Crisis*.

Then came the Palme Commission on security and disarmament issues, followed by the World Commission on Environment and Development, published in 1987 under the title, *Our Common Future*, and chaired by the Prime Minister of Norway.

In recent years, thick reports on the state of just about everything, accompanied by voluminous statistical annexes, have become increasingly fashionable. Each year since 1978, the World Bank has produced a *World Development Report* dealing with major international themes and containing a lengthy series of 'World Development Indicators' – tables which spell out, country by country, the state of the world's economy. UNICEF publishes an annual *State of the World's Children* and the Worldwatch Institute has since 1984 published an annual *State of the World Report* detailing 'progress towards a sustainable society'. This report, published in 20 languages, ran to a hundred thousand copies in 1990. In the mid 1980s, a Washington-based research group, The World Resources Institute, began publishing a series of studies on the management of natural resources and protection of the environment. Late off the starting block but by no means least, UNDP published its first annual *Human Development Report* in 1990 on 'the human dimension of development', a counterpoint or supplement, depending on the perspective of the reader, to the World Bank's more economics-oriented effort.

The season of light; the season of darkness

The Pearson Report, maligned in its day by some as a neo-colonialist apology, relegated now to back shelves in libraries, and long-gone from used-book stores, stands up moderately well. When it appeared in 1969, more than half of the countries of the Third World had been independent for less than a decade, a decade characterized by optimism and expanding economies. The average annual rate of growth in the Third World actually exceeded that of industrialized countries. Growth in African export earnings, for example, was equal to that of East Asia and almost four times higher than South Asia. Agriculture, which had stagnated for several years, appeared to be on the threshold of a 'green revolution'. School enrollment in the Third

5

World had tripled in fifteen years, and great strides had been made in reducing deaths due to plague, cholera and smallpox.

As a product of its time, written by men (there were no women on the Commission) who had lived as adults through the depression of the 1930s, the Pearson report can perhaps be forgiven for viewing poverty largely in terms of employment, for ignoring women, for simplifying the idea of technology transfer and for the slightly hysterical edge on its approach to the issue of population. The report noted somewhat prematurely that 'Malaria has been virtually eliminated by a worldwide campaign under the leadership of the World Health Organization'.

It is, nevertheless, a prescient document on several counts. It warned against a stagnation in official development assistance, and urged a clearer, more efficient, more developmental approach. It recommended the untying of aid, greater emphasis on programme assistance and a downplaying of projects for which recurrent costs would not be available later. It worried about the 'brain drain' from the South to the North, and about the cost and effectiveness of the 100 000 technical experts and volunteers working in the South. It noted the positive contributions of voluntary agencies. It urged a strengthening of multilateral agencies, and it invented the now-famous aid target: 'We recommend that each aid-giver increase commitments of official development assistance to the level necessary for net disbursements to reach 0.7 per cent of its gross national product by 1975 or shortly thereafter, but in no case later than 1980'.[2] Warning of growing interest payments on a 1968 Third World debt of $47.5 billion (compared with $1300 billion in 1990), the Report suggested a greater grant element, and more concessional loans from aid donors.

It warned of other problems ahead. It gave two estimates of world population by the turn of the century: a low of six billion and a high of seven, based on different assumptions about fertility and life expectancy. That 1991 estimates predicted a population closer to the lower figure – about 6.4 billion in 2001 – should not detract from the alarm with which a 1969 world saw a doubling of its population in only thirty years.

The Pearson Report recognized the problems of growing urbanization and malnutrition, but saw solutions largely in terms of increased investment in jobs. Scale was not a factor in the recommendations except by inference: large problems suggested large solutions. The fast-approaching 'green revolution' was problematic only in the sense that it would require increased levels of investment to support it. Given what transpired in the following decade, one of the Report's more ironic recommendations has to do with foreign private investment as a means of funding some of the development requirements of the Third World. There is none of the concern that would follow in the Brandt Report about the role of multinational corporations. And the basic contradiction between such investment and what the report called 'unsuitable technology' is ignored. Direct private investment is enthusiastically encouraged: 'We recommend the removal, in developing countries, of legal and other barriers to the purchase by institutional investors of bonds issued or guaranteed by governments of developing countries'.[3]

One of the Report's strongest sections deals with trade. The first United Nations Conference on Trade and Development (UNCTAD) had been held five years earlier and had made clear that the development of poor countries would require important adjustments in industrialized countries. In 1969, all but ten per cent of the export earnings of Third World countries was derived from primary products, and half of the countries earned more than 50 per cent of their income from a single primary commodity – jute, sisal, rubber, tin, copper, aluminum, sugar, bananas, coffee, tea, cocoa. It was unequivocally clear to the Pearson Commissioners that diversification and trade were key areas of development potential, and the naïvety and good sense in their recommendations, viewed across a quarter century of futile negotiations, is almost touching. They recommended the removal by industrialized countries of excise and import duties on primary products from developing countries; the financing of buffer stocks to curtail the damaging effects of price fluctuations; the abolition of quotas during the 1970s; and the development of a general, non-reciprocal scheme of preferences for manufactured and semi-manufactured products from developing countries – before the end of 1970. This, the Report states in an ironic choice of words, 'implies a willingness on the part of industrialized countries to make *structural adjustments* which will enable them to absorb an increasing range of manufactures and semi-manufactures from developing countries'.[4]

The age of wisdom; the age of foolishness

Ten years later, when Willy Brandt handed his Commission's report to the Secretary General of the United Nations, the world was a harder, less optimistic place. The post-war boom was at last over. Rocked by one oil crisis and gripped by a second, industrialized countries were in the depths of a recession. 'We are aware,' the Commissioners wrote, 'that this report is being published at a time when rich countries are deeply worried by the prospects of prolonged 'recession' and the diminishing stability of international relations...

7

In the short period since our Commission first met, in December 1977, the international situation has gone from bad to worse. It is no exaggeration to say that the future of the world can rarely have seemed so endangered'.[5]

The Brandt Report, much more hard-hitting than the Pearson Report, made depressing reading. It was deeply concerned about peace, an issue beyond the remit of the Pearson Commission. It understood that environmental issues were of primary concern, and that dependence on non-renewable sources of energy had to be curtailed. It recognized the fundamental importance of women to almost every issue of development. It discussed the unacceptability of Third World poverty in a way that the Pearson report had not.

Brandt wasted little ink on the achievements of the previous decade, because apart from a few spectacular instances, such as the final eradication of smallpox, there was little to report of a positive nature. Although there had been progress in some countries – Netherlands, Denmark, Sweden, Norway – towards the Pearson aid target of 0.7 per cent of GNP, others (the United States, Britain, France) had actually reduced their aid percentages. 'This failure,' Brandt noted, 'points to a marked lack of political will ... Governments with poor aid performances often plead budgetary constraints and balance of payments difficulties, but it is clear that these are not insuperable obstacles. When GNP in industrial countries increases by 3 to 4 per cent a year, the allocation of one-fortieth to one-thirtieth of the annual *increase* in GNP to foreign aid would close the gap between 0.3 and 0.7 per cent in only five years'.[6] Official development assistance spending in 1979 represented about 5 per cent of the $450 billion devoted that year to military spending.

In the area of international trade, the decade following the Pearson Report had its promising moments. Although the 1973 oil crisis had a devastating impact on most Third World economies, it also underscored the urgent need for a comprehensive approach to the commodity problem. Years of international lobbying and negotiation culminated in the 1976 UNCTAD IV meeting in Nairobi, which discussed an 'Integrated Programme for Commodities'. This plan formalized and detailed many of the recommendations on trade made in the Pearson Report and proposed a 'common fund' to support buffer stocks and other price stabilization measures. By 1979, however, few of the recommendations had been accepted or ratified by industrialized countries. Tariffs and quotas continued to be the order of the day; prices of primary commodities went up and down like umbrellas on a rainy day. The North basically ignored a series of proposals put forward by the South, and countered with few of its own. It was, the Brandt Commission said, a dialogue of the deaf. 'The

8

air is thick with alibis for inaction ... the result is frustration and deadlock'.[7]

The importance of economic diversification and of increased manufactures in the South was not an idea the average Third World economist or planner needed to have repeated. Despite the oil crisis and Northern hostility, efforts in this direction during the 1970s had continued. In 1955, manufactures had accounted for only 10 per cent of non-fuel exports from the Third World. By 1965 the figure had risen to 20 per cent, and by 1975 it was 40 per cent. Although these exports originated in only a few countries, the number of successful exporters was increasing. As with Pearson, for Brandt, 'adjustment' to this new situation was a process that *industrialized* countries would have to undergo. Adjustment was not expected to be painless, but it would be far from serious. EEC studies had already shown that imports from the South were not causing unemployment in the North. A study on adjustment in Britain demonstrated that increased importation of Third World manufactures between 1970 and 1977 had displaced fewer than 2 per cent of the 1970 labour force, while increased exports to the Third World had created as much new employment.[8]

The 1979 conclusion of the 'Tokyo Round' of the General Agreement on Tariffs and Trade (GATT) talks, however, did little to ease the situation for the South. On manufactured goods the proportion facing OECD tariff and non-tariff barriers in 1979 was 30 per cent, compared with only 11 per cent between OECD countries, and a rate of only 4 per cent in 1974.[9] What this meant in terms of Southern job creation can be seen from the scale of tariffs on different degrees of value added. By 1982, for example, the average tariff barrier in 11 major developed countries on iron ore from the South was zero. It rose to 2.4 per cent on unwrought iron, 9.3 per cent on iron and steel plate, and almost 20 per cent on knives and forks. Unsawn timber entered the North free, but the simple act of sawing it into planks drew 2.2 per cent protection, and turning it into a chair added 11.5 per cent to the protection.[10] European Community protection on fresh pineapples is 9 per cent. On tinned pineapples it is 32 per cent, and on pineapple juice it is 42 per cent.[11]

The Brandt Report was much clearer than Pearson on the role of technology in development. It raised questions about farming systems that had been over-mechanized and over-fertilized, at the expense of jobs, the ecology, and ultimately, food production. It echoed other studies which demonstrated the poor results of huge irrigation projects. In India, for example, 72 major irrigation projects commissioned between 1951 and 1965, with a combined command area of 13.4 million hectares, had delivered water to only a quarter of

9

that area by 1966.[12] The 'green revolution' had indeed increased food production in some countries, but often to the accompaniment of impoverishment for smaller farmers. And net food increases had grown more slowly than the population in 58 out of 106 developing countries between 1970 and 1978.

Many countries in the South, taking their cue from Northern economists, equated development with growth, and growth with industrialization. Massive investments were made in industry, on the premise that these investments would form important linkages with other sectors of the economy, by supplying other industries and agriculture, or by increasing the demand for their products as inputs. For some, for a while, the strategy worked, but for many it did not. In Ghana, for example, where the experiment was embraced on a grand scale, manufacturing as a percentage of Gross Domestic Product rose from 10 per cent in 1960 to 14 per cent in 1970. Most enterprises were highly capital intensive, however, and were completely dependant upon imported raw materials, spare parts and foreign technicians for their survival. Capacity utilization was dismal. Prices rose, exports were not realized and production fell, yet between 1972 and 1977, the industrial sector sponged up between 42 and 55 per cent of the available foreign exchange – 95 per cent for the import of industrial raw material, and the balance for spares and accessories.[13]

The Brandt Commission pointed out that almost all advanced technology originated in industrial countries where it was developed for a different set of economic and production circumstances. Worse, the North accounted for 96 per cent of the world's spending on research and development, while much of the 'transfer' of technology to the South, or the 'choice' of technology, rested with Northern investors – multinational corporations – and with 'experts' involved in aid projects.

E.F. Schumacher, a professional economist who had worked closely with John Maynard Keynes and who had been a major intellectual influence on British economic planning during and after the Second World War, had begun as early as 1961 to articulate the challenge of technology in terms of the essential problem it was supposed to solve in the Third World: poverty. He wrote of the industrial estates that could be found in almost every developing country 'where high-grade modern equipment is standing idle because of lack of organization, finance, raw material, supplies, transport, marketing facilities and the like ... a lot of scarce capital resources – normally paid from scarce foreign exchange – are virtually wasted'.[14] He spoke of the importance of economic evolution rather than unworkable quantum leaps, and of the need for choosing and developing 'middle' or 'intermediate' technologies. He advocated technologies that could be effectively adopted by those people in the Third World left behind by a modern sector serving and providing affluence to a tiny proportion of the population. Support to large-scale industry would simply worsen the growing problems of rural unemployment and under-employment, and would stimulate further growth of cities, many of them already nightmares of poverty and disease.

The Brandt Commission foresaw two major crises. The first was debt. It noted the international banking system had successfully channelled OPEC surpluses, in the form of loans, to poor countries, much as Pearson – without foreseeing the oil crisis – had suggested. But the Brandt Commission noted ominously that many countries were in arrears and it spoke of the crisis posed by constraints on the growth of export earnings to meet increased debt service commitments. The second crisis had to do with energy: 'the political dangers arising from the energy situation are underlined by fears ... that force might in some circumstances be used by powerful countries to ensure the security of future oil supplies ... putting world peace in jeopardy'.[15]

Despite assurances that the worst did not have to happen, the Report culminated on a gloomy note: 'A number of poor countries are threatened with the irreversible destruction of their ecological systems; many more face growing food deficits and possibly mass starvation. In the international community there is the possibility of competitive trade restrictions or devaluations; a collapse of credit with defaults by major debtors, or bank failures; ... an intensified struggle for spheres of interest and influence, leading to military conflicts. The 1980s could witness even greater catastrophes than the 1930s.'[16]

The spring of hope; the winter of despair

The Brandt Commission recommended a major North-South world summit aimed at an intellectual reorientation, structural change and increased practical co-operation in the interest of enhanced international peace and development. The meeting, which took place at Cancun in Mexico, in October 1981, was attended by an impressive 'who's who' of leaders and thinkers from both North and South. But Cancun was an inconclusive failure, and industrial countries, still gripped by recession, further tightened self-serving measures.

The 1987 World Commission on Environment and Development, commonly known as the *Brundtland Report* added high octane ecological fuel to the increasingly explosive mix of poverty, debt and trade imbalance. In addition to the other calamities heaped on the poor of the Third World, in the 1970s almost 25 million people had been affected every year by drought and 15.4 million suffered from floods. Unchecked pollution, declining energy and mineral resources, deforestation and plunder of the oceans highlighted the symbiosis between ecology and economics. The Brundtland Report saw – in pollution, in dwindling resources, in the droughts, floods and famines – the clear and devastating hand of man, rapaciously exploiting new-found power to alter planetary systems at a rate that outstripped the capacity of science to assess the effects, and outstripping the capacity of fragmented political systems to check the damage.

Awakened by numerous public attacks on its structural adjustment lending, the World Bank devoted its entire 1990 *World Development Report* to the issue of poverty. What the report revealed was bad. Despite a problem with definitions and statistics, it was clear that the number of poor had increased in both real and relative terms since the Pearson Report. By 1990, between one and one and half billion people, twenty per cent of those on the planet, were living in absolute poverty – spending most of what they earned on food, and yet still eating less than enough to remain healthy.

During the 1980s, the Pearson aid target, 0.7 per cent of GNP, had proved as elusive as ever. Few of the large donors came close to a half of one per cent. Moreover even the World Bank was publicly beginning to question bilateral aid effectiveness. It noted that in 1987 41 per cent of all aid went to middle and high income countries.[17] Two thirds of all OECD member countries' aid was tied to their own goods and services, thus reducing effectiveness (or increasing costs) by 20 per cent or more. There was continued emphasis on large, capital-intensive projects rather than support to social sectors. And many aid programmes were much more related to commercial or strategic initiatives than to development. The Bank estimated that in 1986, for example, only eight per cent of the USAID programme could be identified as 'development assistance devoted to low-income countries'.[18]

'Structural adjustment' became the Rosetta stone of World Bank and International Monetary Fund thinking in the 1980s. A concept which began life as a potentially thorny problem for the North rather than the South, structural adjustment had, by 1990, changed meaning entirely through a combination of factors. First, primary commodity prices began to collapse at the beginning of the 1980s. ('Collapse', of course, means that the prices Northern importers would pay had collapsed.) Between 1980 and 1982, for example, the price of sugar fell 78 per cent, rubber 37 per cent and copper 35 per cent. Many developing countries were consequently forced to live with fewer resources, lowering consumption unless they had access to foreign capital through loans, investment or aid.

Secondly, the Brandt warnings on debt began to come true in Poland in 1981, and in Mexico the following year, presaging a debt and banking crisis of massive proportions. As global inflation, Western interest rates and foreign exchange fluctuations all increased, developing countries had to adjust yet again. The economic recession of the early 1980s, the debt crisis and commodity collapse led governments and financial institutions to focus increasingly on short-term problems such as debt servicing, inflation and falling foreign exchange receipts. In 1990, the Philippines was spending 36 per cent of its central budget on debt servicing and 22 per cent on social services. In Jordan, the respective amounts were 39 per cent and 18 per cent.[19]

Most developing countries suffered from a combination of declining exports, rising debt servicing costs, and severe domestic inflation, with a consequent balance of payments crisis. The doctor's prescription, 'structural adjustment', referred to the macroeconomic policy reforms required to accommodate these worsening economic conditions. IMF and World Bank structural adjustment loans were intended to reduce the impact of the external shocks by promoting more durable economic structures and by building the foundations for more sustained economic growth. Typically, structural adjustment programmes included currency devaluation, reductions in government spending, and trade and exchange liberalization.

Industrialization and diversification into the export of manufactures – another aspect of adjustment programmes – assumed access to external markets. Trade liberalization and reduction of tariffs and quotas *by industrialized countries* were therefore important elements of Bank, IMF and OECD discussions on adjustment. In fact, however, it was this element of the adjustment process – not the conditions imposed on and accepted by Third World countries – that most often met with failure.

In order to judge how official development assistance and adjustment have affected economic growth and poverty reduction in the Third World, the entire range of interactions between North and South must ultimately be examined. If countries are expected to shift the emphasis of their development policies increasingly towards manufacturing, expansion of trade, and liberalization, there must be concomitant adjustments within developed countries. There must be a rational approach to industrialization and questions of technology. This was clearly recognized by the Pearson and Brandt Commissions; it has underscored the existence of UNCTAD since 1964; it is ritually reinforced by the OECD, and is acknowledged at all GATT

13

meetings. For every step forward over thirty years, however, there have been five steps backward.

Primary commodities still account for more than 70 per cent of total exports of low-income countries, although real prices for most have continually worsened over the past three decades. As products in developing countries undergo increased fabrication, tariffs in industrial countries tend to escalate, especially around tobacco products, rubber, leather, paper, cotton, jute and iron. It is estimated that distortions to grain, livestock products and sugar markets in developed countries cost producers in developing countries $28 billion annually, the equivalent of 35 per cent of the annual exports of food and agricultural raw materials from *all* developing countries.

Cotton is grown in 80 countries worldwide, and for many it is an important export crop. A natural evolution of the cotton economy is diversification into textiles, a relatively straightforward industry and one – not without coincidence – which helped start the Northern industrial revolution. Processing and textile manufacture seem to fit the structural adjustment nostrum perfectly: comparative advantage, diversification, greater value-added, increased manufactures, increased exports, increased foreign exchange earnings. Northern countries, however, through the 1960s and 1970s, devised a mechanism that worked against this single most-promising Southern growth industry. Known as the Multi-Fibre Arrangement (MFA), it works directly against the GATT principle of *non-discriminatory* trade liberalization by restricting Southern textile imports into the North.

It is estimated that the gain to developing countries of the removal of quotas and tariffs under the Multi-Fibre Arrangement would have been $11.3 billion, roughly one third of *all* official development assistance from *all* OECD countries in 1987. In Bangladesh such a move would have resulted in an increase of 44 per cent of *all* exports in 1986.[20] Instead, the opposite happened. Growing from none in 1979, Bangladesh had developed 700 clothing export factories by 1985. Despite pressure from donors, from the World Bank and from the IMF to diversify, to industrialize and to move away from primary commodities; despite Bangladesh's heavy donor-dependence; and despite the fact that its exports to the North were negligible (1.8 per cent of all US clothing imports in 1985), in that year the US, followed by Britain, Canada and France, imposed quotas which resulted in the closure of 500 of those 700 factories.[21]

Other studies have shown that removal of all Northern trade barriers to Southern exports would result in a 10 per cent increase in their exports, worth $50 billion, or 20 per cent more than all overseas development assistance. It is further estimated that the cost of such a

14

move to developed countries would be the equivalent of a three per cent reduction in GNP.

In underlining the importance of consistency between Northern economic policies and the aims of development assistance, the Organization for Economic Co-operation and Development (OECD) states that 'failure to arrest the pressures for *managed* trade and unilateral trade measures would seriously undermine trade and investment prospects for developing countries and put in question the credibility of OECD Members' advocacy of trade policy reform in developing countries.'[22] Adjustment, then, runs the danger of becoming not a one-time economic housecleaning, but the continuation of a long downward spiral of belt-tightening in the face of intractable Northern trade policies.

International concern about the social impact of initial adjustment programmes, particularly their impact on vulnerable groups such as women, children and the poor, led to calls for a different approach. 'Adjustment with a Human Face', is what UNICEF called for in an important 1987 study of adjustment programmes, demonstrating that economic reform programmes clearly put social services in jeopardy, especially in Africa. The Bank itself, perhaps not yet fully awake to the magnitude of the issue, admitted dozily that 'when structural adjustment issues came to the fore, little attention was paid to the effects on the poor. Macroeconomic issues seemed more pressing, and many expected that there would be rapid transition to new growth paths'.[23] By the late 1980s, international financial institutions were attempting to mitigate the negative impact of reforms on the poor through 'social dimensions of adjustment' programmes. Many, however, were grab-bags of diverse, high-profile welfare schemes: drops of oil for squeaking wheels rather than preventive maintenance for the machine.

In 1990, the Prime Minister of Jamaica, Michael Manley, juxtaposed the problems of adjustment and reform with the debt crisis:

> Countries like Jamaica today stand at the threshold of economic growth. In the past, many leaders, myself included, placed too much relevance on government involvement in the production of goods and services. Now ... we have developed strong private sectors, have for years attempted to implement IMF stabilization programmes and World Bank structural adjustment programmes, but find our economies burdened by debt ... I [do not] expect Jamaica to be permitted to walk away from its debt obligations. However, common sense and conscience surely demand that the major powers ... take an urgent look at those agencies' inflexible rules, rules that have long since outgrown justification and now add to the strangling burdens of countries like Jamaica.[24]

15

The epoch of belief; the epoch of incredulity

The roots of the problems do not lie exclusively in the North or with aid donors, as Michael Manley acknowledged. Many Third World governments have been easily beguiled by promises of the quick development fix, the 'high tech' solution, by unrealistic reliance on Western development models and by the potential for graft that accompanies travelling salesmen and investors. In Africa, the importance of small farmers has been ignored at the ultimate expense of agricultural production, while pricing policies designed to maintain political support from the urban elite have hastened the downward economic spiral. Rural infrastructure has suffered throughout Africa, and in some countries has all but collapsed.

Arms sales, both cause and effect of political instability, are a major contributor to Third World debt. Sub-Saharan African governments spent $2.2 billion on arms imports in 1983, compared with $1.7 billion on health. The African arms market was a gold mine for the Soviet Union, which accounted for 46 per cent of all arms agreements between 1976 and 1983. In 1985, North American arms sales and military assistance to 40 African countries totalled $400 million.[25] In 1987, Bangladesh spent twice as much on defence as on health. Almost 22 per cent of the Indian budget went to defence, four times more than was devoted to education and health combined. In the same year, defence spending in Pakistan was more than eight times higher than combined education and health spending.

Weak public institutions, poor managerial and financial control, and lack of political accountability are in part a cause, in part a result of underdevelopment. Between 1960 and 1986 there were 144 successful coups in the Third World, half of them in Africa. Between 1945 and 1990 there were 100 wars and civil conflicts in the South.

Overly regulated economies encourage corruption. The Indian Government has initiated several studies of 'black money' and has found 'pervasive tax evasion on legal economic activities and widespread corruption and abuse of all forms of public discretionary authority'.[26] The export of capital by individuals and corporations, known as 'capital flight', is a serious drain on the resources of many Third World countries. Although it is hard to measure, it is estimated that an amount equal to half of all the money borrowed by Mexico, Argentina and Venezuela between 1975 and 1990 was reinvested abroad. In the Philippines it may have been as much as the equivalent of 80 per cent of the national debt between 1962 and 1986.[27] It is perhaps not surprising, therefore, that the legitimate economic and political complaints of Third World governments are often disregarded in the North as rock-throwing from people living in glass houses.

The problem with statistics is not a new one. In 1874, Mark Twain noted in *Life on the Mississippi*, that the Lower Mississippi River had shortened itself by 242 miles in the previous 176 years. 'That is an average of a trifle over one mile and a third per year,' he wrote. 'Therefore, any calm person, who is not blind or idiotic, can see that in the Old Oolitic Silurian Period, just a million years ago next November, the Lower Mississippi River was upward of one million, three hundred thousand miles long... There is something fascinating about science. One gets such wholesale returns of conjecture out of such a trifling investment of fact.'

Depending on their perspective and the points they want to make, futurologists tend to over-emphasize some points and neglect others. In the 1960s, for example, those most worried about the 'population explosion' stressed the likelihood of higher rather than lower growth estimates. The prediction of disaster helped reinforce the demand for drastic action.

The Club of Rome's first report, *The Limits to Growth*, published in 1972, contained a variety of doomsday scenarios which showed, depending on the model and timeframe chosen, that a conjunction of unchecked resource depletion, increasing pollution, a finite capacity to produce food, and continued population growth would sooner or later – perhaps as soon as 1990, and probably before 2050 – lead to irreversible global collapse. The report gave substance to the warnings of others, such as U Thant, Secretary General of the UN, who said in 1969 that, 'Members of the United Nations have perhaps ten years left in which to subordinate their ancient quarrels and launch a global partnership to curb the arms race, to improve the human environment, to defuse the population explosion, and to supply the required momentum to development efforts. If such a global partnership is not forged within the next decade, then I very much fear that the problems I have mentioned will have reached such staggering proportions that they will be beyond our capacity to control'.[28]

Because some of what was predicted did not happen, a number of healthy babies were thrown out with the bath water. *The Limits to Growth* suggested, for example, that world mercury resources would be depleted by 1983; tin would be gone by 1985, zinc by 1988, and copper and lead by 1991. It is estimated, however, that known reserves, if used at 1988 consumption rates, will give zinc and tin until 2009, mercury and lead to 2010 and copper until 2029.* Known reserves of natural gas in 1988 were three times higher than they were in 1970.[29]

---

* This is not to deny the problem, nor its geographic specificity. Zambian copper, for example, on which the country's economy is heavily reliant, is not expected to last beyond 2006.

And in more ways than one, the world seemed awash with oil: in 1988 it seemed that there was enough to carry the world through to 2029, but the next year, Saudi Arabia, with 16 per cent of the world's known supply, adjusted its reserve figures upwards by 55 per cent. World food production, although geographically very uneven, has more than defied the worst predictions of the 1960s. World cereal crops, which provide about half the calories in the human diet, increased 88 per cent between 1965 and 1989, and by more than 100 per cent in the South.[30] The world may have been late in acknowledging the effects of pollution, but an array of international agreements, control efforts and research, much of it initiated in the 1980s, is beginning to rectify previous mistakes. It might appear, therefore, at least superficially, that the more optimistic futurologists had been at least partially right after all. American architect, engineer and technology guru, R. Buckminster Fuller, for example, had written in 1967 that 'Humanity's mastery of vast, inanimate, inexhaustible energy sources and the accelerated business of doing more with less of sea, air, and space technology has proven Malthus to be wrong. Comprehensive physical and economic success for humanity may now be accomplished in one-fourth of a century.'[31]

Some of these issues will be dealt with in greater detail in the following chapters. But the truth is that nothing like 'comprehensive physical and economic success for humanity' was achieved in the twenty-five years foreseen by R. Buckminster Fuller. Much was accomplished in providing better health and education. Life expectancy in the South increased by 16 years, and adult literacy rose by 40 per cent. But by the early 1990s, there were a billion people living in absolute poverty. Or, so bad were the measurements, perhaps the number was as high as one and a half billion.

Even the most optimistic projections for the future are bleak. In 1990 Willy Brandt reconvened the members of his commission, adding Gro Harlem Brundtland, Benazir Bhutto, Julius Nyerere and Robert McNamara to the panel. 'The number of the world's poor has continued to increase,' they wrote in their 1991 report.

> Despite sustained growth in the industrialized countries, the 1980s saw a worsening economic environment for developing countries. Increasing protectionism, falling commodity prices, volatile exchange rates and high interest rates are parts of an environment that was shaped outside the influence of the developing countries. This contributed to precipitating the debt crisis, and the ensuing severe reduction in net capital flows that the developing world has experienced. In addition, aid levels have stagnated, at best, during the course of the decade.[32]

The Pearson Commission Report had begun with the words, 'The widening gap between the developed and developing countries has become the central issue of our time'. More than half of the two decades that followed the publication of that report saw unprecedented growth and prosperity in the North, while increasing millions in developing countries moved further into poverty. If, indeed, the widening economic gap between industrialized countries and the Third World had become the central issue of our time, the fact seems – in the West at least – to have gone largely unnoticed.

CHAPTER II

Poverty in the South

We have always known that heedless self-interest was bad morals; we know now that it is bad economics.   Franklin D. Roosevelt

THE OBJECT OF much study over the past three decades, poverty continues to exercise an army of researchers. Study and research notwithstanding, the data base for measuring and analysing poverty remains inadequate and unreliable. The World Bank's 1990 World Development Indicators, for example, contain income distribution figures for only six low-income and 12 lower-middle income countries. The figures are five or ten years out of date, there is no time comparison, and the data, derived from various sources and using different criteria, is not readily comparable.

The World Bank's 1983 report, *Accelerated Development in Sub-Saharan Africa* shows six different estimates of growth in Gross Domestic Product for six Sahelian countries during the 1970s. Estimates for Niger, for example, ranged from a low of 0.9 per cent, to a high of 4.7 per cent. Discrepancies ranged from 23 per cent to 1300 per cent! In Bangladesh there were two different sets of national accounts in the 1980s, one prepared by the Bangladesh Bureau of Statistics, the other by the World Bank. These varied by as much as 20 per cent.[1] In 1982, the Government of India estimated the percentage of its population living below the poverty line at 37 per cent. The World Bank's estimate was 44 per cent, a difference of over 50 million people. By 1989, the divergence between the Government of India and the Bank had risen to 116 million, more than the populations of Britain and France combined.[2] In 1990, the World Bank estimated the worldwide number of those living in absolute poverty at one billion (using 1985 data), while UNDP a year later estimated the number at 1.2 billion, with another billion living close to the edge of desperation.[3]

Part of the problem is an understandable difficulty in gathering accurate data on 'the poor'. A further problem is what Robert Chambers calls 'the misfit between methods and practice of research'. Many academics and evaluators tend to shy away from poorer regions and poorer people; they avoid the difficult seasons, thus missing important seasonality factors. 'An exaggerated impression of well-being can also be given by the averages beloved of researchers.'[4]

Financial, political, administrative and statistical biases contained in many official surveys may further obscure the bottom end of the poverty picture. Anthropologist Polly Hill observes that statistics gatherers are not necessarily professional, knowledgeable people. Many are under-trained, lonely, under-supervised, over-worked, ignorant, bored, under-paid and strangers to the area in which they work. Their data is 'extracted from unwilling informants by resorting to many convolutions, blandishments and deceits, including sheer guesswork... Then, at later stages, the field material is commonly fudged, cooked and manipulated by officials at higher levels, the main purpose being to ensure that the trends will be found satisfactory and convincing by those with still greater authority.'[5]

Another factor contributing to the problem is a general lack of interest among big development agencies in the impact of their work on poverty. Of the interest groups within a donor agency, few have anything to gain from an investigation of the poverty impact of aid projects. This lack of interest in poverty extends to Third World governments as well; few exert any pressure for investigation of the income distribution effects of aid.

Measurements and definitions

Poverty, defined in dictionaries as 'the condition of being without adequate food, money, etc.', is usually regarded as a distinct condition: one is either poor or one is not. Attempts to measure poverty, however, and to define the 'poverty line' – the line which divides the poor from the non-poor, have engaged economists and planners for more than a century.

The household is often used as the basis for data collection, although this method has its drawbacks. Households of different sizes are not differentiated. Per capita consumption in a large household would differ from that of a small household; thus a low income household need not necessarily be poor. It may simply be small. Differences in consumption patterns between adults, children and the elderly are similarly ignored. Women often eat last, and least. This sometimes severe gender bias in consumption patterns is also obscured in household data. When derived from household data, per capita income levels present difficulties similar to those of household consumption indicators. In addition, variations in seasonal and annual incomes, especially for rural areas, are difficult to capture in such statistics, as is income from informal and sporadic sources. Income in one area of a country may buy a very different level of goods from that in another.

Calorie intake has become a common method of measuring

poverty: the absolute poor are sometimes defined as those consuming less than 2250 calories per day. When measured on a household basis, however, this technique has the same drawbacks as other household surveys. Data requirements are high and the objectivity of calorie-based definitions has been challenged. Calorie requirements will vary with age and occupation, may be generally lower in warmer climates, but are higher for pregnant women, lactating mothers and those suffering from infections and parasites. The FAO has attempted to overcome this weakness by calculating an average 'basic metabolic rate' – the energy expended for the function of human organs when a person is in a state of absolute rest.[6] Indicators of health and nutritional status to determine the incidence of stunting and wasting have proven useful in determining the effects of poverty on children. UNICEF, for example, promotes the 'Under Five Mortality Rate' as the most important indicator of the state of a nation's children.

Location and concomitant factors such as climate, soil condition and ethnic or religious make-up will also affect the poverty profile. In the Ivory Coast, for example, poverty in the West Forest is, in absolute terms, a quarter of what it is in the savannah and the East Forest. In the savannah, where a large percentage of expenditure is devoted to food, non-food consumption indicators show, erroneously, that people there are better off.[7] The same phenomenon holds true elsewhere, most glaringly in the part of India known as the 'poverty square' – eastern Uttar Pradesh, Bihar, Madhya Pradesh and the neighbouring parts of other states.

Although the use of per capita GNP figures to compare the relative well-being of countries has been widely criticized, and a range of complementary comparative 'development indicators' created, per capita GNP has remained remarkably resiliant as the primary measure of comparison. But GNP figures simply do not reveal much about the poor; for example in a hypothetical country of ten people, in which five receive an income of $100 per annum and five receive $10 000, the average annual income would exceed $5000.

A special distinction must also be drawn between the poor and the poorest 10 to 20 per cent who, in places such as India, Bangladesh and the Sahel, have considerably different problems and behaviour than the further 25 to 35 per cent who fall below the 2250–calorie line.[8] The ultra-poor, for example, devote virtually all increases in income to food; other poor people do not. The ultra-poor are much more prone than others to illness, functional impairment, medical risk and inadequate mental and physical performance. These problems make them less able to work and more prone to employment instability. If they are to be assisted, the ultra-poor cannot be lumped into the general category of 'absolute poverty'.

22

A major difficulty with most measurements is that they are concerned with the *incidence* of poverty, but provide little information on the flow of people into or out of poverty. In addition, there is more to poverty than levels of income and consumption. As important are questions of power, status, recognition, freedom of choice, degree of participation and self-esteem. Given the complexity and the many dimensions of poverty, however, the tendency to over-simplify is perhaps understandable. According to Robert Chambers, 'Planners and politicians need measures to tell them how well (or badly) they and the economy are doing in their attempts to reduce deprivation... This makes it all the easier to ignore complex realities and concentrate on single numbers.'[9]

Chambers expands the discussion by dividing deprivation into five dimensions or conditions: poverty proper (lack of income and assets); physical weakness (under-nutrition, sickness, disability, lack of strength); isolation (ignorance, illiteracy, lack of access to government services, remote location); vulnerability (to contingencies, to becoming poorer); and powerlessness:

> To varying degrees these are tackled by government programmes, but vulnerability and powerlessness are neglected compared with the rest... Members of elites find physical weakness, isolation and poverty more acceptable and less threatening aspects of deprivation to tackle. They also appear more measurable than vulnerability and powerlessness which are less tangible, and more social and political. So there is a convergence between elite interests in limiting interventions to physical aspects of deprivation, and professional interests in measurability. Together they conspire to concentrate planning, programmes, policy and debate on physical weakness, isolation and poverty, and to neglect vulnerability and powerlessness. Not surprisingly, normal professional and elite paradigms of deprivation are predominantly physical.[10]

In 1990, the United Nations Development Programme (UNDP) took some preliminary steps to correct the information problem in its first Human Development Report. It contained what UNDP called a 'human development index' (HDI) which combined national income statistics with adult literacy and life expectancy to provide a more comprehensive overview of longevity, knowledge and living standards.[11] This changed the picture presented by the GNP figures alone, which had positioned Switzerland, Japan, Norway, the United States and Sweden in the top five rank, in that order. The new figures placed Japan, Canada, Iceland, Sweden and Switzerland in the top rank. Somewhat surprisingly, several developing countries, including Barbados, Cyprus, Uruguay and South Korea, did as well as European countries like Portugal, the Soviet Union and Hungary.

When adjustments were made to the Human Development Index

in 1991 for gender-related issues such as female literacy and mortality, the ratings changed again, in some cases dramatically. Japan fell to seventeenth place, while Finland, Sweden, Denmark, France and Norway moved into the top five. A further calculation was made to determine *progress* on the human development indicators over time. It was found that some countries – Niger, Mali, the former Yemen Arab Republic – had tripled their HDIs between 1970 and 1985, while in others, such as Burkina Faso, Senegal and Afghanistan, they had doubled. Obviously, those countries near the bottom might make significant progress in percentage terms and still remain low, but even those with higher starting points, such as Mexico, Colombia and Chile achieved increases of 20 per cent or more. Cast a different way, to show relative wealth – the distribution of income – Japan again rises to the top, followed by the Netherlands, Sweden, Switzerland and Norway.

The UNDP figures also attempted to incorporate factors relating to human freedom, outlining 40 basic rights (freedom of association, the press, courts) and freedom *from* such things as forced child labour, unlawful detention, and torture. In a preliminary study of 89 countries, the report found that only 18 achieved a 75 per cent rating or better, and that in 38, only one quarter of the basic freedoms existed.

Poverty: a profile

The reality of poverty cannot be captured in statistical household surveys or bizarre calculations of 'the energy expended for the function of human organs when a person is in a state of absolute rest'. The poor are real people, with real ideas, fears, needs and real hopes for their children, if not themselves. Many find themselves in poverty because sustained drought or ecological degradation has wiped out their animals or damaged the land improvement of generations. Women – abandoned, widowed, divorced – and other people impoverished by events, may have moved onto land that is marginal, or even dangerous, in terms of soil, weather and ecological conditions. Isolated households in both rural and urban areas are the last to benefit from the flow of goods and services, and the first to suffer when they are diminished. The poor face each day and each new problem in poor health, with few resources, little education and limited knowledge.

It is estimated that two-thirds of the rural population of Africa and one third of the urban population remain below the level of absolute poverty. Infant mortality rates averaged 104 per thousand in 1985, compared with 71 per thousand for the Third World as a whole and only 8 for OECD member countries. Child death rates were twice as high as those for all developing countries. 65 per cent of the urban population and 26 per cent of the rural had access to safe water, compared with 75 per cent and 42 per cent respectively for all developing countries. Life expectancy was almost 20 per cent lower in the region than for the Third World as a whole.

Asia withstood the economic downturn of the late 1970s and early 1980s better than other regions, and some countries maintained reasonable and even impressive growth rates. In East and South East Asia population growth declined and there has been a steady increase in per capita incomes, with concomitant decreases in poverty. Nevertheless, Asia contains half the world's population, and 75 per cent of all Asians live in China and India, countries with low per capita incomes. There is growing landlessness, and an estimated 500 million people in the region live below the poverty line, mainly in India, Bangladesh, Pakistan, Indonesia, Burma, Nepal and Sri Lanka.

Although Latin America is the wealthiest Southern region in terms of per capita GNP, estimates of those living in absolute poverty range from 20 per cent to 40 per cent. Many Latin American countries have suffered the ravages of hyper-inflation. During the early 1980s, for example, Bolivian inflation reached 40 000 per cent a year. As in Asia, the broad statistics conceal national and regional variations. Generally, there have been increases in urbanization and in the incidence of landlessness. Real per capita GDP has fallen, while per capita food consumption in the region as a whole has declined. The rural poor have been especially hard hit by a drastic decline in public sector resources.

There are serious problems involved in estimating the number and incidence of rural people in absolute poverty. The rural poor are not a homogeneous group. They include tenants, sharecroppers, landless labourers, artisanal fishermen and other vulnerable groups, among whom there are wide gradations of income. Income levels, however, give little indication of how the income is spent – whether on food, clothing or social obligations such as weddings or funerals. People's priorities and strategies for survival change, depending on their economic proximity to desperation.

The positive correlation between land – or security of land tenure – and income, though not perfect, has been well documented. Because it is calculated in different ways, the definition of landlessness affects the estimation of numbers. The term may mean hired agricultural labourers who do not rent or sharecrop; it is sometimes used to describe those occupying an amount of land too small to sustain a household, and implies those without significant off-farm assets. It is estimated, however, that 10 per cent of Indian households are *totally* landless, and that the number in Bangladesh is probably in the vicinity of 30 per cent and rising. If estimates of those living on 'wasteland' and small homesteads were included in these figures, the number of functionally landless would be significantly higher. Estimates of the total landless population of the South, excluding China, place the total at 13 per cent of all rural households, with a further 60 per cent owning too little land to maintain a subsistence living.[12]

IFAD estimated that in 1970, 1.95 million rural Ghanaians were below the poverty line. By 1984, the figure had risen to 6.4 million. 1984 was a particularly bad year for Ghana, following a severe drought, a drop in commodity prices and a massive repatriation of people from Nigeria. However in 1986, when the economy had adjusted to some of the shocks, the number of rural poor stood at 3.8 million. This figure represented a 95 per cent increase over the previous 15 years, and accounted for 54 per cent of Ghana's farm population.[13]

In virtually every country there are more women than men at the lowest levels of income, and generally, households headed by women are among the poorest in society. 'Households headed by women' is a common but misleading term. What it usually means is that the male who is normally designated as head of the household in most surveys has died, deserted or migrated in order to find work. Female-headed households are poorer than the others because there are fewer income earners (in male-headed households, women often add to family income). It is also true because women are often employed in work that yields low economic returns. The number of rural households headed by women, particularly in Africa, the Caribbean and Latin America, is increasing. In countries such as Kenya, Botswana and Zambia, a third to one half of the households may be headed by women at any given time.

Poverty imposes a particularly heavy burden on rural women because of their dual role in the economy – both inside and outside the home. An often overlooked feature of Third World agrarian systems, particularly in Africa and Asia, is the crucial role played by women in agricultural production. In much of Africa, where subsistence farming predominates, most tasks associated with subsistence food production and processing are performed by women.

Not all households headed by women are poor, but among the majority that are, poverty is often inter-generational, passing from mother to daughter. Women are usually less well educated, have fewer employment opportunities and receive lower wages than men, even where they do similar types of work. They have less access to land, capital and technology, all of which diminishes the efficiency of their production, both in the home and outside. Most development programmes, however, aim at improving the productivity of the male worker; men are usually given access to credit and are taught modern methods of production, while women continue to rely on traditional methods. Consequently differences in labour productivity between men and women continue to widen. In times of economic adversity, women's participation in the formal and informal labour markets increases, although their income levels, compared with those of men, remain low. The majority of refugees, worldwide, are women and children.

The multiplier effect of women's poverty is well known: the children of poorer women, for example, are nutritionally less well off than those of women who earn an adequate income.[14] There is increasing acknowledgement of rural women as primary producers, recognition of the obvious links between the food crisis and the marginalization of women, and of the negative impact of excluding rural women from the benefits of technological advancement. Nevertheless, progress in achieving quantitative and qualitative improvements in the status of women remains slow and inadequate.

In most Third World countries, children – especially those in the poorest families – assume a wide range of responsibilities before adulthood. For them, absolute poverty is compounded by an unequal distribution of even the least scarce resources. Because of their greater need, poverty places children – particularly young children – at far greater risk than adults. Basically, children are the victims of adults. They are unable to protect themselves from abuse, or to change the conditions in which they live. They are weaker and more vulnerable than adults, and their plight is clearly the responsibility of adults. Their rights, their problems, and the solutions to their problems lie entirely in the hands of adults.

Beginning with its 1987 'State of the World's Children' report, UNICEF has provided – in its 'Under Five Mortality Rate' – an indication of development based on the welfare, rather than the economic performance, of a large part of the population. The result is a complex picture with two significant features: first, there have been dramatic improvements in the general condition of life in most Third World countries over the past three decades; secondly, millions of children continue to live and die in appalling conditions. And in many cases, the positive trends of past years are being reversed by worsening economic conditions and the techniques chosen to deal with them. An estimated 15 million infants and children die each year, 5 million of them between birth and the age of four.[15] Although death rates are generally declining, birth rates remain high, which means that the number of children is high and growing quickly. It is estimated that of all children under 16, about one third, or over 500 million are living in absolute poverty.[16]

There is a direct correlation between child mortality and high fertility. Where child death is a common feature, parents generally expect to have more children. Thus, poverty and high rates of population growth reinforce one another. Historical trends show that population growth rates decline naturally with development, but for many countries the luxury of time no longer exists. Population growth eats directly into economic improvements, in many cases simply negating them.

It is possible to project the size of a country's eventual stable population using current trends or projections in birth rates. In Bangladesh, for example, it is calculated that the population will rise from 109 million in 1988 to 346 million before it stabilizes. Kenya's population, growing at 3.8 per cent each year, will grow from 22 million in 1988 to 62 million by 2025, and will stabilize at 113 million later in the century. Although the figures are only hypothetical, the trends are not, and the human catastrophe they imply is genuine. Of the 40 low-income countries for which comparative data is available, population growth rates actually *rose* in 34 between the period 1965–80 and 1980–8.[17] More must obviously be done to slow or reverse growth rates, and there are concrete examples of what is possible. Growth rates in India, for example, showed a slight decline between 1965 and 1988. But Japan and China offer more dramatic examples. Between 1949 and 1956, the Japanese population growth rate dropped from 2.2 per cent to 1.0 per cent, and Japan today has already reached its hypothetical stable population size. In the 1970s, China saw its economic development threatened by a population growth rate of 2.6 per cent, and within a decade, through programmes of incentives, disincentives, improved health and education, and access for parents to family planning services, the rate dropped by half.

A major issue in the alleviation of rural poverty is the question of environmental sustainability. Rural poverty and environmental degradation are closely linked. Traditionally, the technologies and farming practices of rural people have often protected and sustained fragile local environments. But pressures of population and changing priorities can make major inroads on tradition. Simply put, poverty contributes to the depletion of natural resources, which in turn exacerbates the suffering of the rural poor.

Environmental degradation is manifested in many ways. The search for fuelwood, overgrazing, inappropriate land use, changes in crops and cropping patterns, and population growth have all put serious additional pressures on the land, pressures which lead to erosion, desertification and a depletion of nutrients in the soil. Localized pressures are reinforced by commercial pressures. Large-scale ranching in Botswana, clearance of the rainforests in West

28

Africa and Brazil, commercial logging in Indonesia, Thailand and the Philippines have all led to serious, and in some cases irreversible, changes in rural and national environments. Environmental degradation in the Himalayas is thought to be a factor in the devastating and unprecedented floods that have taken place in Bangladesh in recent years.[18]

Some of the causes of, and solutions to, environmental problems are economic, social or technological; others are political and institutional. For example, in many countries, security of land tenure is a critical element in the willingness of small landholders to change practices that are generations old, to take risks or to make long-term commitments. The basic challenge for the future is not only to halt further degradation, but to restore and improve the productive capacity of the environment so that small farmers can meet the food requirements of growing populations.

Urban poverty

The statistics on Third World urbanization and misery are as shocking as they are dramatic. The urban population of the South grew from 286 million in 1950 to 1.1 billion in 1985, expanding at a rate double that of the total population. Pushed off the land by rural poverty, drawn by the lure of better income, the urban poor live in squalid slums, two thirds of them as squatters, without clean water, access to sewage facilities, medical attention or schools. Many of the slums in which they live are provided with no services whatsoever, and many are regularly razed in the hope that this will discourage more people from coming. It does not. The urban population of the Third World grows each year by 45 million. Between the mid-1980s and the turn of the century, another *billion* people, representing two thirds of the total Third World increase, will have to be accommodated in cities.

In the poorest countries as much as half the urban population lives in absolute poverty; in India the number is about 40 per cent, and in 'lower middle income' countries such as Morocco and the Philippines, it is as high as 30 per cent.[19] While Asia has some of the world's largest cities, the rate of urbanization is generally low. In Africa, however, the urban population, at 23 per cent of the total by the late 1980s, is expected to reach almost 50 per cent by the end of the century. In Latin America, two thirds of the population already live in cities. Many of today's squalid Southern slums echo Hobsbawm's comment on British cities of the 19th century: 'The city was a volcano, to whose rumblings the rich and powerful listened with fear, and whose eruptions they dreaded.'[20]

The correlation between human misery and economic stagnation is abundantly clear: cities with inadequate infrastructure create bottlenecks for economic expansion. Longer travel time from home to workplace, inadequate or costly transport of goods, uncertain delivery of raw materials, inadequate education, child care and health services, environmental decay, and water and power shortages all reduce productivity.

Caution must be used in interpreting the figures, however. Michael Lipton argues that,

> The rural sector contains most of the poverty, and most of the low-cost sources of potential advance; but the urban sector contains most of the articulateness, organization and power. So the urban classes have been able to 'win' most of the rounds of the struggle with the countryside; but in so doing, they have made the development process needlessly slow and unfair. Scarce land, which might grow millets and beansprouts for the hungry villagers, instead produces a trickle of costly calories from meat and milk, which few except the urban rich (who have ample protein anyway) can afford. Scarce investment, instead of going into water pumps to grow rice, is wasted on urban motorways... Resource allocations, within the city and the village, as well as between them, reflect urban priorities rather than equity or efficiency.[21]

Lipton further argues that there is an 'optical illusion' in urban migration. Many of the newcomers, he says, are 'turnover migrants': in some countries as many as 10 to 30 per cent of rural males between the ages of 15 and 30 will spend 10 years or more in the cities, working and saving, before returning home. Some of the apparent rapid expansion can also be accounted for by the growth of metropolitan areas to take in rural populations; and some by the reclassification of towns as they cross the line which distinguishes rural from urban. These phenomena, combined with a need to justify disproportionate government and donor spending in urban areas may account for a variety of doubtful statistics. For example the population of Dhaka, which stood at 800 000 in 1970, was estimated at something between five and seven million in 1990.

A World Bank study shows that the incidence of 'ultra poverty' – the poorest 10 to 20 per cent in, for example, India, Bangladesh and the Sahel – is much higher in rural areas than in cities. UNICEF studies show that city dwellers have much better access to safe drinking water than most rural families and that a sick person in rural areas is two to six times less likely to receive medical attention than a city dweller.[22] The figures, of course, conceal the fact that urban slum dwellers may have little real access to doctors. They also conceal the fact that most 'rural' doctors are based in provincial towns rather than villages.

The impact of urban problems affects the urban poor dispropor-
tionately, but it can be argued that it doesn't damage them nearly so
much as the villages they come from; migrants are usually the better
off, the more educated, the more mobile. When they move, the
villages lose in two ways. They lose the skills and energy that depart
with the migrants, and the arrival of these people in the city reinforces
the existing bias towards urban dwellers. Lipton argues that 'over-
urbanization' fosters an output structure that is costly in building and
industry, employs ever fewer people, and mainly benefits the already
well-off. It survives largely on arbitrary price and investment advantages created by government. The remedy, he argues, is not to seek
ways to restrict migration or limit the rewards of urban living to
those already there, but 'to remove the arbitrarily assigned advantages
that render urbanization artificially attractive: to neutralize the
pricing, investment, educational, medical and other policies that are
currently transferring income from villages to the towns, and encouraging the ablest villagers to follow.'[23]

The future

Taking Mark Twain's prediction about the length of the Mississippi
River into account, what are we to make of projections regarding
Third World poverty through the last decade of the century? In 1990,
the World Bank projected a decline in absolute poverty from a
billion, to approximately 700 million people by the turn of the
century.[24] Given an anticipated population growth of one billion
during the decade, this projection indicates remarkable improvement
in both real and relative terms. The Bank's projection, however, is
based on strategies very similar to those recommended by the
Pearson and Brandt Commissions (and generally ignored by both
Northern and Southern governments), and on growth projections
that are both optimistic and misleading.

The Bank's recommended strategy includes 'efficient, labour-
intensive growth based on appropriate market incentives, physical
infrastructure, institutions and technological innovation', and 'adequate provision of social services, including primary education, basic
health care, and family planning services'.[25] The Bank's projections
are based on an assumption of growth in industrialized countries of
three per cent per annum and a similar growth in real aid flows. It was
projected that interest rates would fall and commodity prices would
rise. There would be a successful conclusion of the Uruguay Round
of GATT trade talks, economic reform would continue in China, and
India would maintain its growth momentum.

The writers must have been late for a very important date when

31

they made their projections in 1990. Those relating to growth, technology and social services will be addressed in subsequent chapters. But to project a decade of growth in industrialized countries, many already entering a serious recession, was, of course, speculative at best. A year later, in its 1991 World Development Report, the Bank had revised its estimate of industrial country growth downward by almost 17 per cent, from 3 per cent to 2.5 per cent for the decade. Real GDP growth in developing countries declined from 4.7 per cent in 1988 to 2.2 per cent in 1990, the lowest in a decade.[26] The hope for an early increase in aid flows, pinned to a certain extent on the vague idea of a post-Cold War 'peace dividend', was already being dissipated on support for eastern Europe, and would soon run afoul of Iraq's adventure in Kuwait.

If, indeed, the rate of growth in India, where half the world's poor live, is important to poverty reduction, then the projection was at least partially invalidated before the ink was dry. During the 1980s, India's growth rate was 5 per cent, and in 1988–9 it rose to a remarkable 9 per cent. But much of it was accomplished at the cost of bigger budget deficits and increased borrowing. From $19 billion in 1980, foreign debt rose to $70 billion in 1991, and the debt service ratio tripled. Political instability, double-digit inflation, high interest rates, heavy tax increases and a scarcity of foreign credit combined to produce a profound deterioration in the economy, unparallelled in a generation. In 1990, the Bank's estimate of India's population in 2025 was 1.35 billion, but only 12 months later the United Nations Fund for Population Activities projected a figure that was 92 million people higher.[27]

Although there was no reason in 1990, when the Bank made its projections, to think that some Third World commodity prices would not rise, there was no particular reason to think they would not fall again either, just as badly as ever. The real promise, in the absence of the international stabilization measures recommended by Pearson, Brandt, UNCTAD and others, was one of constant fluctuation and instability. There was, in fact, a strong perception in the North, voiced by Peter Drucker, that 'the primary products economy has come 'uncoupled' from the industrial economy ... primary products are becoming of marginal importance to the economies of the developed world'.[28]

A year after the World Bank's projection of a decline in poverty from 1 billion to 700 million during the 1990s, UNDP projected a *growth* from 1.2 billion to 1.3 billion. Regardless of the projections, the prognosis on poverty is not good, certainly not good enough to justify continuing along the same gradualist path that has guided governments and aid agencies for the past three decades. For a large portion of the world's population the question is not so much one of development, as of rescue. It is not so much a question of reducing poverty, as of attempting to halt its spread. To continue business as usual, combined with band-aids and short-term emergency measures is to condemn millions of children to an early grave, and increasing numbers of adults to stunted lives of permanent misery.

Schumacher acknowledged that poverty had existed from time immemorial. 'But,' he wrote, 'miserable and destitute villagers in their thousands and urban pavement dwellers in their hundreds of thousands – not in wartime or as an aftermath of war, but in the midst of peace and as a seemingly permanent feature – that is a monstrous and scandalous thing which is altogether abnormal in the history of mankind.'[29]

CHAPTER III

The best of the West; thinking big

Growth, like a rising tide, will float all boats.   John F. Kennedy

DESPITE OCCASIONAL DIVERSIONS, conventional economic theory of development since the Second World War has been dominated by the concept of growth. It posits that there is a stage in a country's history during which the required conditions for sustained and fairly rapid growth must be consolidated, following which, such growth is more or less assured.[1] Growth rates depend upon the level and efficiency of capital investment in physical infrastructure and the industrial sector. More investment in more productive sectors will create higher growth and speed the development process. Aid can help to consolidate growth and accelerate the development process by filling gaps, raising investment levels and increasing absorptive capacity. Because technology is such an important part of the growth process, aid can be of invaluable assistance in the transfer of technology from the North to the South.

The sorcerer's apprentice

In the old German tale, an apprentice learns the sorcerer's arts, but cannot control the consequences of the spells he casts. In 1969, the Pearson Commission Report, though still uncritically equating development with growth, admitted uncertainty as to what actually promoted growth. 'The growth process is still mysterious, and no decision-maker can be absolutely certain that any of the effects of any particular change in policy such as devaluation, import liberalization, export subsidy, land reform, or labour-intensive rural programmes will produce precisely the effects planned.'[2]

The 'trickle down' theory held that general economic growth would trickle down to the masses in the form of jobs and opportunities, along with better distribution of other benefits of growth. The theory remained credible until the mid-1970s, when research began to demonstrate that economic growth by itself was no guarantee of a reduction in poverty. While growth had been accompanied by improved equity and poverty reduction in some countries – Malaysia and Indonesia, for example – in others, such as Brazil and Pakistan, it had not. When it became evident that the trickle down approach was not reaching the poorest well enough or fast enough, two responses emerged. The first, in the early 1970s, led to greater direct focusing of aid projects and programmes on the poor, through a basic needs approach and integrated rural development projects (IRDPs).

Proponents of this approach held that growth was not a sufficient condition for reducing absolute poverty, and that particular initiatives were required to address the special needs of the poor with respect to education, primary health care, better nutrition and access to safe water. They also argued that poverty-oriented development initiatives were sound economics. Poor farmers are highly responsive; the poor are a resource, and without an educated and healthy labour force, economic progress is impossible.

The limited success of this approach, however, combined with the oil crises of the 1970s and recession in the early 1980s, led to the emergence of a second response, which was essentially a restatement of aggregate growth theories, with new emphasis placed on structural adjustment. With many Third World countries in a state of economic near-collapse, the question became one of restructuring economies so that self-sustaining development would occur.

The debate between those who advocate 'wealth creation' and those who stress 'redistribution' is characterized in much development writing as though the two ideas were mutually exclusive. Social injustices that lead to extremes in the distribution of wealth should, arguably, be altered or removed; but this is not to imply a halt to the creation of wealth. Similarly, the creation of wealth does not have to mean the concomitant creation of workhouses and debtors' prisons. In much current literature, however, strategies for growth and equity continue to be juxtaposed, as though there were always trade-offs to be made in opting for one over the other. Reviewing the relationship between economic growth and poverty alleviation, a major 1988 World Bank Task Force concluded:

Long term aggregate growth, while necessary, is not sufficient for the alleviation of absolute poverty at the desired speed. Benefits of national growth do not always accrue to those who are below the poverty line. In many instances, the poor do not possess the physical and human assets which would bring them higher returns... This helps explain why the number of people living in absolute poverty has increased in low-income countries even while respectable growth rates were achieved over the past three decades... Areas of complementarity between the twin objectives of efficient economic growth and the alleviation of poverty exceed those areas involving serious trade-offs. Pursuit of both objectives is therefore possible, indeed essential to lasting, stable and humane development.[3]

35

Although it is now widely accepted that growth-oriented strategies must be supplemented by clearly defined poverty alleviation efforts, the greater emphasis in most development spending remains on growth.

The 1987 Brundtland Report observed that sustainable development requires more than growth; it requires a change in the *content* of growth, making it less dependent on energy and making it more cognizant of the capital stock on which it depends. The Report used the example of income from forestry operations. Only the value of timber extracted and the cost of extracting it are measured in national accounts. The cost of regeneration, or the losses accruing from non-regeneration are ignored. Depreciation, commonly calculated in national accounts, is not extended to minerals, timber, oil, gas and other natural resources. Countries dependent on natural resources are, therefore, in effect, mortgaging the future in order to pay for today's growth statistics. The Brundtland Report concluded that 'in all countries, rich or poor, economic development must take full account in its measurements of growth of the improvement or deterioration in the stock of natural resources.'[4]

The Washington-based World Resources Institute has taken the process a step further in a calculation of what such an approach would mean in Indonesia. Often cited as a developmental success story, between 1971 and 1984, Indonesia's Gross Domestic Product grew at an annual rate of 7.1 per cent, higher than that of most OECD member countries. However, by subtracting estimates of net natural resource depreciation in only three sectors – oil, timber and soils – the study brings the growth rate down to 4 per cent, a level more consistent with that of other Third World countries.[5]

If other factors had been taken into consideration, such as the future effect on agricultural potential of soil erosion, the figures would have been reduced even further. In Indonesia, the erosion of hillsides on Java, Bali and Madura averages 54 metric tons per hectare each year, a problem far from exclusive to Indonesia or the Third World. In the United States in the 1980s, the government converted 13 million hectares of farmland to woodland and grassland before it became wasteland, such was the rate of topsoil loss.[6] In such instances, the cost in lost production is a calculation that is not difficult to make. Similar calculations could be made with regard to lowering of water tables, and for pollution, such as acid rain, which eats into the income of future generations.

Infrastructural development

All countries trade. All countries import things they do not produce, and export commodities and products for which there is an external demand. For the South, especially for the majority of countries without oil, the terms of trade have deteriorated steadily over thirty years while access to Northern markets has been systematically blocked. Many countries concentrated on import-substitution by placing high tariffs on imports in order to encourage the development of local production. But those countries which embarked on aggressive import-substitution policies usually found that extended protection for local production, especially where imported raw materials were required to sustain an industry, led to inefficiencies, inflation, and in extreme cases to economic collapse.

Northern commercial bank lending for investment all but disappeared with the debt crisis of the 1980s, while structural adjustment lending and IMF stabilization programmes became increasingly conditional on opening economies to more, rather than fewer, competitive forces. Third World countries were urged, therefore, to exploit their comparative advantages, instead of investing in risky new areas. As Chapter I showed, however, efforts to exploit the most competitive Third World advantage, cheap labour, has resulted in an effective Northern blockade against Southern manufactures, most notably textiles.

Many countries have exploited cheap labour in another way, by taxing agricultural production. Because revenue for public spending is low in countries where the tax base is small, this makes sense at one level. Inevitably, however, high agricultural taxes simply discriminate against the producer, ultimately reducing production. Great emphasis has therefore been placed on internal growth-oriented policies and programmes, and on efforts to increase production for internal consumption, particularly in agriculture. Having failed to achieve anything like a world trading system to match its rhetoric in GATT or UNCTAD, the North – in the form of bilateral and multilateral aid agencies – joined this battle for growth and development in the fields and cities of the Third World.

Infrastructural development in many parts of the South predates ancient Greece and Rome by centuries, and has continued up to the present day. It has been an especially intense area of endeavour, however, since aid agencies first arrived in the South. Irrigation, roads, railways, communication facilities, schools and hospitals have all been seen as essential precursors to, or components of, growth and development. There are myriad studies to show that, as a generic approach, infrastructural improvement is important to development, and few would dispute the contention. A study of 58 countries over the period 1969–78 found that a 1 per cent increase in irrigation, for example, was associated with an aggregate increase in crop output of 1.6 per cent.[7] A Bangladeshi study showed that households in villages benefitting from public infrastructure – roads, schools, banks, electricity – had significantly improved income from better crop production and more wage labour than villages which had not been exposed to the new services.[8] The deterioration of the Ghanaian road network during the 1970s had profound effects on the overall economy: journeys took three times longer than necessary, at a significant additional cost in fuel. Bad roads caused more frequent vehicle breakdown and write-off. Shortage of vehicles made distribution of food and agricultural inputs such as seed and fertilizer difficult or impossible. Lack of transportation to move cocoa to the port meant that exports, and therefore foreign exchange, declined. Roads were the dog that chased the cat, that ate the rat, that killed the mouse that lived in the house that Jack built.

The levels of investment, efficiency, and technology behind any infrastructural development are critical to its success and, like the measurement of growth, to the all-important question of *who* actually benefits from it. The Bangladesh transport sector is an example of infrastructural development that has consistently avoided dealing with these questions.

At the time of Partition in 1947, Bangladesh – then East Pakistan – had only 287 miles of paved road, mostly in towns and cities. An urgent programme of road and bridge building was undertaken, and by 1970, the network of paved roads had increased to 2000 miles. Damage during the War of Liberation, however, was enormous: 270 road and rail bridges were destroyed or damaged; rail and rolling stock were destroyed, river routes and port facilities were blocked or wrecked. Logically, the transport sector became a focus for the large aid efforts which followed the independence of Bangladesh in 1971.[9]

By 1974, most of the damage had been repaired, but investment in the transport sector continued to grow. Because of the alluvial soil, the vast number of rivers and the annual threat of floods, road building in Bangladesh is enormously expensive – 60 per cent higher, for example, than in India. During the 1970s the transport sector absorbed 17 per cent of public expenditure, and by 1980 it was estimated that ongoing and planned road construction would occupy the country's construction industry fully, until the end of the century. The highly inefficient railway sector had by 1980 become, in the words of one study, 'a millstone around the government's fragile financial neck'. The World Bank warned strongly against any fleet expansion and recommended 'drastic action'. Nevertheless, road construction, railway fleet expansion, the importation of cars, trucks and buses, and the establishment and growth of an international airline continued apace, much of it funded through general balance of payments support made available by international donor agencies –

30 per cent of it through blue-ribbon bilateral aid programmes.[10] Canadian aid to the railways – largely in the form of locomotives and rolling stock – was, in the early 1990s, Canada's largest aid project anywhere.

Considering how most Bangladeshis relate to transportation, the situation was ludicrous. In 1986, nearly 94 per cent of all commercially operated vehicles and boats in Bangladesh were non-motorized. There were four times more rickshaws than all motorized vehicles and boats combined, and for every motorized vessel, there were 100 traditional wooden 'country boats'. These country boats provided 60 per cent of the employment in transport, and the combined carrying capacity of country boats, rickshaws and bullock carts was double that of the mechanized sector. The reason was simple: 70 per cent of Bangladesh's villages are between five and ten miles from access to any form of motorized transport.

This is not to suggest that roads and railways should be ignored; rather it is to point out the overwhelming indifference of government and aid agencies to the importance of the non-mechanized sector. As one study points out, in their approach to the transport sector, government and aid agencies 'effectively exclude 95 per cent of all vehicles and craft ... [which] account for 80 per cent of all employment in a country beset by chronic and worsening unemployment, and account for 75 per cent of the value-added by transport operations'.[11] In other words, the transportation needs of the poor are more or less ignored. Of all projects in transportation, government-funded or otherwise during the mid 1980s, only one out of 334, representing 0.004 per cent of all public investment in the transport sector, had anything to do with non-motorized transport.

The dam busters

Massive dam projects are another form of infrastructure development. With varying emphases on irrigation, flood control and power generation, they have captured the imagination of planners and absorbed great amounts of development spending over the past forty years. Dams offer poor countries a one-off technological solution to some of the most intractable of development problems. Results, however, have been very mixed in most cases, and disastrous in many. Egypt's Aswan High Dam, inaugurated in 1970, had all the usual objectives of a large dam project: power generation, irrigation and flood control. It improved the lives of many poor Egyptians, but the side effects that came with it had not been anticipated: pollution of drinking water because of increased requirements for fertilizer, destruction of the country's sardine industry because of disruption to the aquatic food chain in the Nile Delta, the spread of bilharzia.

The Akosombo Dam in Ghana, completed in 1972, has rarely functioned to projected capacity and created a wide range of ecological and human problems in the catchment area. Worse, however, were the downstream effects. In the two decades after the dam's commissioning, a growing swath of beach in neighbouring Togo has disappeared, damaging roads, port facilities, fishing villages and threatening Lake Togo, an important wildlife habitat and source of human drinking water. The Kainji Dam in Nigeria halved fishing and dry season harvests from traditional floodplain agriculture.[12] Perhaps the most extreme case of growth-oriented dam projects are those that have reduced the flow of the rivers feeding into the Soviet Union's Aral Sea to a trickle. Once the world's fourth largest freshwater lake, the Aral sea has shrunk more than 40 per cent since 1960, becoming a polluted, saline disaster area. Its once vibrant fishing industry has disappeared.[13]

Fifty years of large dam building in India has also produced mediocre financial and agricultural results. Instead of projected yields of four to five tons per hectare, serviced areas rarely produce more than two.[14] In an international study of forty large dam projects, the Inter-American Development Bank found that only one, the Koussou Dam in the Ivory Coast, had met with a measure of success. At the cost of displacing 100 000 people, the Koussou Dam, however, was not expected to achieve more than 30 per cent capacity.[15]

The massive environmental damage done by the Itaipu Dam on the Parana River between Brazil and Paraguay and by the gigantic Mahaveli scheme in Sri Lanka, funded by Germany, Canada, Britain and the United States, can hardly be calculated. In human terms, 50 000 people in the former were forcibly relocated, many without adequate compensation. In Sri Lanka, the combined resettlement and new settlement projections exceeded a million people, and in the mid-1980s became a destabilizing factor that contributed to the country's devastating civil war. Between 1979 and 1985, 40 World Bank-financed projects for agriculture and hydro-electric power development resulted in the forced resettlement of 600 000 people in 27 countries, with devastating consequences for their health and livelihoods.[16] It should be pointed out that many of these projects, if not most, were conceived and requested by Southern governments, not the development agencies and lending institutions. This does not, however, absolve banks and donors from complicity, especially when the technology, the expertise and the final decision in almost all cases lay in the North, rather than the South.

With each new dam proposal, planners and builders assure an

increasingly critical environmental movement that lessons have been learned and that past mistakes and miscalculations will be avoided. Public skepticism is well placed, however. Quebec's $70 billion investment in two James Bay hydro-electric projects had a number of unforseen by-products. One was the release of methyl mercury from the ground into the waterways. Fish, the staple food of the Cree and Inuit who live in the area, have been rendered unfit for human consumption. By the time they are completed, the James Bay projects will have flooded 14 000 square kilometres of land, an area larger than Jamaica, in order to provide cheap electricity, largely for the use of new or proposed aluminium smelters, and for export.

Instead of waiting for the results 'next time', a Canadian non-governmental organization, Probe International, undertook a preemptive investigation of a new dam proposal, with a professional vengeance. The project, the Three Gorges Dam on the Yangtze River, promised to be the world's biggest-ever power development. It had been proposed by the Chinese Government as far back as the 1920s, but adequate funding and technical capacity had not existed until the late 1980s. An $11 million study, carried out under the auspices of the Canadian International Development Agency between 1986 and 1989, examined the Chinese proposal and recommended that the project go ahead.

Opposition was considerable. Forced to resort to Canada's Access to Information Law, Probe International eventually obtained a copy of the 13–volume report, and submitted it to an international panel of 11 eminent professionals and academics in the fields of engineering, economics, environment, hydrology, biology and soil science. Given their environmentalist credentials, the outcome was perhaps predictable. The results were published by Probe International in book form in 1990: *Damming the Three Gorges; What Dam-Builders Don't Want you to Know.*[17] The book investigates the Canadian findings and recommendations on resettlement, flood control, the environment, navigation, design and safety and on economic aspects of the proposal. The panel found that the lessons of the past had not been learned. Economic, human and ecological costs had been underestimated or under-stated, while projected benefits had been exaggerated. One of the panel members, Vaclav Smil, author of several books on energy and the environment in China, wrote, 'this is not engineering and science, merely an expert prostitution, paid for by Canadian taxpayers'.[18] CIDA withdrew from the project.

Disintegrated rural development

Beginning in the late 1940s and growing throughout the 1950s, 'community development' gradually became a cornerstone of development policy and programming. The concept grew from early successes in India to become by 1960 the basis of national, regional or localized programmes in dozens of countries of Africa, Asia and Latin America. Community development included both economic and political development objectives, and was viewed as a process which involved the direct participation of people in the solution of their common problems. Community development facilitated the transfer of technology to the people of a community for solutions to common problems. The *process* in achieving the goals was an important element in the concept.

Attention shifted away from community development in the 1960s, however, when it became clear that it was not meeting the political or the economic expectations placed on it. The proceeds of community development and the institutions it created were often co-opted or 'hijacked' by local elites, and where the process did activate communities, it worried governments that were uncomfortable with criticism from below. With the Asian crop failures of the 1960s and the advent of high-yielding seed varieties later in the decade, development agencies redirected their focus and spending towards agricultural research, extension, credit and systems for supplying seeds, fertilizer and other agricultural requirements.

Then, in the early 1970s, Robert McNamara, veering from the traditional World Bank growth track, made a number of speeches pledging to redirect more aid towards the poorest. 'Increases in national income,' he told his Board of Governors in 1972, 'essential as they are, will not benefit the poor unless they reach the poor. They have not reached the poor to any significant degree in most developing countries in the past, and this in spite of historically unprecedented average rates of growth throughout the sixties.'

The concept of 'integrated rural development' gained increasing currency among bilateral and multilateral organizations during the 1970s. The idea differed from previous community development approaches in stressing the integrated nature of requirements – education, health, rural infrastructure, access to credit, fertilizer and other inputs. Integrated rural development programmes complemented a 'basic needs' approach initiated by USAID in 1973, aimed at redirecting efforts towards meeting the basic needs of the poorest. Between 1975 and 1983, annual bilateral and multilateral spending on agricultural development, in which the integrated and basic needs approaches predominated, increased from $6.9 billion to $11.6 billion (at constant prices). World Bank agricultural projects during the period 1979–83 totalled $10.9 billion.[19]

By 1988, however, the wheel had turned full circle again, and the concept of integrated rural development had become the subject of debate and controversy. A seminal 1988 World Bank document on poverty alleviation states the about-face with startling clarity: 'Rural development has become a bad word in the Bank's vocabulary, as well it should be, given the poor performance of rural development projects'.[20] Many projects had failed to generate expected economic returns, the report states. 'Their organizational structure was unsustainable following the withdrawal of external funds; benefits [as with previous community development efforts] were being siphoned off by the not-so-poor farmers; they perpetuated inefficient public sector control over marketing activities; and, most importantly, extractive macroeconomic and sectoral policies undermined project intent... Many favourable project investments made under favourable commodity price conditions suddenly became unviable once world prices began to fall.'[21] An example occurred in Thailand where, although rice exports rose by almost 330 000 tons in 1986, earnings declined by $112 million because of a drop in world prices. World prices subsequently recovered, but the dip led the World Bank and other lending institutions to halt investments in irrigation.[22] The Bank's review goes further, in saying that the strategy itself was flawed in that it focused on farmers with productive assets, ignoring those for whom the programmes were intended. A further criticism turns on the problem of 'scaling up'. There are many examples of successful small integrated rural projects, but few have been replicated without losing their purpose in bureaucracy and governmental control.

Criticism notwithstanding, some projects, including a British ODA-funded project in Orissa and nine supported by IFAD in Africa demonstrated considerable success.[23] A possible area of relatively unplanned success for integrated rural development programmes has been their 'social profitability' and the important positive 'externalities', or spin-offs which they can spread through the economy. If these were properly accounted for, many projects might compare much more favourably with others.[24]

Many integrated rural development programmes, however, were clearly unsuccessful. A 1984 EEC Court of Auditors report studied 12 agricultural projects in Senegal, Mali and Mauritius and concluded that not one was profitable; that they could survive only with continued external inputs and that only half could be made viable – with radical alterations in approach.[25] Similar conclusions were reached on a variety of USAID and British rural development projects. Many had become massive enclave operations, planned, managed and financed by outsiders, heavily reliant on approaches and technologies that simply could not be made to function efficiently, or which actually exacerbated the problems they sought to solve. In Sri Lanka, for example, successive waves of tractors, provided under

British aid programmes and subsidized by government had the effect of contributing to unemployment and the economic polarization of rural communities. Estimates calculate the displacement effect of one tractor at between 500 and 1000 person-days of work per annum in Sri Lanka.[26]

In a review of the short-term results of over a thousand projects, a 1985 World Bank study found that the failure rate in Asian agricultural projects was 5 per cent, while in West Africa it was 33 per cent and in East Africa, 50 per cent. Five years later, the longer-term results were considerably worse.[27] Commenting on fifteen years of rangeland management projects, the FAO concluded that a billion dollars had been 'largely wasted'.[28] According to the World Resources Institute, some of the reasons are straightforward:

> Aside from policy and institutional problems, cultural differences among donors and recipients may help explain project failure ... misreading economic or social conditions was a factor in virtually every project in which new technology was rejected. The introduction of technology that was unfamiliar or required major life-style changes was a major cause of rejection.[29]

The failure among integrated rural development programmes is an indication of the complexity which led to the development of the concept in the first place; it is not necessarily a valid justification for the general donor retreat from rural development, especially if there was genuine concern – as the critical evaluations suggested – for the poorest. As in the 1960s, the second retreat was justified largely on the failure of the projects to achieve a reliable food surplus, when an equal, if not more important premise was *equity*. In justifying the retreat, however, some writers have gone so far as to suggest that growth and equity are antithetical.[30]

Roger Riddell argues that in their eagerness to achieve quick and tangible results from their interventions, donors project an image suggesting they know the answers and that the answers lie comfortably and consistently within the context of the assistance they have to offer:

> At the same time, and paradoxically ... donors have constantly changed the details of their programme approaches (often in line with fads and fashions ...), while also failing to learn from past experience ... Neither the exaggerated claims of the donors nor the partial responses of the critics focus sufficiently on the fundamental issue of how to promote rural development in the extremely hostile environment of most Third World Countries.[31]

The twenty-ninth day

Abundant examples similar to the dams and integrated rural development projects can be found in other sectors and sub-sectors: a health industry fixated on hospitals; education systems focused on schools and especially on universities, more than on what goes on inside them; a major bias in spending on urban areas rather than on the countryside where most people live. The result has been far from satisfactory in terms of stated objectives. Unstated objectives – such as the commercial imperative, and hidden persuaders – like the world view of bureaucrats and engineers – will be discussed in future chapters. Basically, however, the costs of a very high proportion of mega-projects have been out of all relation to their achievements. The high hopes attached to them for development and poverty reduction have not been realized.

Now the bad news. Even if the large-scale, quick-fix, technology-bound approach so favoured by Southern governments and Northern aid agencies had worked, there are new doubts about the entire reliance on growth, whether growth in the classical economic sense, the 'growth with equity' concept fostered by the World Bank, or the 'sustainable growth' of the Brundtland Report. Population growth is exponential, rather than linear. The year advances in linear fashion, one day at a time. But population, the food required to feed it, the resources required to grow the food, and the side effects of the process (such as pollution), grow exponentially – by a constant percentage of the whole. It took almost 250 years for world population to double after 1650. The next doubling took a little over a century. By 2000 the process will have occurred in only thirty years.

The problem this presents for a world with finite sources of energy and raw materials is illustrated in an old French riddle: in a certain lily pond, there is a single lily plant, which doubles in size each day. On the thirtieth day it will cover the entire pond, choking all other forms of life, but in the early days it seems not to present a problem. Action to cut it back is planned for the day that it covers half the pond. What day will that be? The answer, of course, is the twenty-ninth day.[32]

Like all parables and riddles, this one has its limitations. But in underscoring the importance of conservation, it also alludes to the need for greater equity both within countries and between countries. Economist Herman Daly makes the distinction between growth and development. 'When something grows,' he says, 'it gets bigger. When something develops, it gets different.' He argues that continued exponential growth, based on the exponential depletion of resources in a finite ecosystem, simply cannot happen.[33] If it is true, as scientists tell us, that the global economy currently uses one fourth of the world's net primary product of photosynthesis, then growth by a factor of four is probably utopian. Beyond that, to the factor of between five and ten suggested in the Brundtland Report, is impossible.

This theme has been consistent in the writings of the Worldwatch Institute for years. In its 1991 *State of the World Report*, for example, it argues that 'a commitment to the long-term improvement in the human condition is contingent on substituting environmental sustainability for growth as the overriding goal of national economic policymaking and international development'.[34] Daly acknowledges that, politically, it is very difficult to admit that growth, with its almost religious connotations of ultimate goodness, must be limited.

> But it is precisely the non-sustainability of growth that gives urgency to the concept of sustainable development. The earth will not tolerate the doubling of even one grain of wheat 64 times, yet in the past two centuries we have developed a culture dependent on exponential growth for its economic stability. Sustainable development is a cultural adaptation made by society as it becomes aware of the emerging necessity of non-growth... To delude ourselves into thinking that growth is still possible and desireable if only we label it 'sustainable' or colour it 'green' will just delay the inevitable transition and make it more painful.'

This is not to suggest an abandonment of either the poor, or the concept of growing incomes and increased material consumption in the South. Greater efficiencies in the use of existing resources, the diversion of expenditure from non-productive enterprise (such as arms) to productive use, the development and application of more appropriate technologies, increased rates of regeneration and the development of renewable substitutes, all offer considerable room for optimism. The counterpoint to the growth issue is that negative rates of growth will not advance the cause of development or contribute to the alleviation of poverty. Neither will worthless currencies and double- or triple-digit rates of inflation. But if left to chance, the relationship between sustainability and development in the Third World, and the relationships between the North and the South will remain as dysfunctional as they have been for the past generation. A rising tide does not float all boats; those fixed to short anchor chains are submerged.

Thomas Huxley observed that it is the customary fate of new truths to begin as heresies and to end as superstitions. Robert McNamara's revelation – that increases in national income will not benefit the poor unless they reach the poor – began as an economic heresy. Today it is as much a superstition as a truth, one to which more lip service than attention is paid. The new heresy is an old phrase, the logic of which is becoming more obvious: there *are* limits to growth.

46

CHAPTER IV

The third sector and the Third World

A government, by itself, is equally incapable of refreshing the circulation of feelings and ideas among a great people, as it is of controlling every industrial undertaking. Once it leaves the sphere of politics to launch out on this new track, it will, even without intending this, exercise an intolerable tyranny.   Alexis de Tocqueville

DURING THE FIRST 'Development Decade' and into the 1970s, non-profit activities in the Third World were generally regarded by governments, and by bilateral and multilateral development agencies, as peripheral to development. Donor agencies regarded non-governmental organizations as well-meaning, but largely irrelevant; governments regarded them as unnecessary. In the late 1970s and early 1980s, however, interest in non-governmental organizations (NGOs) grew, reflecting a combination of factors: the growth and greater professionalism of the non-governmental or what is sometimes called the 'third sector' in the United States; a disenchantment with the large and often unsuccessful integrated rural development projects of the 1970s; and disappointment at the lack of direct and visible impact by larger agencies and Third World governments on poverty. There was also a greater emphasis among OECD member countries on the private and non-governmental sector as an aid delivery mechanism.

Historically, NGOs have actually been at the forefront of several important areas of Third World development, including primary health care, women's and gender issues, credit for the assetless, and participatory approaches to development. The concepts of inter-mediate and appropriate technology grew entirely from the non-governmental sector. NGOs are almost exclusively responsible for placing environmental issues on the development agenda. They have an ability to reach the poor, often in remote areas; they are innovative; they adapt easily to new conditions and situations; and they operate at low cost. Above all, the strength of NGOs lies not so much in paying for development projects, as in the mobilization of people into organized group action for self-reliance and self development.

The financial contributions of NGOs should not, however, be overlooked. Oxfam's gross income in 1988–9 was £66.7 million, and Save the Children Fund took in £50.4 million.[1] In the United States, CARE raised over $41 million in 1990. In 1987, flows from NGOs in Northern countries reached $5.7 billion. This is the equivalent of 14 per cent of all bilateral flows, including bilateral contributions to multilateral institutions,[2] and in absolute terms compares favourably with the total *development* spending of some bilateral agencies.

There is a less flattering side to NGOs, characterized by amateurism, opportunism, and self-righteousness. Sheldon Annis points out that 'NGOs are so frequently lost in self-admiration that they fail to see that the strengths for which they are acclaimed can also be serious weaknesses. In the face of pervasive poverty, for example, 'small scale' can merely mean 'insignificant'. 'Politically independent' can mean 'powerless', or 'disconnected'; 'low cost' can mean 'under-financed' or 'poor quality'; and 'innovative' can simply mean 'temporary' or 'unsustainable'.'[3] Self-evaluation has generally had a low priority within NGOs, partly because resources have been plentiful, and partly because there has been little relationship between performance and survival.

Some Third World observers are increasingly concerned about the development of local NGOs on other, more basic ethical, financial and political grounds. Some charge that the professionalization and institutionalization of NGOs contradicts a traditional or religious voluntary ethic: career development workers negate the virtue and integrity of voluntary service. Others worry that the voluntary sector increasingly diverts external bilateral funding away from government plans and priorities, and that some NGOs are fronts, or could become fronts, for unwanted political activity.

The historical context

Humanistic service and the philosophy behind it is neither new, nor does it emerge from a particular place or time. At its most basic, even in primitive ancient societies, it grew from the elemental obligation of the family, tribe or clan to ensure that its members were fed, housed and clothed. Four thousand years ago the Code of Hammurabi ordered Babylonians to see that 'justice be done to widows, orphans and the poor'. Humanism, focusing on family and society rather than the individual, predominated in ancient Chinese philosophy. The Confucian code of ethics, based on goodness, benevolence and love for all, was developed in the sixth century B.C., and the subsequent advent of Buddhism imbued it with spiritual underpinnings that have survived 2500 years. Hinduism stressed the transitory nature of life on earth and the importance of doing good works in order to gain release from the cycle of rebirth and therefore achieve salvation: 'If a man does justice and kindness without sin, his reward is stretched into other lives which, if his virtue persists, will be reborn into a loftier place.'

Basic Jewish law, originating 3300 years ago, stressed the importance of tithing one tenth of a person's income to charity. Greek philosophy and ethics have influenced western thinking for over 2500 years; it was in the Golden Age of Greece that the common sharing of political authority – democracy – was developed, based on a financial system of contributions rather than taxes for education, health, culture and the welfare of the aged. Christ prescribed charity as a means of salvation: 'If thou wilt be perfect, go and sell what thou hast, and give to the poor, and thou shalt have treasure in heaven.' Seven hundred years later, charity became one of the five obligatory duties of Islam through a special tax on property and income for redistribution to the poor.

Through the Dark and Middle Ages in Europe, the Christian church became the dispenser of benevolence and charity, establishing hospitals, schools and universities, and by the twelfth century in England, it controlled half the country's entire public wealth. With the advent of Protestantism across much of Europe, a 'work ethic' developed which equated poverty with sin, and established its alleviation among the helpless as the responsibility of the state, or of parishes and villages. Among the able-bodied, poverty was basically regarded as a punishable evil, a concept resulting in workhouses, debtors' prisons and widespread misery. The Elizabethan Poor Law of 1601 codified this approach and influenced charitable thinking and deeds in North America for two centuries, and in Britain for three.

In nineteenth century Europe, it was reformers and reform movements rather than governments who brought about changes in working conditions, public health and child labour. The pressure of these reformers, the almost uncontrolled proliferation of charitable societies, and the political threat of a potentially revolutionary underclass gradually urged greater welfare initiatives on government. Germany's pioneering social welfare programmes of 1880 were followed by France's 1893 National Law for Free Medical Assistance for the poor, and by Britain's old age pension scheme of 1908 and the National Health Insurance and Unemployment Insurance Acts of 1911.

It is in North America, however, where government was slower to respond to welfare needs, that the importance of the nonprofit sector can be seen most clearly. In 1986, for example, it was estimated that in the United States there were 873 000 philanthropic nonprofit organizations and a further 370 000 nonprofit (but not philanthropic) organizations. These organizations employed approximately seven million people, more than the federal and all state governments combined. Roughly a quarter of all Americans over the age of 18 did volunteer work of some sort *every week*. In 1980, American business donated $2.3 billion to nonprofit organizations, while nonprofits returned twenty times that amount, or $42.6 billion to the economy through the purchase of business goods and services, creating in the process 1.4 million jobs in business and manufacturing.[4]

It is the societal role of the nonprofit sector rather than the economic, however, which has had the greatest impact in the United States. To appreciate this societal impact, it is helpful to go back 150 years, to the 1835 visit to America of the French political writer, Alexis de Tocqueville. In his opus, *Democracy in America*, de Tocqueville commented again and again on the unique American propensity to create and join voluntary organizations:

> Americans of all ages, all stations in life, and all types of disposition are forever forming associations. They are not only commercial and industrial associations in which all take part, but others of a thousand different types – religious, moral, serious, futile, very general and very limited, immensely large and very minute. Americans combine to give fêtes, found seminaries, build churches, distribute books, and send missionaries to the antipodes. Hospitals, prisons and schools take shape in that way. Finally, if they want to proclaim a truth or propagate some feeling by the encouragement of a great example, they form an association. In every case, at the head of any new undertaking, where in France you would find the government or in England some territorial magnate, in the United States you are sure to find an Association.[5]

It was de Tocqueville's observation – less than 50 years after the effective independence of the United States – that these associations formed the basis of America's development and the roots of her democracy: 'In democratic countries knowledge of how to combine is the mother of all other forms of knowledge; on its progress depends that of all the others. Among laws controlling human societies there is one more precise and clearer, it seems to me, than all the others. If men are to remain civilized, or to become civilized, the art of association must develop and improve among them at the same speed as equality of condition spreads ... The more government takes the place of associations, the more will individuals lose the idea of forming associations and need the government to come to their help. This is a vicious circle of cause and effect ...'

It is in international development and in the redefinition of 'the art of association' and 'community' that the nonprofit sector takes on immediacy for Third World countries; for until recently, most of the prominent non-governmental organizations operating in Africa, Asia and Latin America, were foreign rather than local. American foundations have played a critical role in the reduction or eradication of malaria, yellow fever, cholera and hookworm, and in the development of high-yielding varieties of wheat and rice. Oxfam and others have acted as the world's conscience on human disaster, and have shouldered much of the responsibility for subsequent international relief activities.

It is arguable, however, that voluntarism does not travel well. International NGOs are an extension of the most basic elements of their donors' altruism. But originating in a foreign country, they can hardly be described as an expression of local concern — either collective or individual. They have other shortcomings: cultural insensitivities; and technical and administrative weaknesses. Even those organizations that support local NGOs cannot avoid imposing their views of development, their priorities, and their bureaucratic requirements on the recipient.

There are other, more systemic problems. The vast majority of people in Europe and North America who make donations for international development want their money used for the immediate and direct alleviation of poverty. Conditioned by a generation of disaster appeals, they are much less interested in structural change, macroeconomics and vaguely ominous concepts of 'empowerment'. Torn between a short-sighted, emotional donor base and Third World realities, NGOs have tended to staff themselves with generalists rather than specialists. One study of NGOs observes that 'NGOs are typically rather cautious in their attitudes towards professionalism, an attitude which derives partly from their dependence on short-term fund-raising, but partly also from their pride in their value-orientation, and the desire not to impose intellectual barriers which might serve to dampen the ardour of their ordinary membership.'[6]

A typology of humanistic service

Dr Johnson observed that definitions are tricks for pedants. Perhaps that is why the fast-growing body of literature on different types of NGOs is not very helpful. In addition to definitions, there have been several attempts to rename the sector – Private Voluntary Organizations is favoured in the United States, but there are others: Private Development Organizations, Private Organizations, Private Service Contractors, the Third Sector. But the term, 'non-governmental organization' seems intent on not going away, for good reason. David Brown observes that NGOs see themselves, by and large, as being what governments are not: 'not bureaucratic, not rigid, not directive and not stultifying of local initiative. This image plays an important functional role in freeing NGOs from established political hierarchies, though it does at the same time ignore the extent to which many of their projects are inter-dependent with governments' own activities.'[7]

The evolution of humanistic service varies in education, health and social services from country to country, over time, and according to the pace of development and the predominating ideology. David Korten has classified international NGO development into four 'generations'. First generation NGOs concentrate largely on relief and welfare. Second generation organizations focus on small-scale, self-reliant development activities, and third generation organizations concentrate on sustainable systems development. Fourth generation organizations are broad-based 'movements' such as the Chinese literacy movement of the 1920s, or the environmental and women's movements of today.[8]

Samuel Martin classifies the evolution in societal rather than organizational stages. Stage One is characterized by a high degree of direct personal involvement and responsibility for the delivery of humanistic service. Small, community-based self-help efforts and personal voluntary service fall into this category, which was most common, in most countries, until the early years of this century. Stage Two grows out of necessity – the institutionalization of humanistic service because of greater needs, and greater concentrations of people. Responsibility remains with individuals – but through the formation of associations.

Stage Three evolves from convenience rather than conviction: the demand for services, the proliferation of associations and the intensification of fundraising lead to the federation and professionalization of associations, and – often reluctantly – to government funding or to replacement by government agencies and departments. And Stage Four is the ultimate humanistic delivery system, in which a society decrees that all members will be provided with an appropriate level of health care, education, cultural enjoyment and social well-being; charities and voluntary organizations become redundant and cease to exist.[9]

The stages are not immutable, however, nor is one necessarily superior to another. Time, societal values and resources will make that distinction. In fact most of Europe in the middle ages – under heavy church rather than governmental domination – had reached a form of Stage Four, only to move backwards to Stages One, Two and Three through the nineteenth century, re-emerging at Stage Four after the Second World War. Conservative political ideologies in western Europe, and the collapse of eastern European communist regimes which espoused Stage Four services (but provided considerably less), suggest a return towards greater reliance on a Stage Three approach. The movement from Stages One to Three can be seen more clearly in the development of African organizations such as the Organization of Rural Associations for Progress, which within four years of its 1980 beginnings, had linked over 300 small Zimbabwean associations. The Federation of NGOs in Senegal began in 1978 by linking some of the most elementary village-based self-help groups in the country, and within ten years had a membership of over 200 000.

Because of their motivation and donor base, Northern NGOs tend to be highly individualistic and territorial, and often have a strong welfare orientation. Proliferating at a staggering pace in the past twenty years, the most successful fundraisers among them usually make their appeal to the donor's sense of personal responsibility and the direct delivery of services to those in need.

Historically in the South, the altruistic ethic has manifested itself in a community-based approach to humanistic service, very much of the Stage One type. During the colonial era, branches of larger metropolitan charitable organizations as well as new, home-grown varieties were planted or transplanted, and often flourished. Many, especially mission-based activities, operated in the fields of education and health. Throughout much of the former colonial world, these have now been taken over by governments.

This left the field open to a newer breed of more secular international NGOs, usually working in the less well-defined areas of social welfare, rural development and relief. It is predominantly in the more recent emergence of development-oriented *local* NGOs, however, that one is likely to find more profound societal impact. AWARE in India, reaching 2000 villages, has had considerable impact on state government thinking about land tenure issues for tribal people and scheduled castes. In Sri Lanka, Sarvodaya – covering a third of the country's villages – was one of the few national institutions, including government, that was able to function in all parts of the country during the devastating civil war. The highly successful Aga Khan Rural Support Programme covers 80 per cent of the villages in Pakistan's Northern Areas with extension, technology transfer and credit facilities. Similar spin-off government-supported organizations are being developed in Punjab and the North West Frontier Province.

The influence of Grameen Bank is legendary, not only in Bangladesh, but in other countries such as Malawi, Sri Lanka and Malaysia, where local versions have been initiated. The Bangladesh Rural Advancement Committee (BRAC) has developed a non-formal primary education programme which was operating 3800 schools for more than 110 000 children by the end of 1990. The BRAC dropout rate was only 5 per cent, compared with 80 per cent in government schools. Similar comments on quality, quantity and impact could be made about the Self-Employed Women's Organization (SEWA), the Mysore Resettlement and Development Agency (MYRADA), and the Working Women's Forum in India, the Proshikas in Bangladesh, PRODEM in Bolivia, ORAP in Zimbabwe and others. For each of them, there are at least two or three more next-generation NGOs coming up that show every sign of being able to reach similar levels of coverage and effectiveness. Without pushing the analogy too far, it could be argued that these Stage Two and Stage Three organizations represent the same phenomena – a generation or so after the independence of their countries – that de Tocqueville so admired in the United States of 1835.

Proliferation, duplication and replication

Although NGOs are not a new phenomenon, until recently they have taken up little time and attention in the corridors of the world's bilateral and multilateral aid agencies. Even now, decades after the founding of organizations such as CARE, Oxfam, NOVIB, Helvetas, Redd Barna, and years after the emergence of strong Third World NGOs such as BRAC, Sarvodaya, MYRADA, it is not uncommon to find consultants from governmental agencies doing surveys, studies and enquiries aimed at figuring out what relationship should be developed with these organizations in order to 'strengthen' or 'professionalize' them.

One of the most serious problems in the NGO sector is the proliferation of organizations, both in the North and the South. Today there are a hundred British non-governmental organizations concerned with and involved in Third World development, and Canada, with less than half the population, has more than twice the number. Although there is some co-operation between organizations, usually having to do with disaster appeals and other fundraising efforts at home, most NGOs operate in isolation from one another. Within the British and Canadian development communities, the multiplicity is justified on the grounds of diversity, on the grounds that as community-based organizations, they inform, educate and sensitize their different 'constituencies' to important issues, and create a foundation of understanding and public support for larger bilateral development programmes.

There is another way of looking at it. The proliferation, regardless of its positive attributes, is costly, selfish and sometimes destructive. Inevitably, each organization must have staff, offices, typewriters, photocopiers, telephones, meetings, newsletters, and above all projects. The projects necessitate overseas offices, staff and travel to the Third World, as well as some means of demonstrating to individual donors that the organization is carrying out useful and unique activities. For most Northern NGOs this means the need for 'partner' organizations in the Third World, many of which exist solely at the discretion of their Northern benefactors. It means that for many NGOs life is a project mill in which

54

opportunities for learning, specialization and professionalism are limited.

The same multiplication exercise is now taking place in the South. In Pakistan, for example, some 4000 NGOs are registered with the Social Welfare Department and there are a further 21 000 registered co-operative societies. A UNICEF study identified 900 non-registered groups in the Karachi area alone. Between 1978 and 1988 in Kenya there was a 150 per cent increase in the growth of local NGOs, and a 260 per cent increase in the registration of foreign NGOs.[10] As Sheikh Mujibur Rahman, the first President of Bangladesh, once observed, where there are bees, there is honey. Before 1972, the number of foreign NGOs operating in then East Pakistan could be counted on the fingers of one hand. Although there were many East Pakistani social welfare organizations, there were few, if any, which could be called development organizations. In 1990, there were 240 registered Bangladeshi organizations approved for receipt of foreign funding, and a further 79 registered foreign NGOs with resident representatives and 'programmes' in Bangladesh. This figure did not include the thousands of village-based organizations that are registered with the Department of Social Welfare. Nor did it include embassy-operated NGO funds or international NGOs which supported activities in Bangladesh but which maintained no presence there of their own.

The proliferation in the South is justified in the same way as it is in Europe and North America: any organization that helps the poor to improve their lot is justifiable. But at what cost? It is arguable that underlying the laudable intentions and grand statements about community participation and self-help, lies a fundamental unwillingness on the part of NGOs, North and South, to share, to subsume organizational identity and ego into a larger pot for the greater good. For all the attempts at co-ordination of NGOs, for all the umbrella organizations and clearing houses, and for all the talk of NGO solidarity, mergers of NGOs are few and far between.

Like theories of social development, 'empowerment' is an intangible thing, a process open to broad subjective interpretation. It is hard to quantify, and from the perspective of institutional donors, difficult to evaluate. The Bangladesh Rural Advancement Committee (BRAC) has struggled with questions of empowerment and replication on its journey through the different stages of growth. BRAC began in 1972 as a small, localized relief operation in Sylhet, but its workers quickly discovered that permanent solutions to the alleviation of the crushing poverty of Bangladesh's rural landless, lay in the ability of these people themselves to mobilize, manage and control local and external resources. This approach, or rather this phraseology, is used by many, if not most, NGOs to describe what they do. 'Empowerment' has become so common, in fact, and covers such a wide variety of activities, sins and omissions, that like many phrases in the development lexicon it has become virtually meaningless.

For BRAC, the difference lay in the learning, the mistakes, the success, and finally in broadening the application. By 1989 it had grown into a multi-faceted development organization with 2800 workers. It had organized 3900 self-reliant groups in 2000 villages. Its principal health programme, the introduction of oral rehydration therapy, had by January 1988 reached an estimated 10.4 million households – more than exist in Sweden, Norway and Denmark combined – and had then been expanded into a comprehensive child survival programme. Its savings and credit programmes had, between their experimental beginnings in 1979 and June 1988, generated Tk43.6 million in savings, and BRAC had provided Tk220 million ($7.1 million) in credit for productive enterprise. The on-time repayment rate was 93.9 per cent.[11]

What BRAC had proven was that it could do things well. It had also demonstrated that it could grow. Its formula – developed tested and applied – worked. The landless rural poor could, largely through their own efforts, be mobilized for their own self-help. BRAC had also achieved that most singularly elusive of development objectives: replicability. What it had not achieved, however, was the means of moving on, of withdrawing after a period of time and starting afresh in new areas. And that very fundamental problem led to the development of a unique proposal.

BRAC felt that its basic village mobilization and development package, including its conscientization, group formation, health and education activities, along with a good degree of savings and credit, could be implemented, on average, within a period of three years. It had discovered however, that without follow-up, without some sort of continued presence, group cohesion withered; lessons learned were forgotten; borrowing patterns changed and deteriorated.

This is not surprising. Given centuries of societal degradation, given the irreconcilable factionalism of village life, given mistrust, corruption and degrading poverty, it is unrealistic to project any kind of withdrawal from successful activities within decades, much less years. In 1990, therefore, BRAC initiated a half-way house: after the basic mobilization is achieved, after there is a prescribed level of savings and a proven credit operation in a village, BRAC's *subsidized* activities are withdrawn, and a nonprofit 'BRAC Bank' takes their place. Subsidized activities are converted into a commercially viable, *self-sustaining* operation, paid for by the villagers themselves through interest on their loans.

Bilaterals and multilaterals

In its basics, the BRAC story provides a striking reason why bilateral and multilateral donors have begun taking a greater interest in NGOs. As the aid failures of the Second Development Decade piled on the corpse of the First, as a private-sector orientation became more fashionable in development thinking, eyes began to turn more frequently towards NGOs. Praise and money followed. In the 1980s, received wisdom held that there were still problems with NGO management, with replicability of NGO projects, and in co-ordination between NGO goals and broad national or sectoral development priorities. But it was recognized that the field orientation of NGOs, their flexibility and focus on community participation, local leadership and self-reliance, gave them a genuine comparative advantage in many areas critical to the development process. Their costs were lower; they worked directly with the poor; they could move in areas where angels – not to mention governments and bilateral agencies – feared to tread: war zones, politically sensitive areas, emergencies. They could respond quickly, pioneering innovative approaches in public health, community participation, the role of women, appropriate technology and non-formal education. Almost as importantly, as Northern taxpayers and journalists grew more critical of official aid shortcomings, it was recognized that NGOs could play a vital role in the development of an informed, concerned and positive constituency for aid programmes at home.

Growing bilateral and multilateral interest in Southern NGOs coincided with a relative decline in funding from Northern NGOs to their larger Southern counterparts. This was in part because in recent years, many Southern NGOs have begun to outstrip their Northern partners in sophistication, size and absorptive capacity. Some Northern NGOs argue that the BRACs, Sarvodayas and AWAREs should somehow have become self-financing by now (although this was seldom a topic of discussion or funding in the growth years, nor is it something Northern NGOs themselves practise). Others argue that the most appropriate role for Northern NGOs is to foster the development of newer, smaller groups coming up as second and third generation organizations.

A less charitable observation of the Northern NGO abandonment of their large Southern counterparts is that big, competent, well-managed Third World organizations deprive Northern NGOs of much of their *raison d'être*. Having no particular management or technical expertise to offer, the 'partnership' is often reduced to cheque-writing, and in some cases, development education at home. Northern NGOs, beholden to a diverse and fickle donor base of their own, one weaned on famine appeals and starving-baby advertising, want what they think or know their donors find appealing: annual reports should list a dozen different initiatives under 'Ethiopia' or 'Bangladesh' rather than just one. Variety is the hallmark of meaningful, busy, professional charities.

Meanwhile, the bilateral agencies' discovery of Southern NGOs, which began with praise, was soon augmented with money. It seemed a logical confluence of interests. To many Southern NGOs, bilateral institutions represented a new source of untapped funding and possibly a means of reaching governments – their own and those of the donors – with a grassroots development message. From the donor point of view, large Southern NGOs offered a new perspective on development, a window hitherto jealously guarded by Northern NGOs. Now, through Southern NGOs, they could undertake experimental projects, or pilots which might prove instructive later in larger government-to-government undertakings. NGOs were also an inexpensive, effective means of delivering official development assistance to the poorest of the poor, something that could be used to good advantage in public reports.

The multilateral agencies were not far behind the bilaterals. Using small amounts of money to advantage, UNICEF, for example, successfully promoted its 'Child Survival and Development Revolution' among NGOs worldwide. The World Bank, UNDP and others began to see NGOs as potential allies in the promotion and acceptance of new development approaches, from population planning to social forestry. Used effectively, NGOs could form a critical part of strategic alliances, alliances between governments, NGOs and official development assistance agencies to help achieve key objectives. 'In fact,' states a surprised World Bank policy study, 'World Bank health analysts report that nongovernment providers in many countries (Ecuador, Thailand, Zambia) offer better care than government facilities. In Nigeria and Uganda mission hospitals and clinics have medicines and other supplies when public facilities do not. In Malawi consumers walk miles past nearly free government health centres to get to mission clinics that charge many times as much.'[12]

As relations between bilateral donors and Southern NGOs developed, problems – sometimes severe problems – emerged. One of the worst is an endemic donor fixation on projects, combined with an almost pathological abhorrence of recurrent costs. At first glance, the project approach seems reasonable and practical. In theory, both donor and recipient share an agreed list of priorities, activities and time frames. The project begins and ends, and unless there is a second phase, the donor will expect to have initiated, catalyzed or sparked a development which will then be taken up by the local authorities. The

58

concept is clear, the terms of the agreement are straightforward, the recipient is accountable, the product can be evaluated.

This reasonable, businesslike approach to getting the work done is, in actual fact, often excessively costly, sometimes anti-developmental and usually unfair. It undermines the very concept of voluntary, non-governmental organizations; it has in more than one case brought large Southern organizations to the brink of bankruptcy and it seriously compromises the delivery of their services to the very people the donors say they want to help.

The problem often begins before a project has been approved by a donor. In some cases, having raised expectations through feasibility studies, or having been assured by a donor that the approval will come 'very soon', the NGO will begin a project, financing it temporarily with funds earmarked for other purposes. All donors warn against this. But in the real world, where the future success of a project may depend on hiring a key individual now, or getting started before the rains, sometimes risks are inevitable. Likewise, activities cannot be turned off while an NGO awaits donor approval for a second phase. People do not live their lives on a project basis: farmers cannot delay planting; sick people do cure themselves; schools and clinics cannot close; administrators and trainers cannot be sent on unpaid vacation. It is, of course very bad if funding is not approved, but it is almost worse when some donors refuse to backdate contracts. 'Raise money from your own sources,' they say.

Once signed, some agreements provide for very little, or even nothing in the way of advances, which means that the NGO must actually subsidize the donor. Money arrives erratically and usually late, making any sort of organizational budgeting and cash-flow planning impossible. One might assume that donors are as efficient and as understanding as they expect a recipient NGO to be. This is not so. In 1987, there was a simple bureaucratic delay at GTZ in processing a claim from the African Medical and Research Foundation (AMREF), a large Kenya-based NGO. Two months passed, and then there was a query; not a query of earth-shattering proportions, but enough to hold up not only the items in dispute, but the entire payment until it had been answered. The claim, for approximately twenty million shillings ($1.2m), was so badly delayed that AMREF was forced to eat into all its cash reserves and for two months was barely able to meet its payroll.[13]

In the North, most NGOs have arrangements with their bankers to cover such contingencies. Banks understand that NGOs occasionally suffer cash-flow difficulties, but they know that inevitably, given the volume of project agreements, government support and general public goodwill, the money will come. This is not the case in the

South, where banks are much more conservative, where NGOs are less well understood, where governments place IMF-inspired limits on overdraft facilities. So it was in Kenya, where the AMREF overdraft facility was only eight million shillings – 3.8 per cent of its gross 1987 income, or enough operating funds for about 14 days. In the private sector, one of the most common causes of bankruptcy is exactly this problem – cash-flow. Even the most flourishing business will go under if it cannot meet the payroll. In 1990, the British NGO, War on Want, suffered a financial collapse, and one of Canada's largest NGOs, World University Service of Canada, went into receivership for precisely this reason.

The problem is not exclusive to bilateral and multilateral donors, but where large sums are involved, the cost of confusion can be enormous. Reporting requirements are another major aggravation. Some donors are satisfied with semi-annual reports, but most require them quarterly; some demand them on a monthly basis. With the rare exception of the occasional donor consortium, all have different formats, all want to be treated as special. What this meant for AMREF, on 50 projects in 1987–8, was an estimated 300 different financial reports and nearly 150 narrative reports. With a Project Management staff of nine – limited by the non-availability of funding for institutional support costs – it is no wonder that reports were late, and that they did not always conform to a donor's standard or expectations.

The reporting problem relates fundamentally to the notion of 'accountability', a word which rolls easily off Northern tongues, as though it were a one-way concept. It could, and perhaps should be asked who holds the donor accountable for inexplicable delays, for rigid reporting requirements and sudden changes in policy and approach, for fields unplanted, children unvaccinated, clinics closed, staff laid off.

Evaluation, which in the 1980s became a major growth industry in the development business, is a thorny issue for NGOs. Because they have done so little of it themselves, they are particularly sensitive to outside examination. Precisely because so much of what they do is small and impermanent, because much of it is process rather than product oriented – participation, experimentation, empowerment, attitudinal change – standard evaluative techniques are often inadequate to the task of supplying donors and governments with substantive impact data.

Southern governments; Southern NGOs

An emerging problem in the growing friendship between bilateral agencies and Southern NGOs is that Southern governments have begun to see in it the tip of an iceberg, and they worry. NGOs, operating under none of the constraints faced by governments, reap high praise for their work, while seeming to pinch bilateral donor funds from under the governmental nose. Southern governments demand to be consulted, and when consulted, they often resist. If a bilateral agency funds a local NGO regardless, the stage for conflict is set. Thus, in their enthusiasm to support Southern NGOs, bilateral and multilateral agencies have begun putting the new-found objects of their affection into direct conflict with their own governments. This will not strengthen NGOs, it will do the opposite.

There are three ways out of the dilemma. The first is a redefinition and reconstruction of the partnership between Northern and Southern NGOs. There are many facets to this complex and much-debated issue, some of which will be addressed in subsequent chapters. For that reason, the issue is temporarily set aside, and will be readdressed in Chapter XV. The second way out of the dilemma is to ensure that any bilateral funding for an NGO is clearly seen as *additional* to regular government-to-government programmes.

The third, and most important, is the need for Southern governments to recognize the importance of the NGO sector to a country's social and economic development. Regardless of a government's view of its own role or that of the commercial private sector, neither is likely to meet all needs of all people. Voluntary organizations, therefore, have an important role to play in assisting, complementing, and even challenging government – in meeting needs or working in areas where costs, or economies of scale, make it difficult for government to operate. They can cut through procedure-bound systems that have become paralysed in red tape. NGOs can provide special services to targeted groups – such as street children, refugees or female-headed households – that fall between the strands of an official safety net. In Karachi, for example, where services to slum areas have been beyond the means of the municipal government, the Orangi Pilot Project organized 28 000 families in a low-cost sanitation programme which, between 1981 and 1986, constructed over 80 miles of underground sewerage lines and secondary drains and 28 400 sanitary latrines, with participants investing over Rs30 million ($1.3 million) of their own cash resources.

Rather than diverting bilateral and multilateral funding from government priorities, NGOs have a proven ability to attract large sums of *additional* funding for development purposes, creating jobs both directly and indirectly through the purchase of goods and services from the private sector. Obviously, those countries with a large number of NGOs, such as the Philippines or Bangladesh, stand to gain considerably more in economic terms than those where the sector is underdeveloped or harassed.

NGOs can be particularly important in areas of research and in the testing of new techniques, new technologies, and new approaches to old problems – such as their work in oral rehydration therapy or social forestry. BRAC's non-formal primary education programme has not only pointed out new, cost-effective ways of providing the basic education that is essential to poverty reduction, it has been instrumental in attracting large new sums of multilateral funding into the formal education system.

Perhaps as important in some ways, NGOs can play a mediating role between individuals and the impersonal institutions of government. They offer people an opportunity to *participate* in decisions that directly affect their own interests. They can act as an important brake on inappropriate development models imported by outsiders, and as an accelerator for workable new initiatives – imported or home-grown. NGOs are not an adjunct to, or a conduit for, development activities; in a strong society they are an indivisible part of them.

And yet, despite the obvious advantages and potential of NGOs, many governments remain openly hostile to them – at both political and technical levels. They focus exclusively on the weaknesses and behave as though they are directly or indirectly threatened by NGO growth and achievement, sometimes treating NGO activities as attempts to subvert government policies or as an unwelcome involvement in politics.

It may be that this attitude, less prevalent in Latin America and the Caribbean but common throughout Africa and Asia, is a consequence of the myriad small, unprofessional and unco-ordinated NGOs that have proliferated in recent years. But the legislation and regulatory procedures that have been developed to deal with the perceived problem have, in general, neither stopped nor corrected the phenomenon. Rather they have made life considerably more complex and costly for those doing good work; they have often directed the talent and energy that is available for vibrant development programmes into much less productive palliative activities, and they have stunted the organizational, technological and intellectual development that is necessary to the advancement of any society. It may be that some governments simply fear the criticism that the very existence of an NGO seems to imply. In a weak government, the sentiment is understandable, though not particularly commendable. In strong societies with confident governments, the attitude is sadly shortsighted.

PART TWO

WHAT WE KNOW

Life must be lived forwards, but it can only be understood backwards.
Søren Kierkegaard

CHAPTER V

Technology in history: lies and promises

I am not digging into such things because I think the old ways are necessarily better than the new ways, but I think there may be some of the old ways that we would be wise to look into before all knowledge of them disappears from the earth – the knowledge, and the kind of thinking that lay behind it.   Robertson Davies, *The Rebel Angels*

PERHAPS ONE OF the greatest wrongs in the misguided lexicon of international development is the expression 'transfer of technology'. It implies that technology is something neutral, something that exists outside of society. It suggests that technology can be handed across a desk, picked out of a pattern catalogue (as in 'how to make a car'), or shipped by jumbo jet from the North to the South along with some 'technical assistance' to get it going. One of the greatest failings of aid programmes and of the development strategies of many Third World countries is that development has been seen very much in these terms: as a dam or as fertilizer, as a machine or a technique or a factory that can be shipped south, as though the lessons learned over two millennia about technology simply do not apply to the latter half of the twentieth century.

Technology is a combination of knowledge, techniques and concepts; it is tools, machines, and factories. It is engineering, but it is much more than engineering. It involves organization and processes. It has to do with agriculture, animal husbandry and health. It is often highly resource-specific. It involves people, both as individuals – creators, inventors, entrepreneurs – and as society. The cultural, historical and organizational context in which technology is developed and applied is always a factor in its success or failure. Technology is the science and the art of getting things done through the application of skills and knowledge. It is, according to the American technology historian, Edwin Layton, 'a spectrum, with ideas at one end and techniques and things at the other, with design as a middle term'.[1]

Over the centuries, technology has been 'transferred' through trade and migration, through art and through religion. It has been fostered and held back by commerce, governments and educational institutions. War has played a large part in its development and retardation. It has been bought, copied, stolen, and sometimes developed through independent invention. It has been lost – occasionally on a grand scale, as with the collapse of the Roman Empire. Sometimes it has been stimulated by something very small, such as the iron stirrup which gave Turkish and Mongol armies the ability to use both hands for shooting and, therefore, considerable superiority over Chinese and Hindu horsemen who rode with wooden stirrups, or with no stirrups at all.[2] Sometimes the stimulus – as with the invention of a successful steam engine or commercially viable electricity – has been enormous and of readily apparent import to a wide range of applications. Although justice to the history of technology can hardly be done in a few pages, this chapter will attempt to review some of the lessons that have a bearing on modern efforts to develop and transfer technology in and to the Third World.

Technology, trade and warfare

Trade is one of the oldest and most common means by which technology has migrated. The prolific land and sea trade between China and West Asia between the eighth and twelfth centuries took silk and textiles from China through India and Persia to Arabia. Techniques in hydraulic engineering – dams, canals and water wheels – developed in Roman times, were improved and further developed in Iraq and Iran after the collapse of the Western Roman Empire. They bear remarkable resemblance to similar developments around the Islamic world and China from the seventh century onwards. It is perhaps significant that Sri Lanka, which had developed one of the world's greatest irrigation civilizations by the first century, was strategically located on the trading route between the Islamic world and China. Paper-making technology also moved along the commercial routes from China, while Arab ships and traders spread Chinese steel technology and Indian medical knowledge as far afield as Indonesia, Madagascar and perhaps Zimbabwe.

Early European trading contacts with the Americas resulted in the rapid spread of new food crops and agricultural techniques not only back to Europe, but through Africa and Asia: yams, peanuts, potatoes, maize, corn, tomatoes, tobacco. Asian fruit and vegetables such as oranges, lemons, bananas, asparagus and artichokes made their way through Europe to the Americas. Trade in West African gold contributed to the development of the iron technology necessary for more intensive mining.

Through the ages, war has been a major stimulus to the development of technology. It is perhaps significant that the only manmade structure visible from the moon, the Great Wall of China, was built not for the glorification of God, but to keep marauding armies at bay. The development of better ploughshares was often the direct result of improved sword production. The invention of the longbow and the crossbow owe as much to warfare as to the need for food. The development of iron and then of steel was spurred as much by the demand for weaponry and armour as for agricultural equipment. Gunpowder, invented in China and used initially for fireworks, was carried to the Islamic world by the Mongols once its salutary effect on armies had been noted. Thirteenth century European armies fighting in Palestine during the crusades were quick to see the value of the technology once they too had felt its devastating effect. Gunpowder and improved building technology for fortifications were two of the technologies they took back to Europe with them. Windmills, unknown in the Middle East at the time, were something they left behind.

Gunpowder had a direct and powerful effect on the development of metallurgy, first in the development of alloys. The manufacture of bronze cannon expanded the demand for tin and copper in China, India, Turkey and Europe. In the late fifteenth and early sixteenth centuries, cannons contributed to knowledge about cast iron, first in its use in cannon balls, and then for cannons themselves. Steel production, developed as early as the seventh century in Iran, remained an expensive and time-consuming technology until the eighteenth century. Before that, the best steels, used primarily for swords and muskets, were produced in Persia, India and Java; in the seventeenth century some of the best European gunmakers were actually little more than assemblers, using imported Turkish barrels.[3]

It was not only gunpowder, but the technologies spurred by gunpowder which created the 'gunpowder empires' of the fifteenth, sixteenth and seventeenth centuries – Persia, the Ottoman Empire, the consolidation of Mughal rule in India, the expansion and consolidation of the Chinese and Russian empires. Guns and advanced weaponry gave Europe the means for its mastery over Africa, the Americas and much of Asia and led to the creation of vaster empires than had been dreamed of. As Hillaire Belloc astutely observed,

> Whatever happens, we have got
> The Maxim gun, and they have not.

The arms race is not a concept confined to the twentieth century. Keeping up with the latest in military technology was as important to the small European countries and city states of the Middle Ages as it was in the nineteenth and twentieth centuries. Thus technological advancement in repeating rifles and machine guns put an end to muskets; the internal combustion engine, installed inside an armour-plated box and outfitted with wheels on treads, put an end to the cavalry. The aircraft, still a novelty at the outset of the First World War and used largely for reconnaissance purposes, had within four years become a sophisticated killing machine, its scope and potential radically altered almost overnight. Rockets, first used as weapons by the Chinese in 1150, received their most important boost in the wartime laboratories of the Third Reich. The principle of jet propulsion, applied (without success) on the advice of Benjamin Franklin to an early American steamboat, became commercially viable only after the intensive experiments of the Second World War. Although the space travel and satellite technologies of our times have had enormous peaceful benefits, the research and development behind them have owed more to the Cold War and to military budgets than to the peaceful march of progress.

The stimulus effect

War has obviously been one of the greatest stimuli to the development and movement of technology, but there have been others – the invention of paper, the printing press, the magnetic compass. The development of the Portuguese caravel, which could sail efficiently against prevailing winds (and thus get home from West Africa), was as important to the realization of Portuguese imperial ambitions as the development of advanced weapons.

Resources, both their abundance and shortage, play an important role in the process of technology development and diffusion. The connection between increasing shortages of fuelwood in eighteenth century Europe, and the development of the steam engine is not coincidental. More costly fuelwood had a direct bearing on the need for an efficient steam engine, because steam-powered engines allowed water to be pumped from ever-deeper mines – from which coal, the substitute for wood, was extracted. This new abundance of cheap coal and the development of coke made possible better and cheaper iron smelting. The growing shortage of wood had other effects, particularly on the movement of shipbuilding technology away from Europe. By 1774, one third of all British ships were being built in North America, and following the American Revolution, much of the industry was shifted to shipyards in Bombay and to the Hooghly River south of Calcutta.[4]

The development of the railway was a powerful stimulus to the iron and steel industries in Britain, which for a generation exported engines and rails to America, and for two or three generations to Canada, Russia, China and India. The very technologies which became available because of the shortage of fuelwood led directly to the end of the wooden sailing vessel.

The 'small' innovation can have as fundamental an impact as the large. New techniques in material development and new designs have revived interest in propeller-driven aircraft. Better shapes and different propeller lengths, combined with new materials, led to the

68

development in the 1980s of propeller-driven aircraft that are 40 per cent more fuel-efficient than jets. Improvements in rail beds, tracks, engines and design have given new impetus to the railway in France and Japan. New designs of windmill with 'eggbeater' turbines and blades on a vertical axis, capable of taking wind from all directions, have given wind power a new lease of life. Like the eighteenth century shortage of fuelwood that provided the stimulus for coal and steam in Europe, these modern innovations have their origin in the rising costs of fossil fuel.

The clock, according to the American sociologist, Lewis Mumford, not the steam engine, is the key machine of the modern era. It 'symbolizes the inventiveness of the age,' and has in all ages marked 'a perfection towards which other machines aspire.'[5] The development of the clock had its origin in the studies of astronomy that so fascinated the Greeks, the Chinese, the Indians and the builders of Stonehenge. Su Sung's great astronomical clock in China's Hunan province, commissioned in 1090, was powered by a giant water wheel with 36 buckets. At the same time clocks were being developed in India. The first European clocks emerged a century and a half later, and by the end of the fourteenth century, clockwork had become a relatively sophisticated art. Instruments that showed the position of planets in addition to telling time had been developed as the result of a combination of complex mechanical and mathematical skills. Careful gearing and measurement, the use of bearings and pinions, fine metalwork and precision balance were all essential to the building of a successful clock.

Although European clocks taken to China in the early seventeenth century were dismissed as useless – both the clock and clockwork technology having been lost in the intervening years – clockmakers in Europe had already provided a major stimulus to mathematics, experimental science and reason. Technology historian Joel Mokyr ascribes Britain's capacity for an industrial revolution, in part, to its advanced clock and watchmaking technologies. Watchmakers in Coventry later formed the nucleus of the bicycle industry, which itself became the cornerstone of the British automobile industry. In the United States, clockmakers were among the first to put the concept of interchangeable parts into operation, and with the advent of steamboats and trains running to preset schedules, the clock became essential to the shaping of regular routines. It is perhaps no coincidence that Joseph Saxton, developer of an early gear-cutting machine; John Fitch who developed the first (temporarily) successful steamboat; Matthias Baldwin who built one of the first American railway locomotives; John Kay, who helped Arkwright develop the water frame; Joseph Brown, the inventor of the sewing machine, and Henry Ford all started their careers as clockmakers or clock repairers.

Sewing machines and typewriters have similarly complex histories, although more compressed. The first patent for a typewriter was granted in Britain in 1714, but the first commercial machine was introduced in 1873 by the American company, E. Remington and Sons. Remington, a manufacturer of firearms, had the machines and machinists necessary for precision manufacturing of very small parts. In order to keep the typewriter keys from jamming, Remington developed the QWERTY keyboard, scattering the most frequently used vowels and consonants over three rows, and deliberately giving 60 per cent of the work to the left hand, which moved more slowly than the right. There must be a streak of sentimentality in technology, because 125 years later, the QWERTY keyboard survives, even on computers, long after typewriters stopped jamming, and long after the use of keys ceased to have any mechanical significance.

Technology lost, technology remembered

Technology, of course, does not always move in a forward direction. It can be ignored, lost, forgotten or destroyed. Sometimes old, forgotten technologies are remembered and put to good use again. The Chinese simply lost interest in clocks and many of their other technological advances. 'The greatest enigma in the history of technology,' according to Joel Mokyr, 'is the failure of China to sustain its technical supremacy' after 1400.[6] Highly advanced technologies in irrigation and agriculture, ploughs, seed drills and harrows, the development of blast furnaces, textiles, water power and maritime technology – all stagnated, atrophied or were simply forgotten.

Technologies are sometimes deliberately extinguished. In its early days, General Motors calculated that its greatest potential competition was not from automobile manufacturers, but from other forms of transportation. As a result, in the 1920s, in conjunction with Standard Oil of California and Firestone Tire (which had similar interests), General Motors began to buy up and dismantle electric transit companies across America. Some 44 systems in 16 states were converted to the use of diesel-powered buses and then sold with conditionality clauses which precluded the future purchase of any equipment that did not run on petroleum products.[7]

As new technologies and resources emerge, old ones often die out. When the Portuguese first arrived in West Africa, they were amazed at the quality of brass casting they found, and refused to believe that the brilliant art work of Ife and Benin had not been influenced by ancient Greek or Roman travellers. The lost wax method of brass casting is an ancient one, known in many societies. But such was the quality of work in West Africa that the Portuguese took African craftsmen with them to introduce and expand the technology in Brazil.

There are sites in West Africa with evidence of an iron industry dating back as far as 500 BC, coinciding with the development of the Iron Age in Britain. The earliest sites in Ghana date from the second century A.D., and by the fifteenth century, iron had become a common village industry there, producing a range of agricultural implements and weapons. When fifteenth century European traders arrived in search of gold, this gave a spur to the iron industry, as new tools were needed for mining. But as the European taste for gold increased and as slaves were added to the list of exports, more and more textiles, agricultural implements, tools and firearms were imported. Under the influence of these imports, the traditional iron industry gradually declined, and by the early twentieth century survived only in remote areas of northern Ghana, as little more than a crude cottage industry. Iron technology was lost, but ironically the lost wax method of bronze casting, which in most other societies disappeared, has survived in West Africa. No longer an essential or important technology, it continues largely through handicraft sales. The greatness of the past age is sometimes recalled, however, in the auction rooms of Europe: in 1989 a single artistic Benin bronze realized £1.3 million at Christie's.

History records several cataclysmic instances of massive technology loss. The most prominent European example was the collapse of Rome under the might of invaders for whom the hard-won technologies of previous centuries meant little. The Mongol invasion of China in the thirteenth century cut short an unprecedented era of intellectual, artistic and technological development. The Mongol invasions of Iran and Iraq had a similar effect. The great libraries of Baghdad were destroyed and the country's extensive irrigation and hydraulic systems were laid waste. Two other examples of 'de-industrialization' are relevant. The first coincides with the European arrival in what is today 'Latin America'. Within only 29 years of the first landfall of Columbus in the new world, Spanish armies under the command of Cortez – driven by a lust for gold and a fanatic desire to impose Christianity on everyone they encountered – destroyed the Aztec armies of Montezuma and their magnificent capital, which Cortez himself had referred to as 'the most beautiful city in the world'.[8] Over the next 50 years, 25 million Aztecs - perhaps 90 per cent of the population – died from devastating epidemics of European measles and smallpox.

The Inca of Peru, noteworthy for the organization they applied to society, were next. The Inca were proficient in mining and metallurgy – in copper, gold, silver and tin. Their architecture and construction techniques were of a high order; their textile technology, their irrigation and agricultural techniques were in many ways superior to those of the invader. But nine years after the destruction of Montezuma's great city, Francisco Pizarro inflicted the same fate on the Inca ruler, Atahualpa. Within a decade, a once proud civilization lay in ruins, its people working as slaves in the gold and silver mines that would fuel expanding European empires.

India is a more particular case of deindustrialization, because after the consolidation of British rule, industrial development was diverted from an evolutionary path to one aimed solely at serving British interests. The destruction of the Indian textile industry is a well known example. Another is the shipbuilding industry. As long as it suited the Admiralty, particularly after the loss of American shipyards, shipbuilding in Bombay and eastern India thrived. The industry did not provide the stimulus that it did in other countries, however, because when strategic and technological interests changed, shipbuilding was allowed to collapse. Skills which might have emanated from the shipyards were simply never developed. The same was true of railway development which, in Europe and America, provided an important stimulus to other industries. Although a vast network of Indian rail lines had been established by the end of the nineteenth century, the rails themselves were imported and engines were assembled from components made in Britain. As Arnold Pacey notes, 'Indian participation in any skilled role was excluded. India was forced to conform to the concept of 'transfer of technology' in its crudest form, in which one party is seen as a passive borrower of techniques, not a participant in dialogue.'[9]

A more modern example of the push and pull of technology in India can be found in the South Indian state of Kerala, where the traditional or artisanal fishing industry represents one quarter of the entire country's marine fish production. In the early 1950s, a Norwegian aid project was initiated in order to assist in the mechanization of traditional fishing boats, one of which, the *kattumarram* has given its name to the modern catamaran. When initial motorization tests in Norway failed, attention turned elsewhere, reflecting the Government of India's view that the fishery sector was in any case, 'largely of a primitive character, carried on by ignorant, unorganized and ill-equipped fishermen. Their techniques are rudimentary, their tackle elementary, their capital equipment slight and inefficient'.[10]

The Norwegians moved on to larger boats, and using bottom trawling techniques, discovered that the waters of Kerala were one of the world's richest prawn grounds. By 1962, with prawns selling to Japanese buyers for Rs8900 per ton and fish selling for only Rs150, private investment in trawlers had become enormous. But the trawlers caught more than prawns. They disturbed fish breeding grounds and netted enormous amounts of fish, most of which were destroyed in the process. During the 1970s and 1980s, the traditional fishing industry, which employed over 90 000 people, went into serious decline. Catches of oil sardine and mackerel dropped from a peak of 250 000 tons in 1968 to only 87 000 tons in 1980.

In an effort to remain competitive, fishermen took matters into their own hands, and began purchasing outboard engines with state government loans. This provided only temporary respite, however, as their boats were not suited to the vibration of the motors, and the engines were unsuited to the locally available kerosene, which was intended mainly for lamps and cooking. When engines failed, income halted and debts mounted. The Intermediate Technology Development Group (ITDG) became involved with the fishermen at about this time, and assisted in the development and local construction of a more suitable plywood boat. Plywood was a versatile material which provided the fishermen with a cheap alternative to their traditional craft, for which timber was becoming increasingly scarce and expensive. ITDG also became involved in the testing and development of engines better suited to the rigours of Kerala. And the fishermen themselves organized a strong political lobby which sought to have trawling banned in shallower waters and during the fish-breeding monsoon season.

In addition, they experimented with a technology of their own, known in Trivandrum for centuries. In order to draw fish closer to shore, fishermen had traditionally dumped rocks with attached coconut fronds into the sea. People also remembered that a shipwreck, discovered in about 50 metres of water north of Trivandrum in 1949, had become a rich fishing reef. So, in response to the problems of the 1960s and 1970s, the fishermen began to construct artificial reefs of their own, using stones, tyres, concrete rings and anchors.

The impact of change in a fragile natural ecosystem is complex, and can only be judged over time. The preliminary evidence, however, was positive. Better boats allowed fishermen to become more competitive, while the partial success of their political lobbying and the development of more than 20 artificial reefs during the 1980s paid off in terms of fishing yields – which in 1988 and 1989 had returned to the levels of the early 1970s. One external technology had changed life forever along the Kerala coast, while two others helped poor families cope with the damage. But perhaps the most important lesson was that the fishermen were not helpless, nor were they 'ignorant and unorganized'. With scientists now studying the effects of their artificial reefs, an old indigenous technology may have an important contribution to make in finding a solution to the sustainability of livelihoods and the Kerala fishery.

Technology and organization

Warfare has contributed immensely to another important facet of the development and diffusion of technology: organization. New technologies in the Middle Ages demanded that military organization extend beyond short-term battlefield strategies into permanent government structures and systems. The manufacture of new weapons in sufficient quantities could not be left to happenstance; military security required organized production and government support.

Improvements in technology both encouraged and flowed from better organization. The classical world of Greece and Rome, for example, used animal traction inefficiently. It was not until the eleventh century in Europe that people discovered that a horse could pull a load of more than half a ton. Greek and Roman horses, depicted in surviving statuary and art as regal animals with their heads held high, were in fact constrained from pulling heavy loads by a harness that strangled them if they put their heads down. The development of the horse collar proved that a horse could pull as much as an ox and, more importantly, that it could do so at twice the speed.[11] Combined with improved crop rotation techniques and military iron technology – now used for horseshoes and agricultural implements – vast new tracts of virgin land could be brought under the plough, accompanied, of necessity, by the development of organized estate farming. Larger farms, in turn, both justified and required greater investments in infrastructure, particularly irrigation.

The development of textile machinery was important to the British industrial revolution, but a more fundamental factor was the emergence of the 'modern' textile factory after 1760. These factories were made possible by the advent of steam power to drive machinery, but they were as much the product of new concepts of work: in a factory, work could be subdivided, routines could be devised and work properly supervised.

The concept of interchangeable parts, developed during the first half of the nineteenth century in Connecticut's Springfield Armory in connection with the manufacture of weapons, further revolutionized concepts of production and organization. Hitherto, each gun had been made by a single craftsman and no gun was exactly the same as any other. If a firing mechanism malfunctioned, a craftsman was needed to repair it. The idea of a replacement part, each of which would be identical to thousands of others, not only altered the face of manufacturing forever, it changed the role of the maker from craftsman to machine operator. Before the concept of interchangeable parts could be properly developed, however, a number of preconditions were necessary: the development of jigs and fixtures; the availability of cheap and abundant steel; precision grinding, cutting and drilling tools that could perform the same function over and over without variation; a cheap and accurate micrometer.

The subsequent capacity for mass production led to refinements in techniques of organization. In early factories, machines were organized by function: all the drills were in one part of the shop, all the lathes in another, all the grinders elsewhere. Raw materials and work in progress were moved about in batches from section to section. The result was often chaotic, as a batch of parts returned two or three or four times to the drilling section, either waiting for other batches to be finished, or holding them up. New concepts of flow led to a reorganization of the factory so that batches of parts moved along a line of machines placed in sequential order. If drilling was required at three stages of the operation, with cutting and grinding between, the appropriate number of drills would be located before, between and after the grinders and cutters. From this type of 'flowline' to continuous flow was a logical next step, widely adopted by the 1880s: parts no longer moved in batches. Rather they moved one by one, significantly reducing the time that material lay idle.

'Scientific management', a concept that began to develop towards the end of the nineteenth century, broke tasks into their component parts and organized them in the most efficient way. It was an effort to overcome worker resistance to the loss of creativity, and – not least – to deal with the increasingly real risks of social upheaval and revolution. Bigger and bigger became better and better (that is, more and more profitable), once corporations recognized the importance of what industrial historian David Noble calls 'the task of transforming America in a sober and scientific manner ... to analyze, rationalize, systematize and coordinate the entire 'social mechanism', to translate haphazard, uncertain and disruptive social forces into manageable problems for efficient administration.'[12] Such a translation involved economic and social research, market analysis, industrial and governmental planning, labour-management co-operation and ever more streamlined production management.

Combining the operations of two or more machines into a single machine further speeded up the flow-through, but it was Ford engineers, working on the Model T in the summer of 1913, who truly revolutionized the flowline principle. Pulling an automobile chassis gradually along the factory floor while stationary technicians worked on it, the time required to produce a car was reduced from 13 hours to less than six. A conveyor belt installed the following year reduced overall costs dramatically, and enabled Ford to slash the price of the Model T from $950 in 1909 to $360 by 1916. Not surprisingly, the annual production of cars expanded during the same period – from 12 000 to 577 000.[13]

While European and American manufacturers relied on the consolidation of small firms into giant corporations, and on lessons learned in the 1920s and 1930s, organizational concepts were further refined in Japan in the 1970s and 1980s. Inventories were reduced to absolute minimums using the 'just in time' or 'right on time' concept: raw materials, components and finished goods arrived at each processing stage or from carefully integrated sub-contractors at precisely the right moment. Stocks did not accumulate; components did not back up. Departments – from design to market – were integrated with a care and precision unknown in Europe and America. Customer opinion and preference were sought with the determination of a salmon heading upstream to spawn. Quality, innovation and flexibility made deep inroads on the single-minded western industrial notion of 'getting the price right.'

The outcome can be seen in the experience of Austin and Nissan. In 1952, Austin provided technical assistance and designs which allowed Nissan to produce the A40 in Japan. Although Japanese production of the A40 declined over the years of the agreement, as late as 1959, Nissan's own Datsun Cedric was basically just an Austin clone. By 1980, things had radically changed. Japan was producing 11 million vehicles annually, while the US produced only 8 million and Britain had fallen to 1.3 million. In 1983 Nissan became the world's third largest car producer after General Motors and Toyota.[14] In Britain, the Austin marque had only survived on two models (one developed in 1959) by 1989, when it was taken over completely by Rover. There are several lessons in all this, but the primary one is that technology is more than machines. Technological success owes as much to technique, design, good planning and effective organization as it does to engineering.

Technology and institutions

Organization does not exist in a vacuum. It develops within the context of institutions: religious institutions, educational institutions, government, industry, trade unions, the modern corporation. Buddhist pilgrims travelling between India and China in the sixth and seventh centuries were carriers of vast amounts of information – not least through the written word – about such things as agriculture, chemistry, paper making and engineering. In Japan, the casting of giant bronze statues of the Buddha was both a result of and a stimulus to new techniques in metallurgy. Both Islam and Christianity were responsible for generations of advances in architecture and building technologies. Norman architects and masons, for example, were at work on English churches well before the Norman invasion. And eight centuries after their construction, many European Cathedrals remain the largest, most solid and most beautiful buildings in the towns and cities where they were constructed.

In an often brutish world, religious institutions were also places where art, another key aspect in the development and movement of technology, could flourish. Writing, the illumination of scripture and eventually printing – block printing in China, and the printing press in Europe – had strong roots in Buddhism and Christianity.

The importance of government in the advancement of technology cannot be over-estimated. The role of the state is obvious in one of technology's greatest stimuli – warfare and the development of weapons. Government's hand (and money) can be found in technologies and techniques ranging from the development of gunpowder through the organization of interchangeable parts at the Springfield Armory, to the advent of manned flight, space travel, and all modern communications technology – from the telegraph to fibre optics.

Governments have played a major role in the development of shipbuilding through the ages, and thus of exploration and trade. The obverse of encouragement can also be found: the Chinese government's decision in the early fifteenth century to *curtail* shipbuilding and to withdraw the Chinese fleet from further trade with India, Arabia and the east coast of Africa had a profound and positive effect on the development of European exploration in the next few decades.

Governments protect new technologies with patent legislation and through the erection of tariffs against competition. Richard Arkwright is remembered for the invention of the 'water frame' which helped to revolutionize the British textile industry. He is less well remembered for his successful efforts to have the government reduce its excise tax on British-made textiles. Although inferior in quality to calico imported from India, the price advantage this gave British calico resulted in a two-thirds drop in Indian imports in only eight years.[15]

Education has also been important to the development and spread of technology. The great universities of Baghdad, Toledo, Paris, Oxford and Cambridge were, of course, famous seats of learning. But technical education was, until the nineteenth century, something that took place largely outside the formal education system. Skilled workmen learned their profession through the apprenticeship system. It was with the movement away from craft-based industry towards mass production that higher education began to play an increasingly important role in industrial education, and in the production and reproduction of the corporate engineer.

Endowed by industrialists to develop scientific and management studies as early as 1847, Harvard did not actually graduate its first engineer until 1854, and by 1892 had produced only 155.[16] At Yale, agricultural chemistry and other practical subjects were taught in the attic of the chapel until 1860. It was this inability or reluctance of established American universities to go beyond polite learning and to recognize the need for advanced scientific and industrial education that led to the formation of the Massachusetts Institute of Technology in 1861. Over the following century, the relationship between American universities and industry became a close one. Business and industry worked with universities in the establishment of research facilities. Universities received much of their core funding from industry. Professors worked with business and industry in the development of curricula; industry recruited graduates straight from the campus; co-operative courses of study, combined with work in industry, were adopted by dozens of universities and hundreds of companies after the turn of the century.

David Noble echoes Thorstein Veblen in questioning what had become a love affair and then a marriage between higher education and industry:

> Veblen understood that the 'free pursuit of knowledge,' which he considered the 'end for which a university is maintained,' was being thwarted, and its radical potential checked, because it was being incorporated within the larger closed framework of big-business enterprise. The 'pursuit of knowledge' would gain considerable social stature and financial support as a result of the new industry-education co-operation, but it would no longer be really 'free'.[17]

Freedom of inquiry might be maintained and guarded, but it would become a 'controlled freedom', a 'disciplined initiative' operating in support of, rather than against the industrial system. Quelling and co-opting opposition to the industrial system was, understandably enough, a concern very much in the forefront of industrial, if not university thinking during the first quarter of the twentieth century.

The advent of mass production, the unquestioned importance of economies of scale, the apparent inevitability of giantism and the services of its handmaiden, higher education, has exercised thinkers and philosophers throughout the century. In France, Saint-Simon predicted a society run by engineers and scientists, while others saw the beginnings of a new form of government: not democracy or bureaucracy, but *technocracy*. In the 1960s, Schumacher questioned the 'idolatry of large' partly on economic grounds, but as much on social grounds.

By the 1980s and 1990s, however, the idolatry of large was on the wane in much professional management theory – on economic and management grounds as well as social grounds. The arrival on the docks of Europe and North America of better, cheaper and *different* Japanese goods – cars, cameras, electronics, steel, biotechnology, pianos, organs and just about everything else – not to mention the presence of Japanese investors in Western corporate boardrooms, had a profound effect on forcing a reconsideration of technology and how it is organized.

Technology and the individual

The study of history has been much preoccupied with kings and presidents, with wars and revolutions and plagues. Major artists and explorers are remembered, as are some individuals credited with a major invention. But ordinary farmers, seamen, craftsmen and women, entrepreneurs, and the people David Freeman Hawke calls 'the dirty fingernail people' are too often forgotten.

Robert Fulton is credited with the invention of the steamboat in 1807. In fact the maiden voyage of Fulton's boat, *The Claremont*, took place a full seventeen years after scheduled steamboat service had been introduced (and then abandoned) on the Delaware River. Fulton had combined the improved technology of two decades – better brass fittings, an improved copper boiler, significantly better tolerances, greater knowledge of water resistance – with the experience of other steamboat innovators. He also worked within a much improved economic context for steam transport. Encapsulating the essence of technology 'transfer', his response to critics who accused him of stealing from others was, 'Every artist who invents a new and useful machine, must choose it of known parts of *other* machines. I made use of all these parts to express ideas of a whole combination, new in mechanics, producing a new and desired effect, giving them their powers and proportions indispensible to their present success in constructing steamboats.'[18] Fulton is remembered; the hundreds of others who contributed to his success are not.

Samuel Colt, whose name is synonymous with small arms, conceived of the revolver himself, but had every one of his models produced for him by others. After several failures and bankruptcies, he made a fortune through shrewd government contracts, astute arrangements with investors, and high quality products made by genuine tool and machinery makers. A generation later, Samuel F.B. Morse – an artist – gained credit for 'inventing' the telegraph. In fact

Morse's genius was not so much in taking other people's inventions to their logical conclusion as it was in raising funds to promote the use he saw for them. Henry Ford's famous assembly line was simply an improvement on already advanced thinking about the industrial flowline.

From these examples and the many others of schoolbook history – Watt, Arkwright, Hargreaves, Faraday, Bell, Edison – it is not hard to understand why the notion of invention without context and, therefore, of a portability and disconnectedness in technology, has gained currency among aid agencies and those concerned with enhancing the pace of development in the Third World.

Although the remembered 'inventors' followed and worked with a legion of unknown craftsmen and innovators, they do stand out as what today's management literature calls *champions*. Peters and Waterman have written at length about the importance of champions, both within and outside formal structures of business, government and industry.[19] They describe the product champion as a zealot or fanatic – not necessarily an intellectual giant, but a pragmatist, possibly even an 'idea thief' who develops a concept 'and bull-headedly pushes it to fruition'.[20] Champions do not always succeed; in fact most of them fail most of the time. But if success is normally achieved one time out of ten, it therefore stands to reason that ten attempts and nine failures must be experienced in order to achieve the one success.

Success is almost always the result of repeated attempts and experiments, and of a climate which encourages experimentation, a climate, most importantly, which understands and tolerates failure. Champions do not emerge automatically. Peters and Waterman argue that 'they emerge because history and numerous supporters encourage them to, nurture them through trying times, celebrate their successes, and nurse them through occasional failures. But given the supports, the would-be champion population turns out to be enormous, certainly not limited to a handful of creative marvels'.[21]

Technology moves when people move. Nineteenth century American manufacturers were notorious for rapacious industrial espionage, sending spies to Britain, bribing technicians to emigrate, smuggling machines, particularly textile machinery, out of the country. But it was the waves of immigrants from Europe to North America bringing new skills, new ideas, and new ways of approaching problems, who had the most profound general human effect on American technology development over the past two centuries. There is a double irony in this phenomenon for today's Third World. First, there is little permanent migration today from North to South, or (with the exception of refugees) between Southern countries. This means that the movement of technical expertise to the Third World is a historical hybrid, consisting mainly of students returning from studies abroad, or of short term technical experts, usually on aid contracts.

The second irony is that attempts to develop a human technical resource base in the South are severely weakened by emigration to the North. In 1970, UNCTAD estimated that some Third World countries were losing between 20 and 70 per cent of their annual output of doctors to the North. It was calculated that the value of imported scientists, engineers and doctors to the United States in 1970 was $3.7 billion, more than the US spent that year on all development assistance to all countries. A 1991 study showed that the trend has not abated. It is estimated that between 1967 and 1985, India transferred $51 billion to the United States in the form of skilled 'human capital' – trained scientists, doctors and engineers. Between 1974 and 1988, the number of immigrant scientists and engineers in the United States doubled, from 5.8 per cent to 10.5 per cent of the total. The five leading sources of the talent were India, Britain, Taiwan, Poland and China.[22] The further bitter irony in this is that the very embassies which process the Southbound flow of temporary technical experts on aid contracts, also process the permanent Northward emigration of a country's most technically qualified people.

It is in studying the role of individuals that some of the most salient lessons about the development and diffusion of technology emerge. Technological development is not automatic. It is the product of conscious and unconscious choices and decisions, all of which take place within a social and a historical context. The notion that technology can be 'transferred' without modification has few historical precedents to support it. The 'transfer' will almost always involve modifications. And the process of modifying a technology will, in itself, often stimulate other developments. But the implications are clear: in adapting a technology to local needs and conditions, local skills must be available. There must be a supply of 'dirty fingernail people', thinking people who have an intimate knowledge of the material with which they are working. This is one of the most fundamental historical lessons of technology development.

CHAPTER VI

Small is beautiful

*There is only one way by which poverty in the developing countries can
be attacked successfully, and that is by producing more in those nations.
In no one of these countries can human needs be satisfied by the simple
redistribution of existing income and wealth. In these countries, small is
not beautiful.[1]*   Robert S. McNamara, President, World Bank

ON A LATE summer's day in 1977, when snow had already fallen in the
high Alpine meadows, a train made an unscheduled stop in a small
Swiss town. The large man the ambulance attendants carried off the
train on a stretcher was followed by a railway official carrying a
suitcase and a broad-brimmed hat. At the village hospital it was
confirmed that the man, Ernst Friedrich Schumacher, – 'Fritz' to his
friends – had died of a massive heart attack.

German born, Schumacher was largely unknown in the country of
his birth. Educated at Oxford and Columbia and interned as an
enemy alien in Britain during the war, he subsequently became one of
Britain's top economic planners. The *Times*, for which he had once
been chief economic leader writer, published three consecutive
obituaries of Schumacher, and the requiem celebrated for him in
Westminster Cathedral was attended by leaders of government, the
academic world and industry. Born a Protestant, Schumacher was
profoundly influenced by Buddhism, yet died a Catholic. He was
employed for much of his working life by one the largest enterprises
in Europe, but he is best remembered for a single book – about
smallness. *Small is Beautiful*, first published in 1973 and translated
into 12 languages, has sold over four million copies and remains
a bestseller. A friend and confidant of the rich and powerful,
Schumacher was honoured by Queen Elizabeth II, consulted by
Julius Nyerere, Pandit Nehru and Kenneth Kaunda. He took tea with
Jimmy Carter in the White House. Yet his greatest achievements
were almost entirely on behalf of the poor.

Intermediate technology: the concept

Schumacher's tryst with smallness and greatness began unexception-
ably in 1955, when he was 44, during a UN consultancy to Burma.
Charged with advising the government on economic planning and
fiscal policy, he was struck by the richness of Burmese culture, by the
Buddhist religion and by the friendliness and dignity of people who
were, in normal economic parlance, simply poor. He began to see

that the 'economics of materialism', with which his professional life had been preoccupied, had its limitations and his report, focusing on the importance of rural development, spoke of the need to develop local expertise and self-reliance. It was the genesis of a professional conversion that would preoccupy him for the next 22 years.

Five years later, in a 1960 article for the *Observer*, he wrote,

> The West can indeed help the others [i.e. 'underdeveloped nations'], as the rich can always help the poor. But it is not an easy matter, expressible in terms of money alone. It demands a deep respect for the indigenous culture of those that are to be helped – maybe even a deeper respect than is possessed by many of them themselves. Above all ... it must be based on a clear understanding that the present situation of mankind demands the evolution of a non-violent way of political and economic life.[2]

Invited to participate in a series of seminars in India, he came into contact with some of the country's leading Gandhians, and in 1961 began to articulate his first ideas on intermediate technology:

> Economic development is obviously impossible without the introduction of 'better methods', 'higher technology', 'improved equipment' ... but all development, like all learning, is like a process of stretching. If you attempt to stretch too much, you get a rupture instead of a stretch... The only hope, I should hold, lies in a broadly based, decentralized crusade to support and improve the productive efforts of the people as they are struggling for their livelihoods now. Find out what they are doing and help them to do it better. Study their needs and help them to help themselves.[3]

Invited back to India in 1962 by the government's Planning Commission to advise on economic development policies, Schumacher further refined his concept of relevant technologies for rural areas, and began to wrestle with the prohibitive cost of creating workplaces in capital-intensive factories. Although his ideas and suggestions were largely ignored by Indian planners, for whom large-scale industrialization remained a preordained ideal, Schumacher persisted. Some of his ideas were borrowed: small-scale rural industries were already a standard development tool in China, for example. And he was deeply influenced by Gandhi who had coined a phrase Schumacher often quoted: 'Production by the masses, not mass production.'

Gandhi, who had popularized one of the first consciously 'appropriate' technologies, the spinning wheel, had said, 'The traditional old implements, the plough, the spinning wheel, have made our wisdom and our welfare... India's salvation consists in unlearning what she has learnt in the last fifty years... You cannot build non-violence on factory civilization; but you can build it on self-contained villages.'[4]

But much of what Schumacher wrote was strikingly new, especially to a Western school of development thought grounded in classical economics and theories of aggregate demand. In 1964, he presented a paper at Cambridge entitled 'Industrialization through Intermediate Technology' which was widely published and republished, and at last he began to develop a following of people who saw the relevance of his message. Among them were David Astor, editor of the *Observer*, Lord Robens, Chairman of the National Coal Board, George McRobie, a fellow-economist, and Julia Porter, Secretary of the African Development Trust. But Schumacher and his friends were uncertain as to how to proceed with an idea that seemed so *appropriate*, yet which received so little in the way of formal support. The governments of Burma and India had basically ignored the message. Britain's Ministry of Overseas Development was polite but uninterested, and the development establishment of the day was preoccupied with growth and Western models of large-scale industrialization – fuelled by apparently limitless supplies of cheap oil.

One day in May, 1965, a group of about twenty people joined with Schumacher in a meeting room at the Overseas Development Institute, and at last they decided to put their ideas into action. 'We had no money,' Schumacher recalled years later on a California radio programme. 'There were just a couple of friends of mine, like myself professional people with full-time work and families to support. But when you feel that something is necessary, you can't simply go on talking about it – you have to talk for a certain while, but then the moment comes – I tell you, a frightening moment – when you have to take the existential jump from talking to doing, even if you have no money.'[5]

In August, the *Observer* published a lengthy article that Schumacher had written months earlier, entitled 'How to Help Them Help Themselves'. It was as powerful and as succinct as anything he had ever written, and it came at precisely the right moment in the life of the nascent movement.

'Mass unemployment in developing countries,' he wrote,

> ... is being accepted as inevitable and unconquerable, even as 'necessary for sound growth', in much the same way as was the case in advanced countries before Keynes... Unemployment and underemployment in developing countries are most acute in the areas outside a few metropolitan cities; so there is mass migration into these cities in a desperate search for a livelihood: and the cities themselves, in spite of 'rapid economic growth', become infested with ever-growing multitudes of destitute people...

> No amount of brave statistics of national income growth can hide the fact that all too many developing countries are suffering from the twin

disease of growing unemployment and mushrooming metropolitan slums, which is placing their social and political fabric under intolerable strain.

The suspicion has been voiced (and cannot be dismissed out of hand) that foreign aid, as currently practiced, may actually be intensifying this twin disease instead of mitigating it; that the heedless rush into modernization extinguishes old jobs faster than it can create new ones; and that all the apparent increases in national income are eaten up, or even more than eaten up, by the crushing economic burdens produced by excessive urban growth.

Rather than simply increasing aid flows, Schumacher argued that a change in direction was necessary, a change that would take aid agencies 'straight into battle' with the evils of poverty. This could be done by creating jobs in the areas where people live – the rural areas rather than cities. The workplaces would have to be cheap enough that developing countries could afford to create them in large numbers without unattainable levels of saving and imports. The employment should be in productive jobs requiring relatively simple production methods, producing goods for local consumption and relying to a large extent on local supplies of raw materials and finance. This could only be done, Schumacher, said, through a conscious effort to develop an 'intermediate technology'.

Western technology has been devised primarily for the purpose of saving labour; it could hardly be appropriate for districts or regions troubled with a large labour surplus. Technology in Western countries has grown up over several generations along with a vast array of supporting services, like modern transport, accountancy, marketing and so forth: it could hardly be appropriate for districts or regions lacking these paraphernalia.

This technology, therefore, 'fits' only into those sectors which are already fairly modernized, and that means – some special cases apart – the metropolitan areas, comprising, say, 15 to 20 per cent of the whole population. What, then, is to become of the other 80 to 85 per cent? Simply to assume that the 'modern' sectors or localities will grow until they account for the whole is utterly unrealistic, because the 80 per cent cannot simply 'hold their breath' and wait: they will migrate in their millions and thereby create chaos, even in the 'modern' sectors.

The task, he argued, was to establish a tolerable basis of existence for the 80 per cent through an intermediate technology aimed at improving the productivity of traditional technologies, which were often in a state of stagnation or decay. This intermediate technology would be cheaper and simpler than the capital-intensive technology being imported from the West.

Some early critics argued that such a technology would waste resources, would produce less per unit of capital than known production methods, and could never be competitive. 'Dogmatic pronouncements are worthless,' Schumacher retorted. 'Let us have design studies and we shall see.' It would not be a long, expensive or particularly difficult task. Fragments of the technology that he foresaw already existed, both in the North and the South. What was needed was a systematic effort to collect them and develop them into practical blueprints for action.

> What stands in the way? Perhaps a kind of technological snobbishness which regards with disdain anything less than ultra-modern? Perhaps a certain callousness in the attitudes of privileged minorities towards the immense suffering of their homeless, jobless fellow-men? Or is it lack of imagination on the part of the planners in resplendent offices who find ratios and coefficients more significant than people?[6]

Public reaction was overwhelming and positive. Letters and support flowed in. In the following year the Schumacher group – which had been meeting in borrowed rooms – incorporated itself as a nonprofit company and a registered charity. They called themselves the Intermediate Technology Development Group (ITDG), and their first donation – the fee from the *Observer* article – came from Schumacher himself.

Intermediate technology: the movement

If, when ITDG started, there was a single basic criterion of what constituted 'appropriateness', it was low capital cost per workplace. There were likely to be four characteristics of a technology that would make it 'appropriate' to a developing society: it would be small in scale so that it could fit into small market situations. It would be simple, so that sophisticated manufacturing skills, organization and finance would be unnecessary. It would not be capital-intensive, and would therefore keep the cost per workplace down. And it would be non-violent. To Schumacher, the non-violence of a technology was an essential part of its appropriateness; it meant that an appropriate technology would be one that was completely under human control, that it would not have unintended side effects, that it would not cause social or environmental disruption.

Over the years since the basic formula – small, simple, cheap, non-violent – was developed, it has attracted a surprisingly large volume of academic and non-academic debate. Papers, theses and books have been written on the definition alone, arguing about finer points in the meaning of 'intermediate', and about definitions of appropriate: appropriate for whom? Appropriate to what? Who, after all, would be interested in an *inappropriate* technology?

Some observers insist on a clear distinction between 'appropriate technology', and 'intermediate technology'. The development of penicillin, for example, was very appropriate to the health needs it sought to address worldwide, but it was hardly an intermediate technology. Likewise the use of an earth satellite to predict a cyclonic disturbance is far from being an intermediate technology. But to villagers living in the low-lying delta areas of Bangladesh, the warning that this highly sophisticated, expensive technology can provide is more than appropriate. On the other hand, an intermediate technology, if it is going to be practical for development purposes, has to be an appropriate technology, and so sometimes the terms are synonymous.

Intermediate technology is a relative term: a technology that stands somewhere between what is known – the traditional technology – and the modern. Thus in Africa, animal traction, falling half way between the hoe and the tractor, could be seen as an intermediate technology. In Asia, where animal traction is well developed, a power tiller might conceivably be the intermediate technology. But in some cases, neither of these examples might be appropriate. In Africa the most appropriate advance on traditional slash and burn agriculture might be better seeds, the use of fertilizer, an improved hoe. In Asia, the power tiller might not be the next logical progression on animal traction. It might be a better plough, improved irrigation, better organization.

In some cases, the definitions have overtaken common sense. George McRobie, who became Chairman of the Intermediate Technology Development Group when Schumacher died was, like Schumacher, far from dogmatic on definitions. Referring to 'small, simple, cheap and non-violent', he wrote that 'it is by no means certain that all four criteria can be satisfied in every case; *but any one of them, or combination of them, is of value for our purposes.*'[7] Ten years later, however, the definition had become much more elaborate and insistent: 'Appropriate Technology is any productive process, any piece of equipment that meets *all* the following criteria (both emphases are in the originals):

○ it meets the needs of the majority, not a small minority, of a community;
○ it employs natural resources, capital and labour in proportion to their long-term sustainable availability;
○ it is ownable, controllable, operable and maintainable within the community it serves;
○ it enhances the skills and dignity of those employed by it;
○ it is non-violent both to the environment and to people;
○ it is socially, economically and environmentally sustainable.'[8]

The irony in this definition – which combines dogmatism with an imprecision that begs for misunderstanding – is that virtually none of the practical ideas and technologies that Schumacher worked on during his lifetime would have survived it. Schumacher himself was impatient with 'those who get stuck on words; who start arguing with me that small is not *always* beautiful... These people who can't go beyond the words. This I consider an academic disease which is rampant.'[9]

In 1965, the concepts of appropriate and intermediate technology were simply that, concepts. Ten years later there were an estimated five hundred organizations, groups and institutions with an appropriate technology focus, and by 1980 the number had doubled to a thousand.[10] Some were small NGOs, others were attached to prestigious universities – St Gallen University in Switzerland, the Brace Research Institute in Montreal, and German universities in Oldenburg and Berlin. GATE was established in Bonn as the appropriate technology wing of the West German Foreign Ministry, and other institutions sprang up across Europe and North America: Techno-Serve in the US, the Groupe de Recherche et d'Echanges Technologiques (GRET) in France, and TOOL in the Netherlands. Appropriate Technology International (ATI) in the United States had an unusual start: inspired by Schumacher's ideals, and by his widely-read book, it was funded by USAID but was given a direct mandate from Congress as a private, nonprofit organization.

Far from being centred in the North, the idea quickly took root throughout the Third World. With advice from ITDG, the University of Science and Technology in Kumasi, Ghana, established a Technology Consultancy Centre in 1971. The University of Zimbabwe founded a similar institution, again with advice from ITDG, in the early 1980s. Committees, groups and organizations were established in Zambia, Kenya and Tanzania. Two institutions were opened in Botswana – the Rural Industries Innovation Centre at Kanye and the Botswana Technology Centre in Gaberone. There were dozens of others: the South Pacific Appropriate Technology Foundation, the Centro Co-operativo Tecnico Industrial in Honduras, the Centro Meso Americano de Estudios Sobre Tecnologia in Guatemala, and many in India, such as the Appropriate Technology Development Association in Lucknow.

Co-ordinating bodies were established: Volunteers in Technical Assistance (VITA), which predated ITDG by six years, had been established to disseminate knowledge about known, relevant technologies to developing countries. SATIS (Socially Appropriate Technology International Information Services) was founded in 1982 to disseminate information about technology produced by other

88

organizations. And the Manila-based APPROTECH, supported initially by ATI, was formed as an Asian regional information centre on appropriate technology.

Everywhere there were experiments with windmills, solar energy, latrines and energy-efficient stoves. Experimental pumps of every sort began to dot the yards behind workshops – pumps made of bamboo, wood, plastic; pumps powered by the sun, the wind, bicycles and oars. Small biogas plants producing methane from animal waste, a technology developed concurrently in India and China, began to appear throughout the Third World.

It was in some of these in tial enthusiastic projects that the first weaknesses in the Appropriate Technology (AT) movement began to appear. The movement had been formed of an uncritical coalition between two distinct groupings. The first, predominantly concerned with the economic and social development of the Third World, was rooted mainly in the non-governmental and academic communities. The second was largely a Western consumer-based movement made up of people disenchanted with mainstream industrial and technological development. Growing out of the counter-culture of the late 1960s and early 1970s, this part of the movement focused less on the technology and objectives of organizations like ITDG and more on an 'alternative' technology aimed at simpler, less wasteful Western lifestyles.

That Schumacher's message spoke so eloquently to both streams is a mark of its universality. But the Western counter-culture, searching for a return to simpler times, often had little useful to say to the poor of the Third World, armed with rudimentary tools, suffering from ill health in debilitating climates, eking poor livings out of poor soil or earning pennies a day in crowded factories. The Walden Pond school of appropriate technology, which carried over into the environmental movement, forgets – or never knew – that Henry David Thoreau did not brave the harsh frontier. He may have lived a bucolic life in the Massachusetts woods, but even in 1845 the woods were not far from civilization, and the pond was not far from his mother's house where he often had dinner when his own larder was bare. This side of the AT movement – dedicated to 'alternative' technologies – is a protest, often a very legitimate one. But it is neither intermediate, nor is it particularly relevant to the parched maize fields of the Sahel, the harsh Altiplano of Bolivia or the crowded slums of Manila.

This is not to diminish the importance of Thoreau nor, more particularly, of the Northern environmental movement. Much of it, however, has been considerably more concerned with trees, birds and wildlife, than with people. This is natural enough in the North where most people have most material needs taken care of, and where industry and consumerism have paved over a sea of Walden Ponds, converting them into parking lots and hamburger stands. It is far from appropriate in the South, however, where much environmental degradation is caused by poverty rather than the reverse. That is why tree-planting programmes in the South often have limited success until the poverty of people who survive by cutting down trees is taken into consideration. This theme will recur in subsequent chapters which deal with energy and a growing convergence of interest between the development and environmental movements. It will suffice to note here that the idea of 'transferring' capital-intensive technology willy-nilly to the Third World is no more arrogant than attempting to transfer Western environmental worries without adaptation, and without careful reference to the very different circumstances in which Southern people live.

Luddites in reverse gear: the critics

The 'AT movement', sometimes advanced and occasionally retarded by its informal alliance with the alternatives movement, went through two distinct phases in the 1960s and 1970s. The first was a kind of 'messianic phase' during which it was assumed, partly because of a lack of funding, that once the problem was understood, solutions would fall easily into place. It reflected Schumacher's early idea that the task would not be 'long, expensive or particularly difficult'. This proved to be far from true, but in the early years it was easier to indulge in criticism of the prevailing development ethic and its emphasis on Big, than to find cheap, workable technologies that could demonstrate the effectiveness of the alternative.

As the 1960s – the 'First Development Decade' – drew to a close and the failings of the basic growth model started to become evident, however, more funding became available for alternative approaches and for NGOs. Schumacher, no longer out in the cold, now saw that in itself, the message was not enough. In Britain, ITDG began to form groups or panels of engineers and designers, builders, agronomists, health and energy experts who could actually begin to work on testing and adapting ideas. In some cases what they came up with were already existing technologies such as small-scale textile equipment or corn grinding machines, well tested but unknown to potential users. In other cases, such as brick making or soap production, they took traditional technologies and improved them. A third approach was the simplification of a modern technology such as hydro-electric power or the manufacture of nuts and bolts. And in some cases there were completely new technologies such as the use of solar energy.

This second phase of the AT movement, which lasted well into the

1980s, is regarded by some as the 'arrogant phase', a period dominated by technology and hardware – what one AT worker called 'the better mousetrap phase'. It was, to a large extent, characterized by the same arrogance that fuelled mainstream aid agencies, and its failures can be seen rusting behind the workshops of dozens of AT institutions around the world. Part of the problem was a fixation with technology, at the expense of diffusion. Diffusion, it was assumed, would follow naturally enough if an idea was a good one. Alternatively, diffusion was the responsibility of others – government, NGOs or perhaps the private sector. And poor diffusion was a reflection on them rather than on the technology.

Biogas is perhaps the archetypal example. Tens of thousands of successful methane gas digesters were already in operation in India and China when the AT movement began to work on the technology. Through the 1970s, literally thousands of prototypes were developed, redeveloped and field tested in other Asian countries, in Latin America, the Caribbean and all across Africa. The result has been decidedly mixed. In northern Pakistan a local NGO, pressed by donors to introduce the technology into the villages with which it worked, discovered that gas production decreases as temperatures drop. When the gas is most needed for heating and cooking, it simply isn't available. In other countries, it was found that the number of animals required to fuel a digester made it inaccessible to the poorest families. In addition, cows had to be kept in a restricted area so the dung could be collected properly. Attempts to organize several families around one gas plant were often futile – in part because not enough gas was produced for the number of people involved. In some parts of the Third World it was as difficult to get people excited about working with animal faeces as it would be in Pittsburgh or Milton Keynes, a problem that did not exist in China and India where animal dung had long been a traditional source of fuel.

Experiments in Botswana illustrate the problem. Botswana has nothing, if not cattle. But after eight years of expensive experimentation at the Rural Industries Innovation Centre, only 12 biogas plants had been put into field situations. Of those that remained in operation after two years, most were experiencing severe operational and management difficulties.[11]

The generalization that diffusion was given a back seat during this phase of the AT movement's development is not universally true, but it is valid to say that widespread diffusion of technologies which seemed genuinely relevant proved far more difficult than had been imagined. In retrospect, this is hardly surprising. The difficulties, however, fuelled a reaction in the official development and academic communities. Quick to find fault, especially fault that allowed a guiltless return to mainstream economics and the continued export of high-cost Northern goods and services, the attack – which continues – was mounted on technical, economic, cultural, social and intellectual grounds. It was, in a sense, a reverse Luddism. Ironically, these modern Luddites no longer attack modern, job-eliminating technology; they take their intellectual cudgels to innovations which seek to do the opposite.

It is easy enough to find examples of how a particular attempt to develop or disseminate a technology failed. Much of the early AT effort revolved around hardware, developed by engineers who loved tinkering and invention. Economic, social, organizational and institutional concerns were often not their long suit. These issues, correctly enough, were left to others. Many of the AT organizations with which they worked, however, were typical of well-funded NGOs – staffed by generalists, careless about evaluation, with levels of income that bore more relationship to the quality of their fundraising literature than to any actual success or failure taking place eight thousand miles away from the support base.

Some critics began to debunk the notion of 'technology choice', arguing that there is usually only one way of efficiently and economically pursuing an activity, only one readily available choice that makes sense in a given situation.[12] This ignores one of the underlying purposes of intermediate technology, however, which is to rethink and redefine what 'makes sense'. It is also argued, as the McNamara quotation at the start of this chapter suggests, that the AT movement, stuck in unrealistic theories of redistribution, is somehow opposed to growth. It is perhaps worth noting that the concept of redistribution with growth, widely accepted as gospel in the 1970s and popularized in a book of the same name, emerged in part from the World Bank's own Development Research Centre.[13]

Reflecting on the lessons of technology in history, Schumacher argued that technology is both determined by, and is a result of factors within a society; it is not only or always or even very often something that Third World countries can order cold from a catalogue with hopes of instant success. Schumacher criticized the pathological inability of mainstream economists to think beyond *quantitative* growth. 'Instead of insisting on *the primacy of qualitative distinctions*, they simply substitute non-growth for growth, that is to say, one emptiness for another.'[14]

Schumacher was equally critical of Adam Smith's 'invisible hand' concept of the market economy as a tool for guiding the choice of technology in Third World countries. The influence of donors, governments and individuals on the choice of technology can be enormous, as well as enormously destructive. This imposes another kind of invisibility on the choice of technology in the Third World, one that is not well represented by precedent in other times and other places. Whether or not the 'invisible hand' of the market place is a useful idea, where technology choice is concerned, the issue is as much one of invisible attitudes and policis as one of a fettered or unfettered marketplace.

Richard Eckaus, an American economist, has been a long-standing and consistent critic of appropriate technology.[15] Most of his criticisms, however, are best aimed at the movement's fringe elements, at its early beginnings, and at the more generic weaknesses of NGOs. Eckaus argues incorrectly, for example, that appropriate technology is a nebulous concept without clear definition, one unsupported by economic, social or scholarly analysis. He also clings to 'better mousetrap' times, claiming that the movement is technologically determinist, a hardware store in search of customers. In fact most of the best AT organizations have moved away from the mousetrap phase towards what ITDG calls an 'enabling phase', one which seeks to address the *causes* of limited uptake.[16] In some cases this has to do with the technology itself. In others it is the 'invisibility' of attitudes and policies framed in ivory towers, corporate boardrooms and donor headquarters. In others it is a matter of organization. What ITDG, ATI and other institutions have discovered is that techniques of organization are as relevant to the transfer of technology as the technology itself. This has proven especially relevant to poverty alleviation, for example, in the organization of landless people in Bangladesh around a known technology – irrigation pumps, or in the application of vertical integration to a well-known but once moribund technology, silk spinning and weaving.

In a densely packed critique of the AT movement, Kelvin Willoughby concludes, 'Many criticisms of Appropriate Technology are based upon either ignorance of available empirical evidence, distortion of the claims of leading protagonists, or reliance upon examples from the literature which differ from the consensus of the movement but which suit the biases of the critic.'[17]

Small revisited

Since *Small is Beautiful* was published, there have been enormous changes in technology, in raw materials, in production techniques, information systems and product development. In many ways, the gaps Schumacher sought to fill have become wider. But much has happened to revalidate his vision and the messages contained in *Small is Beautiful*. The first is that the appropriate technology movement has matured, and has become more professional. Although some of the weaknesses of the 1970s and 1980s persist, there is a growing body of success stories and much greater sophistication in dealing with the societal and political obstacles which in the past have limited progress.

The second is a growing recognition in the West as a whole that Big is not, of itself, better. Mass production and giant industries grew out of a particular approach to organization and out of ideas about the primacy of price and the importance of economies of scale. There have always been dissenting views, however. In the 1930s and 1940s, for example, Joseph Schumpeter argued that it is the firm rather than the market which is the determinant of success in industry. It is not so much price competition, he said, but 'competition from the new commodity, the new technology, the new source of supply, the new type of organization,' which determines the wealth and progress of a nation.[18] It is the entrepreneurial firm, which seeks strategic innovation in product, process and organization, and through constant improvement, which has the ultimate advantage over hierarchical firms rooted in single-minded price competition.

This lesson, forgotten or ignored in Europe and North America, was rediscovered and used to excellent advantage by Japanese firms in the 1970s. The body of literature available on the reasons for their success confirms Schumpeter's views. But there are other reasons for the Japanese success, one of the most prominent of which lies in the relevance of Small. Price was important, but it was not the only factor, nor was it necessarily the most important factor. The most successful Japanese firms, which by world standards are enormous, have focused clearly on the customer – customer preference, customer need, customer taste. Within the best firms, there is an emphasis on innovation, and on close, personalized co-ordination between divisions, and between managers and the shop floor. Lee Iaccoca's disdain for the remoteness of Ford's luxurious senior management dining room did not develop when he was Vice President of Ford; it occurred to him when he became President of Chrysler Motors, a company that had been virtually bankrupted by Japanese competition.

An automobile has approximately 20 000 parts. According to economist Michael Best, the average Japanese car-maker produces only 30 per cent of the parts itself, subcontracting the rest to smaller firms. The average American car-maker produces about half of its own requirements, and thus operates much larger and more complex plants. But the story doesn't stop there. General Motors deals with 3500 subcontractors, whereas Toyota deals with only 300. The difference between the complexity of the American network and the Japanese is as day is to night. But the major difference is that Toyota's subcontractors, with whom it is able to develop a very close, personalized relationship, subcontract much of their own work to a second tier of 5000 firms, which in turn deal with a further 20 000 smaller third and fourth tier firms.[19]

Within the most successful American firms examined by Peters and Waterman for their bestseller, *In Search of Excellence*, the same principle was at work: the creation of what Western economists have traditionally disdained as 'sub-optimal' units, along with decentralization, encouragement of independent thinking, innovation and new approaches to old problems. 'The message from the excellent companies we reviewed was invariably the same,' they wrote. 'Small *is* beautiful.'[20]

The phenomenon is not unique to Japan. In the US, between 1976 and 1986, the number of new businesses nearly doubled, while GNP grew by only a third. The average contribution to GNP per firm dropped from $245 000 in 1980 to $210 000 by 1987, falling in every industry except retailing and farming, thus putting the lie to the common assertion that growth in small-scale enterprise is simply a shift from manufacturing to service industries. In Britain, between 1982 and 1984, firms employing fewer than 20 people created an estimated one million new jobs, offsetting 750 000 job losses in large firms.[21] Between 1975 and 1990, the top 500 American companies added no new jobs to the economy whatsoever.[22]

Perhaps the most striking example of new industrial thinking can be found in the 'Third Italy', a region between the industrial heartland of the Italian north and the agricultural regions of the south. Characterized by a vast number of small firms, the Third Italy is not unlike nineteenth century Birmingham, or the Connecticut Valley which fostered the Springfield Armory and modern American production methods. Of Italy's 20 regions, Emilia-Romagna has been the fastest growing in recent years. Its 350 000 registered firms have an average of only five employees each, and an estimated one third of the work force is self-employed. And yet Emilia-Romagna has the highest per capita income in Italy and accounts for 10 per cent of Italy's exports. With imports to the region accounting for only four per cent of the country's total, Emilia-Romagna contributes an international trade surplus of $5 billion to the Italian economy every year. Unlike California's high-tech Silicon Valley, the Emilia-Romagna workshops are largely devoted to low-technology indusries in leather, textiles and automobile parts manufacture.

Between the 1970s and 1980s Italy's rate of growth was one of the fastest in Europe, its GNP surpassing that of Britain and France. The numbers came not from large firms, but from the small firms of this Third Italy. The secret, however, lies not only in the smallness of the firms, but in their organization, in their productive associations and consortia, in the physical, monetary and policy support they receive from government. The lessons of the Third Italy are important for small enterprises in many developing countries, where the shadow of a similar phenomenon can be vaguely discerned. This shadow, and the comparisons between the Third Italy and the Third World will be further discussed in Chapter XV.

A third factor which revalidates Schumacher's message is a growing awareness of the informal sector. Unorganized, disorganized, clandestine and usually illegal, the informal sector has been neglected by aid agencies, denigrated by economists and harassed by officialdom. And yet an increasing number of studies are revealing how widespread and how important it is. In most Third World cities, it represents as much as half the workforce; in Bombay it occupies a full 55 per cent of the labour force. In Peru it covers 47 per cent of the population on a permanent basis, accounts for 61 per cent of the person-hours worked, and contributes 38 per cent to the Gross Domestic Product.[23]

A study of 18 countries by Peter Kilby and Carl Liedholm showed that non-farm activity accounts for the primary source of income for 14 to 49 per cent of the rural labour force. In Madagascar and Niger, farm income accounts for only half of rural income, and in Thailand, only 37 per cent of average peasant income is derived from work on their own farms. Of the remainder, 80 percent is from non-farm activity.[24] Actual numbers are probably even higher, as formal surveys often miss or understate secondary labour and the work of women.

Not only are these numbers high, they are getting higher – in both real and relative terms. Indian agriculture, which represented 68 per cent of rural employment in 1977, accounted for only 64 per cent six years later. In Bangladesh, the agricultural sector is expected to absorb only 40 per cent of the additional labour force annually, although some estimates place the figure at less than 20 per cent.[25]

The disaster looming behind these figures is compounded by other statistics which show that the formal sector is not creating jobs at a rate anywhere near the demand, and that the jobs it does create are as prohibitively expensive as they were when Schumacher wrote on the subject in the 1960s. Zimbabwe's 1986–90 National Development Plan, for example, forecast an increase in wage employment of 21 000 workers, with an expected investment of Z$1.4 billion. This puts an amazing price tag of US$26 000 on each job.[26] Estimates of the number of jobs required annually in order to 'mop up the backlog' and to deal with new school-leavers in Zimbabwe range from a low of

160 000 to more than a quarter of a million.[27] At this rate, using the lower figure, it would cost over US$4 billion per annum to create the necessary number of jobs, an amount equivalent to 90 per cent of the country's entire GNP. Meanwhile, as a result of a structural adjustment programme introduced in 1991, Zimbabwe looked forward to job *losses* of 20 000 in industry, 10 000 in government, and a further 2000 in parastatals.[28]

In Kenya, estimates are equally staggering. Even with continued economic growth and investment, it is estimated that only 1.4 million jobs can be created by the turn of the century, leaving approximately 40 per cent of the labour force, or 5.6 million people, jobless.

There are only two solutions, if people are to work. The first is that the cost per workplace in the formal sector will have to come down dramatically, as Schumacher said it must if chaos is to be avoided. The second is that the informal sector will have to expand to make room for large numbers of new entrants. This cannot be done if governments continue to ignore it, hound it and hide it behind tin sheet fences. Donor agencies have begun to realize its importance, and there is a growing number of indigenous lending institutions, especially in Asia – Grameen Bank, SEWA, BRAC and BKK, for example – that have developed successful programmes for lending to people without assets. But lending alone will not formalize the informal sector. Nor will a few hundred takas or rupees or pesos make a poor person financially self-reliant. The policy framework in which a credit programme operates is critical to the productivity of any investment, whether it is a hundred taka or a million. And genuine investment opportunities for poor people, opportunities that go beyond the obvious – poultry, petty trade, handicrafts – require the kind of research and development with which the appropriate technology movement has been engaged for more than 25 years. In a sense, greater integration of the informal sector requires a kind of reconstruction of the economy and of economic thinking. Much of Schumacher's writing was concerned with 'reconstruction', flowing, no doubt, from his experience between 1946 and 1950 as economic adviser to the British Control Commission in Germany.

There is a final phenomenon which revalidates Schumacher's philosophy. That is the overwhelming evidence that the continuing pre-eminence given to indiscriminate growth strategies has done little or nothing to reduce poverty. There are more poor people today than there have ever been, and the numbers show little sign of diminishing. Schumacher's predictions about growing immiseration, about urban poverty and social unrest have all come true with a vengeance that wreaks horror on the lives of increasing millions.

'Our scientists tell us with the utmost assurance that everything around us has evolved by small mutations sieved out through natural selection ... even the Almighty is not credited with having been able to create anything complex. Every complexity, we are told, is the result of evolution. Yet our development planners seem to think they can do better than the Almighty, that they can create the most complex things at one throw by a process called planning, letting Athene spring, not out of the head of Zeus, but out of nothingness, fully armed, resplendent, and viable.[29]

It is perhaps worth returning to Schumacher's comment that today's poverty is 'a monstrous, scandalous thing which is altogether abnormal in the history of mankind.' In the last pages of his final book, *A Guide for the Perplexed*, published shortly after his death, Schumacher recalled the *Divine Comedy*. In it, Dante wakes up to find himself in a horrible dark wood from which he cannot escape without first descending into the Inferno, in order to appreciate the reality of sinfulness. 'The art of living,' Schumacher wrote, 'is always to make a good thing out of a bad thing. Only if we *know* that we have actually descended into infernal regions where nothing awaits us but the cold death of society and the extinguishing of all civilized relations', can we summon the courage and imagination needed for a 'turning around'.

Can we rely on it that a 'turning around' will be accomplished by enough people quickly enough to save the modern world? This question is often asked, but whatever the answer is, it will mislead. The answer 'Yes' would lead to complacency; the answer 'No' to despair. It is desirable to leave these perplexities behind us and get down to work.[30]

CHAPTER VII

Farmers, food and forests

Glendower: *'I can call the spirits from the vasty deep.'*
Hotspur: *'Why, so can I, or so can any man. But will they come*
           when you do call for them?'   William Shakespeare

IN THE SEARCH for new approaches to rural development in the 1960s
and 1970s, it was sometimes forgotten that most innovations in
farming have been made by farmers, not by research scientists. Like
factory workers and mechanics, farmers do not write much history,
and therefore tend to be forgotten, especially when they are poor and
speak a strange tongue. It was 'primitive' farmers, however, five and
even ten thousand years ago, who domesticated almost all the crops
and vegetables in use today, and who domesticated animals for food
and draught power. As any good extension officer knows, the
innovative spirit is alive and well in almost any farming community.

Much of what farmers do is devoted to food production. With
world population increasing by a billion during the 1990s, and likely
to grow by a further three billion in the first quarter of the next
century, food production has become an increasing concern. Almost
three quarters of the people in low income countries today earn all or
most of their income and subsistence from agriculture and related
activities. Agriculture, therefore, faces a double challenge: it must
produce food at a rate of expansion never before known. And it must
provide most of the world's population, including the increase, with a
livelihood.

Return to Oz: the green revolution

During the first half of the century, colonial agricultural research
stations were established in Africa and Asia to work on the development of hybrids and higher-yielding varieties, mainly of cash crops.
The 1950s and 1960s, however, were a period of impressive break-
throughs in food crop research. The first was an adaptable dwarf
wheat, developed in Mexico by Norman Borlaug under the auspices
of the Rockefeller Foundation. Because most of the world's poor live
on a rice diet, Rockefeller, joined by the Ford Foundation, turned
towards Asia, and in 1960 founded the International Rice Research
Institute in the Philippines. Gathering some 10 000 strains of rice
from around the world, scientists began the task of cross-breeding,

and within a relatively short period, combining a Taiwanese variety with one from Indonesia, they developed what became known as IR-8, a rice capable of doubling traditional yields.

National agricultural institutions further developed the new varieties to suit local conditions. The impact was enormous. In 1964, an estimated 200 acres were devoted to high-yielding cereal production throughout Asia. By 1973, 80 million acres in Asia and North Africa had come under the new varieties.[1] Pakistan was transformed from a grain importer into a net exporter in only seven years; Indian wheat production increased from 11 million tons in 1965 to 26 million tons in 1972, a rate of growth unmatched in history. The *additional* rice produced in Asia alone as a result of the HYVs, fertilizer and irrigation is currently estimated at 90 million tons annually.[2]

The shortcomings of the green revolution have perhaps received more attention than its achievements. Critics were justified in their worry about the narrow genetic base of some plants, and their stability against weeds, disease and pests. Because the new varieties were more dependent on fertilizer and pesticides than traditional agriculture, investment costs often put them beyond the means of small farmers. Likewise, the organization of improved irrigation favoured larger farms, while government distribution and credit schemes favoured people with collateral. Many were unable to make the investment, but many others who might have been able to do so shied away. The poor are understandably 'risk-averse': a single crop failure can mean the loss of everything – land, livelihood, family, even life itself.

Nevertheless, there is now a large body of research on how the HYVs have affected the poor, and the message is becoming more positive.[3] Poor farmers *have* adopted the HYVs, and because the new varieties are more labour intensive, there has been a consequent increase in employment. Food prices, which account for the bulk of a poor family's spending – in rural and urban areas — have been reduced as well. The impact of the new varieties on the farming practices of the marginal farmer has, however, been limited. The new strains were developed for average or better than average land, not the remote, infertile patches on which the poorest inevitably live. The increases in food production of the 1960s and 1970s, therefore, mask worrisome statistics: by the turn of the century, an estimated 220 million Third World households, representing more than a billion people, will be functionally landless, or will live on small plots of poor land, overusing the resource base and eking out less than subsistence lives with traditional, low-productivity techniques.[4]

Perhaps as important as these problems is the fact that there has been a marked slowdown in food production since the tremendous advances of the 1960s and 1970s. The biggest gains of the green revolution have already been made in many countries, and in some, food production is barely keeping pace with population growth. In Africa it is not keeping pace. Africa's 1990 'food gap' of 10 million tons could grow to 245 million tons by 2020 if present trends continue.[5] Although this is the type of statistic that Mark Twain would have applauded, it underlines a dramatically negative trend.

Deforestation: cutting down tomorrow

Tropical deforestation is a relatively new environmental issue, publicized in part by the Brundtland Commission. The Brandt Report, issued only six years earlier, devotes only three paragraphs to the subject. Until recently, the most authoritative estimates of tropical deforestation were based on a 1980 FAO study which calculated the annual loss at 11.4 million hectares.[6] More recent studies indicate that the situation is much worse – almost double the 1980 estimate, or 20.4 million hectares annually, an area about the size of the United Kingdom.[7] So alarmed was the government of Thailand at the discovery (from satellite photographs) that its forest cover had declined from 29 per cent to 19 per cent between 1985 and 1989, it suspended logging altogether in the southern Provinces.

The major causes of deforestation are directly linked to poverty – the poverty of individuals and the poverty of nations. This is not a question of 'blaming the poor', nor of absolving the greed of people in the North and the South who cut down trees for profit. It is a simple statement of fact. The world's poorest people generally live in the most environmentally vulnerable areas. In Africa, 51 per cent of the poorest people live on marginal land that is highly susceptible to soil degradation and erosion, floods and other natural calamities. In Asia the figure is 60 per cent, and in Latin America it is an incredible 80 per cent.[8] The most prominent cause of deforestation is related to population pressure, the need people have for greater security, and the conversion of forest land to agriculture. The second contributory cause, logging, does not have to lead to deforestation if it is properly managed. In most countries, however, it is not managed at all. The third is a growing demand for fuelwood, fodder and other products unavailable at affordable prices except from the forest.

The effects of deforestation are widespread. Exposing weak soil to erosion, deforestation often leads to a loss of biological diversity, the creation of permanent wasteland, flooding and the siltation of reservoirs. And the game, birds, berries, nuts, resins, spices, honey, oil and other products associated with the forest disappear. In Indonesia, such products were worth $125 million in annual exports

101

in the early 1980s.[9] Deforestation also affects the global carbon cycle. Second only to the burning of fossil fuels in the production of atmospheric carbon dioxide, deforestation is directly related to the greenhouse effect and global warming. Deforestation and land-use change in the tropics, in fact, account for 33 per cent of annual human-related carbon dioxide emissions. In 1987, deforestation and land clearing by fire in Brazil alone released 1.2 million tons of carbon into the atmosphere, precisely the same amount as was generated in the United States by burning fossil fuels and generating heat to produce cement.[10] Between the mid-1970s and 1988, 600 000 square kilometres of Brazilian forest were cleared, an area larger than France. The benefits, however, were limited, both locally and nationally, as Amazonia accounts for only three per cent of the national income.[11]

As with agronomic research, work on livestock has reflected the priorities of the larger farmer, and of the urban demand for milk and beef. Exotic cattle have been introduced at the expense of research on local varieties, and much work on animals which are the priority of the poor – goats, sheep, pigs and chicken – has focused on improvements in 'factory' settings, rather than improvements that might benefit the very small farmer. Yet the productivity of animals has a greater importance for the poor, whose livelihood or even survival may depend entirely on the health of a single ox or a few chickens.

Sustainability: the myth

'Sustainability' is another of those good words that development agencies have hijacked. It is used to justify and disguise so many things that its meaning has become lost in a swamp of jargon. The dictionary defines 'sustain' in several ways: to withstand; to maintain or prolong; to be supported from below; to provide or give support to – as in supplying necessities; to keep up vitality or courage; to affirm the justice or validity of an endeavour. But the word has come to mean other things in the development lexicon. It has become a euphemism, subjectively used, for virtually everything 'good' and benign. But when hard project funding decisions must be made, it generally comes to rest on the notion of *self*-sustainability – the capacity of a project or endeavour to stand on its own feet financially when external support is withdrawn. This fundamental alteration can lead to programming efforts which are driven by narrow, short-term economic concerns, and which fail to appreciate the broader context within which genuine sustainability must exist.

Genuinely sustainable agriculture is directly related to the sustainability of resources. Renewable local resources, such as land, air and water are sustainable only as long as they are used properly. Erosion, upland deforestation, chemical pollution or incorrect water usage can all have detrimental effects on them. Non-local resources such as seeds or fertilizer are another factor. If adequate and timely supplies can be maintained at stable prices, there is no reason to assume that these detract from sustainability. Changes in national or international prices, however, can have a major impact on sustainability. Structural adjustment programmes, for example, which emphasize agricultural subsidy reductions may damage sustainability, especially at the margins where farmers and consumers are less able to withstand price increases. Removing a subsidy on fertilizer in Sri Lanka, for example, had a direct negative impact on both producers and consumers.

Food production cannot be divorced from imports or, therefore, from the exports needed to pay for them. Even if they could do without imported fertilizer and pesticides, countries need roads and trains and trucks in order to distribute seeds and fertilizer, and to move agricultural produce to market. They need fuel, bitumen for roads and steel for rails and agricultural implements. All of these things reflect wage rates and inflation in industrialized countries. All reflect the price of oil, which moved from $3.22 a barrel in 1973, to variations on a theme ranging between $20 and $40 a barrel over the next two decades.

The idea, therefore, of perfect national food security, of a country which requires no imports to sustain its own food production, belongs to another time and another place. In other words, countries must export. Yet since 1950, the prices of what most poor countries export have declined in both real and relative terms, falling to record lows in the mid-1980s. This has resulted in greater emphasis on export crops, in usually futile attempts to do more than tread water. In 1960, for example, a ton of bananas could buy 13 tons of oil. By 1972, it could pay for only 1.6 tons. In 1960, a ton of sugar would purchase 6.3 tons of oil. By 1982, the same ton of sugar would purchase less than three quarters of a ton of oil.[12] Thailand increased its exports of rubber by 31 per cent between 1984 and 1985, yet because prices changed, it earned eight per cent *less* in rubber revenues, a drop from $262 million to $242 million.[13] The price of coffee dropped from $2.20 a pound in January 1986 to $1.37 by July, 40 per cent of what it had been a decade earlier. A coffee plant does not produce its first crop for three years. Price fluctuations of this nature, therefore, have a devastating effect on farmers, and on the economies of countries like Jamaica, Uganda and Colombia, where coffee is an important export.

Increased emphasis on cash crops can reduce the amount of land available for food production, but it has other, sometimes more far-reaching effects. The government of Indonesia, for example, encouraged an increase in cassava exports by doubling the farmers' price in 1985 and again in 1987. The result was that many Javanese farmers switched from mixed farming to cassava, removing terraces and water conservation structures that had been built at great cost and which, in the past had prevented erosion.[14]

As a concept, therefore, agricultural sustainability requires careful thought, especially by donor agencies. It is far more than an investment in a self-financing enterprise. There are complex trade-offs that must be considered: trade-offs between export crops and food production; trade-offs between productivity and equity; trade-offs between short and long-term production; trade-offs between investment and productivity; trade-offs between genuine agricultural sustainability or food security and the prevailing system of international trade.

Agroforestry

This is not to suggest that nothing can be done. On the contrary, as the limitations of the green revolution became more apparent in the 1970s, greater attention was focused on technologies and approaches which would reduce the cost of food production and increase the productivity of people living on marginal lands. In India, for example, huge investments have been made in the construction of earthworks to reduce farm soil erosion. Simply to protect the existing agricultural land base from further erosion, this strategy could cost as much as $14 billion. An alternative, already well established in Fiji and in hilly areas of some Caribbean islands, is under trial, however. It is the simple use of a coarse perennial grass, used in conjunction with contour planting and hedges. The new method is between one-tenth and one one-hundredth the cost of earthworks.[15]

Agroforestry, known for centuries in some countries, began to gain widespread acceptance in the 1980s. Basically, agroforestry is the combination of crops with trees and shrubs that provide nutrients to the soil through their root systems, through the 'green manure' they produce, and their mulch. For centuries, Javanese garden culture has practiced an intensive form of agroforestry, combining horticulture, animal husbandry and tree crops. The *Leucaena leucephala* or 'ipil-ipil' tree was used by the Aztecs, Maya and Inca for inter-cropping with maize, and travelled to Asia on Spanish galleons. In recent years it has become the favoured tree for inter-cropping because of its high nitrogen-fixing properties and its rapid growth. It is also used for applications in hilly areas, such as the tea gardens of Sri Lanka where, in addition to its other benefits, it retards runoff and provides shade to the tea bushes.

A CARE agroforestry project in western Kenya has distributed several million *Leucaena leucephala* seedlings since 1984. Working closely with farmers and with the Kenya-based International Council for Research in Agricultural Forestry, CARE uses schools as a starting point for introducing the concept to a community. Like most other primary schools in Kenya, Nyabeda Primary School in Siaya District receives government support in the form of salaries for teachers. Everything else, including buildings, supplies and upkeep must be provided by the community, by the parents of the school's 600 children, or by the school itself. Some years ago the school started a one acre maize plot for provision of a hot lunch during the school year. Sales of the surplus were used to fund small school projects, such as roof repairs or a new classroom.

In 1985, CARE began to provide support, training one of the teachers, Dishon Omondi, in inter-cropping and seedling production. A seedling plot was established near the school, and on the school farm, maize was intercropped with *Leucaena*. Five years after it began, Omondi ascribed several benefits to the project: the *Leucaena* provided fuelwood and building poles which previously had to be brought by children from reluctant parents; the surplus produced income for the school. Maize yields had improved slightly, but children no longer had to steal manure from home for the school plot, as the green manure from the *Leucaena* and the tree's nitrogen-fixing properties had taken its place. The community was happier, and a by-product was the school's ability to provide some parents with seeds and seedlings. Except for plastic bags for seedlings, Omondi saw little further need for CARE, and could point across the compound to a new 1.5 acre plot that he was starting, using the same techniques. It could be said that the project had become *sustainable*.

CARE saw the success in a different light. Although the technology had been established by 1990, the school had not yet worked out the planting and harvesting seasons correctly, because weather patterns were slightly different from those in other parts of the region. Little work had been done by CARE in documenting the quality and quantity of output – whether in green manure or maize. Clear economic analysis and documentation would be necessary if more individuals, NGOs and government workers were to accept the important extension issues that CARE was addressing. Nyabeda Primary School would require more attention in the next few years if the achievements were to be consolidated and properly replicated elsewhere.[16]

In conjunction with the Pan-American Development Foundation, CARE has developed a similar project in Haiti which in its first four years exceeded its target of three million seedlings by a factor of four. In Haiti the reason for success was not so much an acceptance of the full concept of agroforestry, as the fact that the trees have genuine economic value, serving first as a form of savings, then as a means of cash derived from timber sales when the need arises.[17]

A direct relationship between planting trees and carbon emissions from the burning of fossil fuels was made in 1989, when Applied Energy Services (AES), a Connecticut power producer, sought a means of offsetting 15 million metric tons of carbon dioxide to be released from a new coal-fired power plant. As the result of a World Resources Institute recommendation, AES funded a CARE agro-forestry project in Guatemala, not only because of its offsetting environmental value, but because of its contribution to community woodlots, agroforestry, alley cropping and soil conservation. The project was also expected to benefit an estimated 40 000 Guatemalan farm families.[18] The Netherlands has taken a similar approach to offsetting the negative environmental effects of a new Dutch coal-fired power plant, by establishing projects in five Latin American countries to plant 125 000 hectares with trees.[19] Given the cost, and the potential value of these initiatives, it is perhaps ungracious and unfairly rhetorical to ask why the South and Southern lands (rather than the North and Northern lands) should be used to offset Northern pollution.

'Minimum tillage' or 'zero tillage' farming is another new farming technique, developed at the International Institute for Tropical Agriculture (IITA) in Nigeria. In Ghana, as in much of West Africa, only 20 per cent of the arable land is suitable for mechanized farming, leaving the rest to traditional hoe and cutlass techniques. Once cleared, however, land which for centuries has supported giant stands of hardwood and dense rainforests is sometimes barely able to support a crop of maize. One of the earliest African Appropriate Technology institutions, the Technology Consultancy Centre (TCC) in Ghana, began in the mid-1980s to experiment with 'minimum tillage'. First, in order to avoid disturbing already weak soil, a herbicide is used to kill the weeds. Seeds are then planted directly through the weed and crop residue, which serves both as mulch and as a further weed retardant.

Despite the need for fertilizer* and herbicides, there are major offsetting advantages. In an area where traditional family farming is back-breaking work, the minimum-tillage approach allows for increased food production without adding costly labour, and without the ravages that have been associated with expensive mechanization projects of the past. By reducing weeding, labour requirements drop dramatically, and erosion is minimized. IITA studies have shown that planting maize on a 10 per cent slope under minimum tillage can reduce erosion to one fortieth of that following normal practice, and even on a 15 per cent slope there is virtually no erosion. The TCC experiment resulted in yields that were twice as high as on neighbouring farms.[20]

Although logging for timber does not have to lead to deforestation, selective logging in the tropics is relatively unknown. In a study of forest management in 17 countries, the International Tropical Timber Organization found that only 800 000 hectares of forest was being maintained sustainably. A further 3.6 million hectares were being partially managed in India, bringing the total to 4.4 million hectares. This represents about a half of one per cent of the world's remaining productive tropical forest.

One of the problems in sustainable forest management is the lack of a suitable technology which would allow selective logging. In order to get the logs out of a forest area, heavy equipment is almost always required. Roads must be built, and as a result it is uneconomical not to take as many trees as lax government supervision will permit. Even where it is practiced, selective logging damages the residual vegetation because of the heavy equipment used to cut and move logs. An experiment in selective logging in Surinam found that 9 per cent of the remaining trees were destroyed and a further 16 per cent were damaged.[21] A similar experiment in the eastern Amazon found that while only 3 per cent of the trees were removed from a particular area, another 54 per cent were uprooted or damaged during roadbuilding and in the logging operation itself.[22]

Ultimately, demand reduction, policy intervention and enforcement are the answers to these problems, but technology can help. In

---

* In some industrialized countries, the use of inorganic fertilizers exceeds 700 kg/hectare annually. In Asia, average consumption is 62 kg/ha; in Latin America it is 48 kg/ha and in Africa it is only 11 kg/ha. This implies that there is scope for much greater consumption in the Third World. Two things militate against simply copying the Western approach, however. The first is that the cost is prohibitive. The second is that overuse of potash, nitrates and phosphates in the North has resulted in levels of pollution and contamination that cannot be replicated elsewhere without significant negative impact. ('Thus Fertile and No Further,' *South*, January 1991)

Papua New Guinea, where the forest is seen more as a source of income than as potential cropland, a simple piece of appropriate technology has made a difference. The 'Wokabout Somil', a sawmill produced by a locally owned enterprise in Lae, requires no roads and no vehicles.[23]

Essentially, the Wokabout Somil consists of two blades driven by an 18 horsepower petrol engine. The engine is mounted on a chassis-and-rail assembly that straddles a log lying on the ground. It is the blades that move, rather than the log. The Somil is easy to dismantle and move about the forest, and the logs – cut into timber – can also be transported manually. The Wokabout Somil, of which more than 450 are now in operation, opens new opportunities for local processing industries – in building trades, carpentry and furniture manufacture. And in the hands of people who control a forested area, it offers a unique tool for forest management. In Bau, for example, a village in Morobe Province, a Somil was purchased in 1988 in order to create employment for school leavers. The village realized that conservation was as important as income, and of the 6000 hectares it controlled, 3000 hectares were set aside for conservation. Knowing better, then, what the limitations and potential were, the villagers realized that the forest could support another Somil, and two were operating by 1990, each on a multi-shift basis.

Animal husbandry

Similar low-cost techniques can be applied to animal husbandry and poultry. In Bangladesh, BRAC began a poultry-rearing project in 1985 with destitute village women – 'destitute' being defined in most cases as abandoned, widowed or divorced, landless, and in most cases head of household, with two or three dependents. Starting on a pilot basis, BRAC trained different women in three sets of skills : the first groups were trained in vaccination and the treatment of simple poultry ailments. The second groups, with one cock and nine hens each, were designated as trainers. Members of a third type of group, 'model rearers', were supplied with 3 cocks and 30 hens each. They were to supply others with eggs for hatching. The cost of the chickens and vaccine were covered by loans taken by the women from BRAC's savings and credit programme, and recovery rates exceeded 95 per cent. From small, experimental beginnings in 1985, the poultry programme had reached more than 46 000 women by 1989, and was expected to reach 80 000 by 1992.[24]

A similar approach to livestock development has been undertaken by ITDG in Kenya.[25] Livestock rearing is an important economic activity for large numbers of people, and is virtually the only source of income for the 25 per cent who live in arid areas. Although there are 11 million cattle, 6 million sheep and 8 million goats in the country, production of milk and meat is far outstripped by demand, with poor performance blamed on low producer prices, increasing costs of inputs, a shortage of credit, and livestock diseases.

Government veterinary services have been growing, but they are far outpaced by the need. In Nginyang Division for example, each of the 13 veterinary personnel are responsible, on average, for 324 households spread over an area of 342 square kilometres. Only one of the vets has access to transportation. In Tigania Division, each of the veterinary personnel serves 2000 households in a 50 square kilometre area, and in Tharaka, an officer must theoretically serve 1200 households and an area of 187 square kilometres. Needless to say, those farmers closest to the veterinary station will be serviced; the vast majority will not. As a result of such poor coverage, it is conservatively estimated that Kenya loses over $43 million annually through preventable livestock disease, with eight conditions accounting for 80 per cent of cattle disease and five complaints accounting for 90 per cent of reported disease among sheep and goats.

ITDG surveys indicated that as many as 33 per cent of the cases of cattle disease and 40 per cent of the sheep and goat ailments would not require a vet if farmers were trained in simple preventive and curative techniques. Working with Oxfam, the Kenya Freedom from Hunger Council and other local organizations, ITDG developed and tested training programmes and follow-up courses for farmers who were nominated by interested villages. The 'barefoot vets' received their incentive in the form of small fees charged to the users and through the establishment of a shop which stocked veterinary supplies and drugs. Preliminary results were encouraging. In one district, 27 men were trained as barefoot vets and 24 women were trained to vaccinate chickens against Newcastle disease, a major problem in the area. In a review conducted after the first 18 months of the programme, it was found that about 6000 chickens had been vaccinated and 4600 animals treated. Half the treatments were for one of the most simple of ailments – worms – yet it had been a costly one that people in the area had known little about.

The Turkana rain water harvesting project

Brief highlights of successful projects can do two things. They can show how a different approach to development and appropriate technologies can make a difference. They can show that small, simple, cheap and non-violent approaches are possible, replicable and sustainable. They can also be misleading, for with each of the examples mentioned above, there were discouraging setbacks and failures before success was achieved. For that reason, it is worth examining a second ITDG project in Kenya in greater detail.[26]

The Turkana people, about a quarter of a million in all, live in an arid part of north-west Kenya that is about 50 per cent larger than Switzerland. They are a pastoral people, depending largely on the herding of cattle, sheep and goats, and on small sorghum gardens planted mainly by women during the rainy season. Raiding – attacking other groups in order to expand their cattle herds – has been a common feature of Turkana life for generations. Although officially 'subdued' by the colonial government in 1917, raiding continued, and in 1980, Turkana forays into Uganda returned with more than cattle. They returned with contagious caprine pleuro-pneumonia and rinderpest.

The diseases, combined with a particularly harsh dry season, were devastating. In a year that the Turkana called *Lopiar*, which means 'the sweeping', 90 per cent of their cattle died, 80 per cent of their small stock, 40 per cent of their camels and 45 per cent of their donkeys. Within a few months people were no longer able to feed themselves, and began to flock towards the few small towns in the area. Many starved; cholera broke out; some committed suicide. An EEC delegation visiting the area in 1980 estimated that there were 27 000 completely destitute people in feeding centres, and countless others in severely reduced circumstances. By 1982, the numbers had risen to over 50 000.

Famine was no stranger to Turkana. A 1961 drought had brought Oxfam and other NGOs to the area. They had promoted the resettlement of destitutes on the shore of Lake Turkana, and provided them with gill nets and canoes. Initial success in exporting dried fish to other parts of the country encouraged NORAD to assist in the building of a paved road into the region. And in order to develop the fishery, NORAD also constructed a fish-freezing plant. Before it was finished, however, the fragile ecosystem of the lake began to react to the new industry, and catches plummeted, dropping from a high of 17 000 tons in 1976 to only 600 tons in 1985. The freezing plant was never commissioned and many families returned to cattle. Other pre-1980 projects, involving church organizations, FAO and UNDP, contributed to the development of various irrigation schemes covering approximately a thousand hectares on two Turkana rivers. A NORAD study found that these projects were unable to provide participants with enough income to cover even subsistence needs, denouncing them as 'disguised famine relief camps'.[27] Other studies found that at $61 000 per hectare, the Turkana irrigation projects were among the most expensive in Africa.*

---

* Even World Bank irrigation projects, rarely the least expensive, seldom rose above $10,000 per hectare in the 1980s, and usually averaged between $1000 and $5000.

Nevertheless, when *Lopiar* struck, irrigation again came to the fore. The reasons were simple. First, although the previous schemes had been prohibitively expensive, it was thought that more appropriate technologies could do the same for significantly less. Secondly, pure relief without some sort of end in sight contradicts everything aid agencies believe in. And third, nobody (except the Turkana) was interested in a return to cattle.

So huge amounts of food were trucked in, and people were employed in Food For Work schemes, building bunds and levelling gardens that could produce sorghum during the rainy seasons. Over 100 kilometres of contour bunds and embankments were built in the first three years, but construction was so poor that many failed to collect water, and others were simply washed away with the first rain. In order to limit the psychological damage caused by the disaster and to separate the hoped-for development aspects of the programme from what had become a thinly disguised relief programme, a separate 'water harvesting and draught animal demonstration project' was established, funded by Oxfam and supported with technical assistance from ITDG. Adrian Cullis, who had been a Voluntary Service Overseas worker, had worked with the Salvation Army in the same area between 1979 and 1981, and had spent time in the Negev Desert studying Israeli techniques of rainwater harvesting, returned in 1984 under ITDG auspices. He introduced several innovations the following year. The failed contour bund was abandoned in favour of a trapezoidal bund, and workers were taught basic levelling techniques with spirit levels. A demonstration herd of donkeys was established. Using a Swiss three-pad collar made from local materials, they were put to work with locally designed scrapers, earth scoops and an Ethiopian-style plough. These were popular innovations because the levelling of a garden and the construction of a single bund could take 15 people as much as seven months of hard work.

During 1985, four gardens were completed in time for the rains, but only two produced a harvest. With yields of about 400 kilograms per hectare, the results were not as good as they might have been, but they did not create the negative impression of earlier efforts. People were prepared to continue working. Then, when Cullis was away from the area recovering from an illness, five of the donkeys died. Project staff had been unable to prevent people from overworking them once the foreigner, whose property they were deemed to be, had left the site. Then, reductions in the food-payment allocations resulted in many of the men going back to cattle, leaving women to work for whatever they could get in the gardens.

Nevertheless, before the 1986 rains, a total of 18 gardens were prepared, and good crops were established. That year it was decided to discontinue food-for-work altogether as a means of getting bunds repaired. People would have to do it themselves, or they would fail. Left to make their own decisions, families at last decided to use their own donkeys for draught work. By 1987, 50 gardens were prepared and the rains were good. But once again disaster struck. Because an external variety of sorghum seed had been available at half the price of the better Turkana variety, most gardeners had chosen the cheaper seed, and yields were poor.

Encouraged by growing local interest in the project, even though the gardens were not producing what had been anticipated, Cullis and Oxfam decided that greater responsibility should be devolved to the garden groups. These groups, in fact, were based on a strong community spirit among the Turkana, and on a traditional system of governance which required careful discussion with the community's elders of any change or new ideas. In 1987 local organizing committees were set up in the three gardening areas of the project, and in 1988 a Management Board with committee representatives was established to run the project. Cullis remained involved as an advisor, but key decisions were now made by the committees and the Board. In 1988, the first year of self-management, 104 gardens – about 20 of them owned and operated exclusively by women – were planted. And 95 had successful harvests. Although some of the harvests were small, the best recorded a remarkable 1300 kilograms per hectare. In all, over ten tons of sorghum were produced, along with smaller amounts of cowpeas, maize, greengram and watermelon.

Sustainability: the reality

By 1990, the Oxfam/ITDG project had begun to demonstrate a number of important lessons. It had shown that it was not necessary to spend the $61 000 per hectare that had gone into the projects of the 1970s; the Oxfam/ITDG schemes cost between $625 and $1000 per hectare.[28] The project also demonstrated that it was important to get the technology right. Small contour bunds, no matter how cheap, were too expensive if they didn't hold water. It showed that success is not a simple process of discovery and action; it results from planning, action, reflection, and further planning. It is also the result of a long process of dialogue with project beneficiaries and community leaders, and of building on their own social organizations. It is the result of encouraging success and of learning from mistakes, of learning from the reactions of people to challenges and failure. It underlines two of the most ignored and yet most badly needed things in development work: *the need for a premium on documenting and understanding failure.*

The project demonstrated that when forced to begin taking financial responsibility for something with potential, people will do so. It also demonstrated that when they are made responsible for their own actions, people can do the right thing. The committees and management board did not abuse the trust placed in them by the donors.

The project demonstrated the importance of time and continuity to success. It had taken eight years for the first significant positive achievements after *Lopiar*. Some of the success was due to the pre-1980 efforts, from which the project was able to learn. But the persistence of Oxfam and ITDG in supporting the project despite continued apparent failure, was critical. Part of the success was also due to something that few aid projects enjoy, the continued presence of a project 'champion'. Adrian Cullis's experience of rainwater harvesting in Turkana spanned more than a decade, as volunteer, as an ITDG field worker, and finally, in the 1990s as a visiting advisor and friend.

The reality of ten or twelve hard years in Turkana puts a new perspective on the definition of agricultural sustainability. Conway and Barbier define it as 'the ability to maintain productivity, whether of a field or farm or nation, in the face of stress or shock.'[29] The stress might be small or large, temporary or permanent. It could be the result of local factors, such as drought, flood or grasshoppers. Or it could come from external forces such as an increase in the price of fertilizer or the withdrawal of technical support. 'Sustainability thus determines the persistence or durability of a system's productivity under known or possible circumstances.'

Time is a key element of success. Many projects are based on unrealistic expectations and are too dependent on the standard development agency time frame of two or three years. Some efforts can take hold very quickly, as in the case of the Wokabout Somil. Others take longer. Good management and 'self-help' are obvious examples of this. People will respond if they see value in something. The opposite has proven to be the case in almost every social forestry project where the external priority – getting trees into the ground – took precedence. Such projects usually fail. But where trees have been tied to income generation or real and visible community benefits, as at Nyabeda Primary School, projects have succeeded.

And any project having to do with land is far more likely to succeed if people own the land they farm or have secure tenure, than if they do not. The structure of land ownership in the Third World is the most important determinant of the distribution of rural income and wealth, and in most countries it shapes the entire character of rural development. In Asia, the positive relationship between security of land tenure and increased productivity has been amply demonstrated, as has the viability of small, owner-cultivated farms. Farmers not only tend to work harder on land to which they have secure rights, they are considerably more willing to take risks and to make the higher investments demanded by high-yielding varieties of rice and wheat. Losing one's land, on the other hand, has fundamental and devastating economic and social implications, including increased vulnerability to debt and coercion, and loss of self-esteem.

Much has been learned about rural development over the past century. Lessons, however, are only useful if the level of integrity in monitoring and evaluation is high, and if the lessons are remembered and applied. Many lessons 'learned' in the 1960s were ignored or forgotten in the following two decades. The lessons illustrated in Turkana and in thousands of similar projects around the world relate to project design, target groups, cost and technology; to external factors, management and political considerations. Briefly stated, they include the following:

○ rural development projects are most successful when they are low-cost and small in scale, when they respond to the needs of a specific target group *and involve the beneficiaries themselves in the planning and implementation process*;
○ there must be a thorough knowledge of the project area – its people, the power structures, the role of women — readily available, conventional data is rarely adequate;
○ projects must have adequate lifespans; planning and scheduling should be flexible, and must be appropriate to the often unstable environment in which they are located; projects must have a capacity for self-correction;
○ rural development must be built around well defined, *appropriate* technologies and methodologies that become available in an appropriate sequence;
○ projects must anticipate relatively low levels of education in rural areas, but must be cautious in their use of high-cost technical assistance.

Some of the original definition of 'sustainability', therefore, remains directly relevant. 'To sustain' still means to withstand, to maintain, to prolong, to be supported from below; to keep up courage; to affirm the justice or validity of the endeavour.

One of the greatest errors that donor agencies make in approaching rural development, is in defining sustainability in terms of their own assistance, and then in unrealistically constraining that assistance. Donor agencies regard their interventions as 'catalytic' – bright ideas which, combined with capital investment, will spur a group or an area onwards into the bright sunlit uplands of sustainability. Then, in a specified period of time – often only a couple of years – having achieved sustainability in one place, the donor can move on to the next. One of the first questions asked in the project approval process is, 'How soon can we withdraw from the project?'

Life, of course, does not work that way. If development flowed so easily from good ideas and capital investment, the Indonesian and Brazilian rainforests would be intact and the Turkana would be living happily on the proceeds of frozen fish exports. Development, especially for poor people living on poor land, has a colder, harder reality to it. Sustainability may require longer-term external inputs; it may require less dogmatism about things like market prices for fertilizer in all places and in all countries. And it may require donor support for the recurrent expenditures that a government, with a weak economy and pressed by too many donor-inspired 'catalysts' in too many places, simply cannot meet.

Politicians and civil servants are usually judged on performance *now*, not in the future. The size of this year's grain harvest, therefore, is often judged to be more important than longer-run development issues. But planners have begun to see that it is as important to ask who is producing the grain, how it is being produced and where, as it is to know how much has been produced. The where, who and how will help answer questions about how much when one looks towards the future. In determining what sort of assistance is required, and over what period of time, sustainability will then be viewed not only in terms of agricultural production, but in terms of sustainable incomes *based* on agriculture.

CHAPTER VIII
Post-harvest technologies

There are no successful projects, only those with less problems than others.
                                                                    A.O. Hirschman

POST-HARVEST TECHNOLOGIES and food processing are essential links in the food chain. Improved food preservation and processing techniques can reduce losses and increase yields, thus increasing net farm output. They can retain greater value-added in the family or the village, rather than elsewhere. Traditional oil extraction techniques, for example, are time consuming and are often very inefficient. Simple improvements can increase yields, reduce workloads – often for women – and increase earning potential. Scaling up from traditional techniques offers one type of advancement, but so does scaling down from more modern technologies. This chapter examines one of the oldest food preservation techniques known: drying, and shows how the economics of scale can be the most critical factor in change. It also shows how scaling down – in Kenyan sugar production and Zimbabwean sunflower oil production – can save money and create jobs in the right sort of economic climate. Examples from Ghana, Tanzania and Malawi demonstrate opportunities and problems in scaling up vegetable oil production.

The cost of drying out

Drying is the oldest method of food preservation, and it remains the most common.[1] For centuries it has occupied the imagination and inventiveness of entrepreneurs, innovators and food technologists. Gail Borden, whose name is almost synonymous today with milk in many countries, had a passion for drying food. He spent six years marketing an unpleasant 'meat biscuit' before inventing milk powder during the 1850s. The meat biscuit is forgotten, but Borden is credited with helping to win the American Civil War for the Union by keeping its armies fed.

Drying retards the growth of bacteria and fungi during storage, and in the case of grain, prevents germination. With the development of new crops and new varieties of wheat and rice in the 1960s, new methods of drying have become an important means of reducing loss and, therefore, of improving incomes. For example the introduction of irrigated rice crops during the dry season in India and Bangladesh meant that for the first time, rice was harvested during the monsoon. Traditional drying techniques, therefore – spreading the rice on the ground in the sun – were no longer as effective as they had been.

Much effort has gone into the development of low cost mechanical and solar driers, but through a process of trial and error, it has been found that there are limits to the potential for scaling up from a traditional technology. Much of the drive behind the introduction of improved drying technologies and better storage facilities has to do with post-harvest losses, which in some of the poorest countries are estimated at 10 per cent, and sometimes as high as 40 per cent. If such losses could be reduced, it stands to reason that both farmers and the national economy would benefit significantly. Economist Martin Greeley disputes the received wisdom of the 1970s and 1980s on post-harvest losses, however. He argues that they are often exaggerated, and that the 'uncritical acceptance of convenient but unfounded guesses' by 'experts' has helped justify huge technology-driven aid programmes, whether focused on 'appropriate' technologies, or simply aimed at selling large grain-storage facilities.[2]

In Bangladesh, the distinction between two types of drying became apparent to ITDG in its development of mechanical driers. The first type of drying is for product preservation. The second has to do with product refinement. Small-scale driers, solar, mechanical or otherwise, have had little success among the poor when preservation is the issue, for several reasons. The first, as Greeley argues, is that losses have been exaggerated. This is borne out not only by new research findings, but also by the observable and historical fact that farmers and consumers vote with their money. The costs associated with new loss prevention technologies, even small ones, are in many cases simply not justified by the benefits. Because the bulk of the food that poor people produce is for home consumption, there is no cash benefit derived from preservation, thus providing no financial motivation, either family-based or communally, for a new drying or storage technology.

The situation is different, however, where there is a marketed surplus, and where the price of a product is sensitive to quality increases. Dried apricots, sold throughout Pakistan, represent a significant source of income for villagers in the remote northern areas where apricots grow. Traditional sun drying techniques are adequate, but the introduction of a simple 'drying tent' produced locally of wood and polyethylene sheet, and a sulphur smoking process, make the product more hygienic and improve its colour. It is the improved colour which has added significantly to the product's appeal and to its price, justifying the small additional cost to producers of constructing a drying tent in the village.

It is in this 'product refinement', the processing of a raw product from one form into another, that newer drying technologies have the most potential. Unfortunately, as with so much modern technology, the gap between what is technically and economically available to villagers in remote areas is highly limited. Modern technology has produced large-scale spray and freeze-drying systems that cost tens of thousands of dollars, and more. But what Fritz Schumacher called 'the missing middle' is as painfully obvious in this technology as in others.

The 'product refinement' message has become most evident through experiments conducted by ITDG and others in Latin America and the Caribbean. Initial experiments to develop a drier in St Vincent, for the production of dried sorrel – used in a traditional drink – were conducted under a British aid programme. The individual who carried out those experiments, further refined the technology on a subsequent assignment in Guatemala. There, a Swiss development organization, working with poor villagers in the highlands, was investigating the possibility of agricultural diversification. The villagers' land holdings were too small to produce enough beans and maize for subsistence, and it was thought that higher value vegetables, produced for sale, might ease their economic plight. The Instituto de Nutricion de Centro America y Panama (INCAP) knew that packet soup manufacturers were importing dried vegetables from Europe for the Central American market. Further research showed that 14 000 kg of parsley alone was being imported, at a price of $8 per kg, almost twice the price of the next best vegetable crop known to the villagers.

The drier that was eventually produced was a simple plywood cabinet containing two chambers with nine trays each, served by a thermostatically controlled heater and blower. Washing and sanitizing systems were developed in order to meet microbiological requirements, and a semi-continuous mechanism also evolved. Because the parsley at the bottom of the chamber dried first, the trays had to be constantly shifted. A simple lever mechanism solved the problem, sliding the bottom tray out and making room for a new tray at the top.

One of the INCAP students, returning home to Peru, asked ITDG for assistance in developing a prototype there. A Peruvian herbal teabag firm, which had been importing its raw material, found its sources cut off by customs restrictions, and had begun to experiment with dried camomile produced in the Andean region. The initial ITDG prototype drier was successful, and because ITDG had made an agreement with the Peruvian firm stipulating that the technology, if successful, would be freely available to other interested parties, diffusion was rapid. Local producers were quick to add further cost-saving refinements to the ITDG version. Cheaper heaters were found, and standard inexpensive cabinets were produced from old crates that had been used to import knocked-down Volkswagen combi-vans from Germany.

Between 1985 and 1991, an estimated 80 driers were commissioned in Peru, almost all in the small-scale private sector, and virtually all developed, installed and maintained without any external assistance beyond the development of the early prototypes and an information package produced by ITDG. In addition to camomile, verbena and lemon balm, the new driers were used for fruit, vegetables and the fixing of dyed cotton cloth.

The success of the technology, which has also been taken up in Colombia and Cuba and which shows great promise elsewhere in Latin America, was based on several factors. It was cheap, simple and locally adaptable. It produced dried fruit and vegetables at one tenth the cost of modern imported tray diers. Equally important, however, the drying of the herbs and vegetables in the successful Latin American cases was only part of a process which started with the growing and ended with packaging (teabags, herbs) or further processing, as in the case of the Guatemalan soup mixes. In other words, the driers became part of a process that already existed; they were a technological and economic refinement. In cases where they were an end in themselves, as with a fish and coconut drying experiment conducted by the Mennonite Central Committee in Bangladesh, rural customers were not prepared to pay the premium, and the product had to be aimed at urban, middle-class consumers.

Scaling down: sugar

There are six basic steps in the production of sugar. First, cane is crushed and juice is extracted. The juice is then clarified, boiled, crystallized and 'centrifuged' to separate the solid sucrose from molasses. Then it is dried and packed. By the end of the eighteenth century, a more or less standard technique had developed, boiling the juice in large open pans and passing the fumes from burning sulphur through it, while adding enough lime to counteract acidity. This 'Open Pan Sulphitation' (OPS) process, however, had drawbacks. It produced brown sugar of uneven quality, and the fuel required for the boiling process was expensive. Normally, heat was derived from burning the cane residue, or 'bagasse', but this usually had to be supplemented with wood or coal.

By the middle of the nineteenth century, a new process had been developed and commercialized. It revolved around the creation of a partial vacuum, which caused the sugar to boil at much lower temperatures. This had two effects. It produced a more uniform, lighter sugar. And the fuel required for the heating process could be derived entirely from bagasse. Other improvements, such as higher extraction rates in the rolling process, improvements in refining, and the automation that came with steam power, combined to make this 'Vacuum Pan' (VP) process the favoured technology.

But there are several reasons why the older OPS system has clung to life, and these explain ITDG's unlikely involvement with sugar, first in India and then in Kenya. The much more expensive and more sophisticated VP system requires high levels of managerial talent, and in most countries the equipment must be imported. The most efficient VP systems consume between 10 000 and 20 000 tons of cane per day, far exceeding demand in many countries. For countries with limited demand, smaller operations would make more sense, especially if the trade-offs between local production and continued import are clear. A 1986 review found 26 countries, 21 of them in Africa, which consumed less than 150 000 tons of sugar annually, and which were net importers.[3] For them OPS has genuine potential. Other countries have a demand that might justify a large-scale plant, but they do not produce adequate supplies of sugar, and are thus obliged to import. But one or more small factories could use even limited amounts of local cane, thus reducing imports. In addition, for poor people in marginal farming areas, small local plants could encourage the introduction of a cash crop and the jobs associated with it.

It was these possibilities, and the continued existence of small OPS factories in many countries that enticed ITDG into the field in the late 1970s. In China, there were an estimated 169 sugar factories with capacities of less than 500 tons per day. In Japan there were 13 with capacities ranging between 300 and 1000 tons, in Costa Rica there were 12, and in India, 35. Much smaller versions in India were numbered in the thousands. The Open Pan Sulphitation process had actually re-emerged there in the 1950s in response to an over-supply of cane and the attractive economies of the OPS system.

There were major problems of efficiency, however, which – in a climate of control and fixed prices – threatened the viability of the technology. The Appropriate Technology Development Association (ATDA) in Lucknow became involved, and with ITDG assistance made two essential improvements to the technology. The first was the development of a screw cane expeller which raised milling efficiency from 75 per cent to 85 per cent. The second was the introduction of larger boiling pans and fuel-efficient furnaces. This had the effect of more efficient and faster boiling, which reduced fuel costs and sugar losses.

ITDG's interest in the technology was predicated on its potential for sugar-deficit countries with a tradition of smallholder cane agriculture, one of which was Kenya. There, in the mid-1970s, two OPS factories had opened and closed in short order. ITDG made an arrangement with a third, the West Kenya Sugar Company (WKS), a private firm located in Kakamega, which had opened in 1981. Using Indian technology, the WKS factory had a capacity of 200 tons of cane per day. Its owners had been encouraged by a favourable investment climate, and by the 800 small farmers near the factory. But the problems that had shut the first two factories became evident very quickly. Because of the different qualities of local cane, crushing efficiency was lower than in India, and because the climate was significantly wetter, the bagasse did not burn as well, requiring greater supplements of fuel. In addition, the factory was located at an altitude of 5 000 feet, which further reduced fuel efficiency. What had seemed economically promising now looked like a potential disaster.

ITDG's technical involvement revolved around improvements similar to those made in India. An improved shell furnace, based on the ATDA design, was developed, which improved fuel efficiency and the utilization of capacity. An Indian screw expeller had been imported and tested by ITDG, but proved unreliable under Kenyan circumstances, and WKS made other improvements to the crushing process. Despite the improvements, however, by the late 1980s, ITDG was beginning to realize that the problems of the sugar industry were not only of a technical nature. ITDG had involved several economists in the project, and through comparisons with the larger VP factories in the country, it was becoming clear that further dissemination would be a business problem, rather than a technical matter.

Depending on prevailing prices, OPS sugar could definitely be competitive with VP sugar. Moreover, the capital investment in OPS per ton of crushing capacity was 60 per cent lower than that of the VP process.[4] Installed in marginal areas, it did add to farm income and create new jobs – 630 during the high season in the West Kenya Sugar Factory. But ITDG's interest was not so much in the success of the West Kenya Sugar Factory, as in the potential for wider diffusion of the technology. This depended entirely on commercial investors taking up the opportunity provided by WKS, and the opportunity remained unpromising. Because the large VP sugar factories were government-owned, they operated in an economic twilight zone. When the price paid to farmers for cane was increased by government fiat, they paid it. When the price of wholesale sugar was held down, they endured it. Original investments were written off. Taxes were postponed, avoided or ignored. Losses were absorbed by the owner (i.e. government), a business technique unavailable to the private investor.

At the time, the policy of ITDG and other AT institutions was shifting towards greater focus on facilitating the ownership of new technologies by the intended beneficiaries – the poor – rather than by surrogates who might offer them only employment. This shift may have been triggered, in part, by the growing realization that the sugar sector policy in Kenya, despite passionate government assertions to the contrary, was firmly biased towards the large-scale, capital-intensive investor. Believing in addition that further investment in sugar would move ITDG too far from its basic objectives, plans for further OPS investments in Kenya and Bangladesh were quietly shelved, and ITDG's interest was downgraded to an information and consultancy function.[5]

The experience demonstrates a fundamental problem in the development of appropriate technology. 'Small' is a relative term, but in the AT world it has been redefined in absolute terms because of funding constraints. In other words, a small cow is still a cow. But with inadequate funds, even if you need cow, you may have to settle for goat. The Open Pan Sulphitation process is small in comparison with the modern Vacuum Pan technique, but it is not cheap. Even a small factory can cost $2 million. ITDG's investment in OPS, at roughly $500 000 over a decade, was enormous by NGO standards, but it was tiny in comparison with the scale of the problem, and with the scale of the potential opportunities. In the absence of an institutional investor – either commercial or aid-related – it was two NGOs, ATDA and ITDG, that shouldered the burden of research and diffusion. If they can be criticized for getting in over their heads, or for dropping out at the half-way point, they can also be congratulated for taking it as far as they did. Appropriate technology is not just limited to small investments because of philosophy, it is limited to small investments because those with money – governments, aid agencies, business and much of the research community – are very often wrapped up in their own vested interests.

Oil in troubled economies

Oils and fats are important nutrients. For people in the North, a reduction of intake is usually warranted; the problem for the poorest people in the South – where cost and availability are serious problems – is how to increase it. Methods of obtaining oil from oilseeds date

122

back to ancient Chinese stone mills and wedge presses, and to the screw presses invented by Romans for olive oil. Today in the South, vegetable cooking oil is derived from coconuts, oil palm, ground nuts, sunflower and shea nuts. Other seeds produce edible and non-edible oils for soapmaking, paints, lubricants and cosmetics, and include neem, rape and mustard, linseed, castor, cotton and sesame seeds. In many countries a traditional, village-based 'women's activity', vegetable oil production has in recent years been increasingly taken over by large-scale business interests.

Traditional oil extraction can be laborious and inefficient. Groundnut oil, for example, which is an important source of revenue for women in many parts of Africa, takes between four and five hours to produce. The groundnuts must be shelled, grilled and winnowed. Then, with mortar and pestle, they are ground into a paste. Boiling water is added until the oil separates; then the oil, skimmed from the surface, is in turn boiled to remove any remaining water. Palm oil production is even more time-consuming. After cracking the nuts by hand, women boil the fruit, let it cool overnight, and then pound it in a vat to which boiling water is added. The resulting liquid is boiled again to remove the water. The process, which takes several hours over two days, is so inefficient that there is usually a 50 to 60 per cent loss of oil. In addition to the hours spent directly on the oil production, women must spend time gathering fuel for what is essentially an energy-intensive process.

Ghana's Technology Consultancy Centre (TCC), seeking a means of reducing the price of palm oil for a soap-making process it had developed, began to experiment with a palm oil press in the mid-1970s. Made from a section of used pipe about 30 cm in diameter, a piston, moving on a large screw, gradually squeezes oil from the cooked fruit. In Ghana, this press had a significant price and performance advantage over models developed elsewhere. For example oil presses produced in Cameroon and at the Royal Tropical Institute in the Netherlands used hydraulic lorry jacks rather than a screw. Widely available, jacks eliminate the problem of having the screw manufactured. In the 1970s in Ghana, however, there were already small machine shops capable of producing the screw from scrap truck axles, but a lorry jack was worth its weight in gold. Lorry jacks, intended for occasional lifting, also proved undependable when used every day.

One of the most important factors in the dissemination of the press was the involvement of the National Council on Women and Development, which made some of the original requests, tested early prototypes and placed the final versions with women in working village settings. The TCC press brought the cost of palm oil

123

production down to half the market price, but significant costs were still associated with the boiling process, and the press had not significantly reduced the overall time required. Gradually, therefore, one improvement followed another. Fuel-efficient boiling tanks, already being used in a TCC soap-making process, were adapted for palm oil. And because TCC was working closely with small engineering workshops, an inexpensive palm kernel cracking machine could be developed relatively easily.

The Ghanaian approach reflected the need for a technology which reduced time and cost. It succeeded because TCC listened to the users, and because it became intimately involved in the entire process of oil production, developing its approach in incremental steps as each new bottleneck or requirement revealed itself. And it succeeded in part because of the availability of light engineering workshops capable of cutting, drilling and grinding steel for prototypes and production models.

In Zimbabwe the situation is very different. There, oil production has been centralized into the hands of one or two major producers in the commercial sector. Farmers who grow sunflowers suffer the vagaries of price fluctuation and see their product trucked away whole, to be returned as expensive, factory-produced oil in bottles with attractive labels. The challenge in Zimbabwe was not the same as in Ghana, where TCC advanced a traditional village technology to an intermediate level in order to save time and money, and to preserve jobs. In Zimbabwe the challenge was to move back a stage, to a less complex, affordable level of technology that could create new income opportunities in rural areas.

ITDG's efforts to develop a decentralized production capacity in Zimbabwe actually began six thousand kilometres away in the Indian city of Rajkot. There, a man named Veljibhai Desai had established a company called 'Tinytech Plants Private Limited' which produced complete packages of mechanized oil-producing equipment: decorticators to remove husks and shells, boilers, kettles, filter pumps, filter presses and expellers. Desai was a good salesman and in addition to the usual promotional material, he would send potential customers a two-hour video showing his machinery at work. He was also a man with a mission, a champion with convictions. 'All the dreadful problems appearing nowadays in the world, such as unemployment, hunger, exploitation, disparity, pollution, urbanization, war etc., are direct result of heavy and centralized industries,' his brochure states. He foresaw a twenty-first century in which decentralized, small production units (some of which he would produce) would be the order of the day. 'Whenever I see any big factory or industry,' Desai continued, 'I am horrified to look at it, because it looks me as DEMON, threatening the extinction of humanity, its culture, its liberty, its freedom, etc. Small is possible,' he wrote, 'Small is inevitable.'

In addition to colourful brochures and videos, Desai produced good machinery. In 1987, following a two-week visit to Desai's factory and some of his satisfied customers in India, an ITDG food technologist decided that the Tinytech equipment might make sense in Zimbabwe. Desai had already sold a dozen of his plants to private companies in Tanzania and Malawi, and at about £3000 for a full set (f.o.b. Bombay), it was between one third and one tenth the cost of similar European or Japanese equipment. By 1990, a Tinytech oil plant was in operation, crushing sunflower seeds in Murombedzi, a small town two hours drive north of Harare. Working with another international NGO which provided the local organizational base, ITDG focused on technical support and economic analysis of the operation.

On several levels, the preliminary results were excellent. In India, such a plant would probably run on a two shift basis. But at Murombedzi, even on a one shift basis, operating for eight hours a day, 24 days a month, a reasonable profit could be projected. Borrowing at commercial rates of interest and using existing prices for seeds, it was estimated that the mill could undersell commercially-produced oil and break even at less than 50 per cent capacity output. Projections would obviously change with alterations in the farmgate price of sunflower seeds and the retail price of oil. But essentially, the project bore out Desai's claim – that his 300 mills in India and Africa had proven small to be possible.

If the transfer of technology were that simple, however, Veljibhai Desai would certainly not need NGOs as his go-betweens. Investors would be clamouring to buy. In Zimbabwe, part of the reason they do not is that those with money to invest do not know or are not interested in small-scale decentralized food production. And those who might be interested have neither the money nor the know-how. Enter, stage left, the development-minded NGO – usually long on ideals and short on business acumen. The problems at Murombedzi started when ITDG's partner NGO began to demonstrate a casual attitude towards production. As a result, the discipline of the eight hour day necessary for economic production slipped.

But an even more elementary business error began to surface early in the production stage. The by-product of sunflower oil – the residue – is an 'oil cake' which, when mixed with bran, can be used for cattle feed. Neither ITDG nor the partner NGO had made provision for selling or using the sunflower oil cake produced at Murombedzi. As a result, as oil production went ahead, oil cake began to pile up in the factory. It piled up and up. Besides having a limited shelf-life, oil cake can be a fire hazard, so when its physical presence began to impede production, Lever Brothers in Harare offered to buy the oil cake, partly because their more efficient machinery could extract a bit more oil from it, but also because they had a market for cattle feed. The partner NGO, having embarked on the enterprise in order to find an *alternative* to Lever Brothers' sunflower oil, rejected the offer. The oil cake continued to mount until, piled almost to the ceiling, work could no longer continue and the plant was forced to cease operation. Eventually an appropriate buyer was found, but there was a lesson in the incident: if a technology is to provide new employment opportunities for the poor, the choice of implementing partners and a clear understanding of *their* objectives and talents are as important as the choice of technology.

At this point in the development of the Murombedzi oil mill, a chance editorial in a Harare newspaper bemoaned the shortage of cooking oil in Zimbabwe. Unwilling to let an opportunity for free advertising pass, ITDG wrote the paper a letter, describing the Tinytech operation. To its surprise, there was a flood of enquiries from commercial farmers, feed companies and aspiring businessmen. Although (as with oil and oil-cake) it would take time to sort the wheat from the chaff, the response provided a partial solution to the next stage of diffusion at an appropriate point in the experiment's development. Unlike the case of sugar in Kenya, the investment had not been beyond the NGO's research budget. Nor was it beyond the capacity of local investors.

An ITDG groundnut oil project in Malawi was more reminiscent of the early Ghana palm oil experiments, except that in Malawi the project was an attempt to develop new skills for a non-traditional product. Working with the US Save the Children Federation (SCF) at a small town in the heart of groundnut country, ITDG established an experimental oil production facility to test the technical and economic feasibility of local production. Two machines were introduced: a simple oil screw press, not unlike the one used in Ghana, and a hand-operated husking machine to remove the nut from its shell. The machines and subsequent adaptations were made by a Lilongwe engineering firm,[6] but the *process* of oil production was as important as the machinery in the development of an acceptable and economic product. The roasting time, the temperature and the precise ratio of groundnut to water were important contributors to the quality of the end product. Customers were unhappy with the amber colour and somewhat bitter taste of early samples, a problem solved by removing the skins before cooking. As each change was introduced, or as new inputs such as bottles and labels were added, the economics of the project had to be carefully recalculated.

By 1991 the technology had reached a half-way point on its way to diffusion. The SCF/ITDG oil could be sold profitably at less than the ubiquitous Lever Brothers product, but there remained three major hurdles before the kind of dissemination that took place in Ghana would be possible. One was the commercial production of hullers and presses. In Ghana there were several small firms capable of developing, producing and repairing such machinery. In Malawi, it remained to be seen whether small-scale workshops which produce a tobacco press that is similar in design, could take up the production challenge.

A second issue relates to programming. A counterpart Malawian organization, like the Ghanaian National Council of Women and Development, would be required in order to help move the technology out into real-life situations. More importantly, if it is to provide genuine opportunities for women, as it does in the SCF/ITDG prototype, women's access to the technology must be addressed and actively protected in the dissemination. A third hurdle to dissemination is the way in which groundnuts are marketed in Malawi. At harvest time, they are normally purchased by the national marketing board and moved to centralized locations. Unless sufficient stocks can be held by the marketing board in rural areas, village oil producers will be forced to buy and store large supplies of groundnuts themselves, adding significantly to their working capital requirements, and therefore to the cost of production.

The Bielenberg ram press

Similar issues and others emerge from the development of an oil press in Tanzania, named after its inventor, an engineer working for Appropriate Technology International, Carl Bielenberg.[7] The Bielenberg press is not a variation or adaptation of known methods of oil extraction, it is a completely new innovation, developed in 1985 in the context of a village sunflower project jointly supported by Lutheran World Relief, ATI and the Government of Tanzania. Unlike the presses in Ghana and Malawi, which use a screw to force oil from the seed, and unlike the Tinytech expeller which works on the shearing effect created by a wormshaft, the Bielenberg Press uses a small, hand-operated piston mechanism, or 'ram'.

Untreated sunflower seeds are fed into a hopper on the top of the press. In the vertical position, a long handle allows a measured amount of seed into a cylinder. The operator than pulls the handle back, activating the piston and forcing the seeds into a small cage. The holes in the cage allow the oil – now being squeezed out of the seeds under great pressure – to drop into a pan below. On the backward motion, the residue is ejected, and a new batch of seeds drops into the cylinder.

The press has several advantages in addition to its efficiency. It is robust, cheap (between $285 and $390 in 1990, depending on the manufacturer), it can be made locally, has few moving parts and thus requires little maintenance. It takes the entire sunflower seed without prior preparation or decortication. Because it is small, it can be moved easily, and unlike many screw presses, does not have to be anchored into a concrete foundation, because the weight of the operator holds it in place.

Within five years, the Bielenberg Press had achieved significant success in dissemination, with over 200 in operation in Tanzania, and experimental or production models in use in Zambia, Kenya, Lesotho, Mozambique and other countries of the region. In a sense, the success was almost too sudden – a case of a technology in advance of its time – for many of the ancillary requisites were not in place when it first appeared. The project was established in an area of semi-arid under-utilized land where there was both potential for increased sunflower production and a market for oil, but there were two production problems. First, sunflower was a new crop to many farmers. But even those who knew it had to be introduced to a new, lighter variety, because previously, sunflower had been sold to the government by weight, and so the heavier variety was preferred.

A second problem in dissemination revolved around ownership. In the early stages, Lutheran World Relief, through the Tanzanian Lutheran Synod, emphasized group, rather than individual ownership. The presses were made available to village groups and Lutheran congregations on a loan basis, with the idea that repayments would pay for the upkeep of the project. Perhaps predictably, especially because no interest was charged, many of the loans were not repaid, and the financial viability of the project became questionable. Many of the group presses were used only sporadically, and efficiencies were low. But when presses were eventually made available to individuals, the situation changed dramatically; it was discovered that where communally-owned presses produced, on average, 1000 litres of oil in a season, those operated by individual families or partnerships averaged 2440 litres.[8]

A third potential problem, manufacture of the machines, had been taken care of by the machine's simplicity, and by the development of simple jigs and fixtures which were supplied to manufacturers as part of a package to ensure uniformity. By 1989 there were three commercial manufacturers in the project area, and a commercial firm had started production in Kenya. With assistance from Africare and USAID, the Technology Development Advisory Unit at the

128

University of Zambia modified the machine to suit local conditions, and began field trials with three dozen presses in 1989.

A fourth problem in Tanzania revolved around the question of oil price and availability. When the project was conceived, most oil was imported; prices were high and availability was a problem. By 1986, however, after the equipment had been developed and the cost of the technology was more or less fixed, import restrictions were lifted, and the price of oil fell. Fortunately this did not seriously affect the profitability of the press, but it signalled a problem frequently ignored in the development of appropriate technology. It is often price distortions and shortages in a troubled economy that make local production and new, appropriate technologies seem cost-effective. Liberalization or sudden changes in the price of inputs can change the situation drastically, often for the worse. When the analysis of the potential for a new technique or technology is being calculated, therefore, provision for such possibilities is essential.

Although there were many reasons for the success of the Bielenberg Press, continuity in leadership, a factor often found in successful projects, was important. Not only were the Project Director and Field Manager present through the startup and maturing periods, the project had access to the inventor of the press throughout its development. Dissemination of the technology beyond Tanzania had considerable support from ATI, through the production of technical manuals, reports, consultancies and workshops.

The IDRC approach

As with the development of the Ghana palm oil press, the Bielenberg Press was like a pebble thrown into a pond. The ripple effect necessitated agricultural extension work with farmers on new crops and seeds; the manufacturing technology had to be simplified and made available to commercial producers through the development of jigs and fixtures. The initial users of the press were inefficient, and a new approach to dissemination had to be developed. For the project managers, some of these ripples must have seemed like tidal waves that required exceptional swimming skills, but they were not dissimilar to the unforseen problems that have faced inventors from time immemorial. Those who can swim, or who learn how to swim, tend not to sink.

The Canadian International Development Research Centre (IDRC) frowns on this ad hoc, chaotic approach.[9] An IDRC specialist observed that the Tanzanian project was lucky to have had good seed when it was needed, and was lucky that farmers actually adopted it. The dissemination package, including agricultural research, manufacturing technology and financing had all worked out reasonably well, but if one were to attempt to apply it on a national scale – in Kenya, for example – some 40 000 presses would be required to meet the annual oil requirement, rather than the 200 in the Tanzania project's first five years.* It is perhaps wrong to dismiss good luck in the development of technology. One of Napoleon's most frequently asked questions about officers recommended for promotion was, 'Has he luck?'

But IDRC had a point. And the way IDRC handled the matter illustrates the difference between the well-motivated, ill-funded NGO approach, and that of a well-heeled research institution, staffed by highly-paid professionals with top academic credentials. Identifying a range of interacting components in the problem of increased oil production in Kenya, IDRC took a systems approach, beginning in 1987 with a consultancy that identified preliminary research requirements. A workshop on the findings drew together government officials and academics – both important to the long-term political and institutional viability of what might emerge.

Then, in 1988, Egerton University was engaged to carry out a comprehensive survey of the oil business, resulting in Phase One of a Vegetable Oil/Protein System Project to investigate the extent and magnitude of small-scale rural oilseed processing. Enthusiasm among Kenyan scientists, administrators and policy makers led to a second, then a third phase in 1989, which had two aspects. The first aspect facilitated 'the integration and co-ordination of an evolving research programme', and the second consisted of satellite projects of applied research, such as the purchase and testing of a Bielenberg Press. This particular effort demonstrated, among other things, that the press was 'well received by the rural population visited, thereby creating an incentive for further investigation'.[10] This finding recalls Saul Alinsky's description of the University of Chicago's Sociology Department. It was, he remarked, a body which would spend $100 000 to discover the location of all the brothels in the city – information which any taxi driver could provide for free.

Along with its preliminary studies, findings and research data, IDRC produced a useful, comprehensive dissemination strategy for those interested in the Bielenberg Press. The strategy could be modified for almost any food processing technology, and its elements are worth paraphrasing. In addition to detailed information on the technical and economic feasibility of the press, the strategy consists of

---

* This recalls a comment attributed to President Kennedy when he heard, in 1963, that there were 200 Peace Corps volunteers in Kenya. 'Two hundred Peace Corps is nice,' he is reported to have said. 'Two thousand would be *development*.'

two basic components. The first is an extension package for buyers or users, and starts with oilseed production technology.

Before investing, producers or extension agents need to know about oilseeds: where to get them, how they relate to other crops, and what they require in the way of land preparation, fertilizer, pesticide and weeding. They need to know about harvesting, and post-harvest treatment, as well as threshing and storage. Ram press users need to know how to operate and maintain the press, and about cleaning, packing and storing the oil and oil cake. Work may be required with consumers or potential consumers in the use and storage of oil and oil cake. Ownership of the press should not be clouded by unprofessional notions about groups. Groups may be able to take a technology and make it work, but the reason will not be because they are a group, but because they have the right mix of skills, discipline and ambition. Hard issues relating to marketing must also be addressed. These include questions of price, storage, packaging, labelling and promotion.

The second component of the IDRC approach relates to the manufacturing, distribution and financing of the press itself – materials, workshops, quality control, prices and distribution. A financing system for both manufacturers and purchasers may be necessary for widespread dissemination, involving financial institutions and government organizations.

IDRC articulated the strategy that ATI and the Lutheran Synod had actually carried out, not in an orderly, theoretical fashion, but in a real-life situation. But like TCC in Ghana, they were small, and IDRC was thinking big. The contradiction remains, therefore, as it did in the case of Kenyan sugar: on the one hand, the 'amateurish' NGO, working against all odds to make a difference, sometimes successfully. On the other, a choice between the professional (and very costly) systems approach, or – as in the case of sugar – nothing. With only 200 in operation, the Bielenberg Press did, arguably, have a long way to go before making the impact that IDRC talked of. And in some cases the systems people have had marvellous success, as with high-yielding varieties of wheat and rice in the 1960s. IDRC's persistence over twenty years in the development of a sorghum dehuller is another success story of this type. But in an attempt to replicate these successes, the few well-funded development research organizations may over-study things. They may be developing expensive templates for a real world that will never use them, leaving poorly-funded, ill-equipped NGOs to do the dirty work, and then criticising them for their limitations.

CHAPTER IX
Energy and power

Genius is one per cent inspiration and ninety-nine per cent perspiration.
Thomas Alva Edison

THE OIL CRISIS of 1973 fuelled an unprecedented interest in the development of alternative technologies. The 1979 oil 'shock' reinforced the drive. Within ten years, however, the price of oil had dropped in real terms to almost its pre-1973 level.[1] Lulled into a somnolent sense of security that was accompanied by growing, rather than depleting quantities of known oil reserves, Northern interest in energy conservation and in new, energy-reducing technologies flagged.

In the South, the situation was somewhat different, in part because the shocks of 1973 and 1979 had been major contributors to mushrooming Third World debt. Countries now had to spend much more, simply in order to keep oil imports at a constant level. Between 1973 and 1980, for example, the oil import bill for non-OPEC African countries rose from $800 million to $8.4 billion. The lending capacity of Western banks, significantly enhanced by the vast increase in petro-dollars suddenly flooding Western financial institutions, fed the demand. African external debt rose from $10.6 billion in 1971 to $68.9 billion in 1982.[2] Big money was badly needed, and big money was readily available. Combined with serious decreases in the value of primary exports, the long-term effect on most Third World countries was devastating.

Confusing objectives

In the mid-1970s, when donor agencies began to take a greater interest in energy issues, they were responding in part to a desperate and collective Southern plea for assistance. It was a recognition that the oil crisis had destroyed the ability of many countries to maintain infrastructure, to sustain the development investments of previous decades, and in some cases, to service their debts. Combined with increased awareness of the global environmental effects of deforestation, support for alternative forms of environmentally-friendly energy seemed a logical new direction for the development establishment.

Many of the projects, however, were far from successful, and ten

132

years of patchy, often unprofessional activity left the Third World littered with windmills that didn't turn, solar water heaters that wouldn't heat, and biogas experiments that were full of hot air before they started. The Third World and poor people were often used as guinea pigs for untested, unreliable gimmicks. It was a classic case of assuming that the 'transfer of technology' was simply a matter of invention, to be followed by widespread uptake by grateful consumers. Unlike other, more mature technologies, alternative energy seemed to attract more than its share of cranks.* The ten-year love-in, which lasted from the mid 1970s to the mid 1980s, helped give appropriate technology and the concept of renewable energy an undeserved bad name.

Given how it evolved, sustainability of interest and funding was perhaps precarious from the outset, especially when so much was expected in such a short space of time. David Inger writes with frustration of the Botswana experience:

> The Botswana Renewable Energy Technology Project dropped out of the skies into Botswana in 1981 and disappeared four years later. In the interim, this USAID project did a lot of damage to the credibility of renewable energy and appropriate technology, and also to local institutions already working in the field. The project assumed that progress could be made in renewable energy technology development and dissemination in three to four years, and to make matters worse, it was badly managed.[3]

No less critical was USAID's 1986 evaluation of its own rural energy projects, which found that they had failed to become 'integral parts of agriculture and rural development efforts, to develop and implement energy technologies as early as possible, to require the minimum of capital investment and to be simple and inexpensive to use and maintain, to be acceptable to the people using them, and to be transferable from one region of the world to another.'[4]

Given this broad range of difficult and complex objectives, given the short space of time involved, and given diminishing Western interest in alternative energy sources, it is perhaps not surprising that bilateral and multilateral donors began to shy away from alternative energy sources in the late 1980s. This was unfortunate, not least because oil prices and supply simply cannot be taken for granted. The 1991 Gulf War was a vivid, expensive reminder of this. But if there is a bite to oil dependence in the North, there is a double bite in the

---

* A failed inventor is a crank; a successful one, however, is a genius. This recalls Schumacher's retort, quoted in his daughter's biography, *Alias Papa: A Life of Fritz Schumacher*, to the suggestion that he was a crank. 'A crank,' he said, 'is a piece of simple technology that creates revolutions.'

South. Its price and availability have an indirect but significant impact on the poor through the prices of almost everything they buy. Ironically, however, few of the poor derive any direct benefits from it. Except for limited amounts of kerosene for lamps, and possibly diesel for irrigation pumps, most of the world's poor have little use for it.

For them, *biomass* – wood, twigs, leaves, corn husks – is the most important form of energy after human and draught animal power. It is perhaps more because of environmental concerns than worry about oil, therefore, that energy has remained a development concern. The story of the fuel-efficient stove is a case in point.

Stoves

In most traditional societies the hearth is the social and physical centre of the home. People cook on the fire, they keep warm by the fire; the fireplace is the focal point of the family. In fact, the Latin word for 'fireplace' is *focus*, which in English gradually came to mean 'point of convergence'. And in the development of fuel-efficient stoves, many important lessons about appropriate technology have found a convergence. A common element in many NGO programmes from Tierra del Fuego to the depths of the Indonesian rainforest, fuel-efficient stoves have in some cases burned more money than wood. In others, they have become spectacular examples of successful technology diffusion.

Almost every description of a stoves project begins with trees rather than people. Made of cement, steel, iron, mud or ceramics, fuel-efficient stoves usually begin their odyssey into the homes of the poor as part of an effort to reduce deforestation. The Ethiopian National Energy Commission, the Ceylon Electricity Board, GTZ/World Bank/UNDP stoves in Niger, the Ministry of Environment in Burkina Faso – all focused first and foremost on reducing fuel consumption and, therefore, the threat to dwindling forest resources.

In fact this first objective of most stoves programmes was almost always misconceived. Successful domestic rural stoves programmes do reduce fuel consumption. But with the exception of already severely deforested areas such as the Sahelian, Andean and Himalayan regions, they rarely have a meaningful impact on deforestation. Usually long after a stove programme has failed or succeeded, it has been discovered that most rural people simply do not cut down trees for domestic firewood.[5] They use agricultural residue, twigs and branches (as opposed to trees), very often from their own land. While urban stoves, on the other hand, do use wood or charcoal, this is often a by-product of logging, and increased fuel efficiency does not usually alter the rate of deforestation.

It was secondary objectives that most often contributed to success in the diffusion of stoves. Increased fuel efficiency which is translated into reduced fuel costs, or less time in the kitchen, or fewer hours spent in collecting firewood have had the most impact. A by-product of many stoves programmes, one rarely mentioned in the objectives of early projects, is improved health. Acute respiratory infections are responsible for nearly a third of all under-five childhood deaths. A study of 15 Third World situations published in the *Lancet* estimates that a child exposed to a regular concentration of 1600 micrograms per cubic metre of particulate concentration from biofuel combustion will have about five extra attacks of acute respiratory infections annually. In plain English, this means that smoke is bad for the health, and too much smoke is very bad. And not just for children. The study also showed that in only four out of 15 cases was the smoke *sometimes* less than 1600 $\mu g/m^3$. In most cases it was more, by a factor of as much as 13![6]

Three success stories

The Zimbabwean *Tso Tso* is generally regarded as a success story by everyone except the person who did most to develop it, David Hancock. Starting with a Californian stove design, one based on charcoal, Hancock quickly found it unsuitable for Zimbabwe, where charcoal was virtually unknown. By combining the factors which women criticized in other stoves, he eventually came up with a metal design that was the right height, which cut down on smoke, and which saved on fuel. One of its best selling points for users, not foreseen in the development process, was the speed with which it boiled water. Time, or more correctly, lack of time is a crucial factor in the lives of Southern women. 'In research work we did try to find out what people wanted, but we were so obsessed with fuel saving that we didn't really hear what was being said,' Hancock recalls.[7]

There were two other factors in the success of the stove, both related to marketing. The first was a reluctant decision to put production into the hands of a commercial metal fabricator. A search for possible informal sector producers proved only that the skills and infrastructure needed were simply not available. The second followed from the first: the commercial producer was able to give the stove a high-quality appearance which added little to the cost, but which added enormously to its market appeal. After unsuccessful attempts to sell the stove outside formal retail outlets, it was also realized that established shops and hardware dealers were the best route to high volume sales.

The *Tso Tso* is an interesting case of an almost accidental but successful alliance between institutions with different objectives. The design of the stove was carried out by the Development Technology Centre at the University of Zimbabwe, funded in part by NORAD. Its manufacture and dissemination came about through a licensing arrangement with the private sector. Quality control, training and information are now being carried out by a Zimbabwean environmental NGO, ZERO. David Hancock's own disappointment with the stove, perhaps too critical, relates in part to over-ambitious early objectives. Although it is fuel-efficient, cheap, sturdy and saleable (over 10 000 had been sold by 1991), it has found its niche mainly in urban rather than rural areas. It has not improved the living standards of the poor, nor has it reduced the burden on the forests. It has, in fact, taken on a life of its own, quite independent of and, Hancock feels, irrelevant to its original objectives.

Perhaps, however, as objectives for a woodburning stove, these were overly ambitious, or maybe even irrelevant. At Sylveira House, a Jesuit Training Centre on the outskirts of Harare, there is a small appropriate technology workshop and a house where several experimental stoves have been installed. There is a *Lorena* stove, developed in 1976 by an appropriate technology organization in Guatemala, a *Tso Tso* and other locally designed mud and ceramic varieties. At lunchtime, three or four women cook their lunch at the house, but they do not use any of the 'model' stoves. They sit on the floor around a traditional grate fire. Sylveira House discovered that by lowering the grate from 15 to 8 inches and by protecting the fire from wind, it was as efficient as any of the exotic designs attempted by donor agencies and the Ministry of Energy.[8]

The Kenyan ceramic *jiko* seems to prove the exception to most of the rules about appropriate technology, and like other stove programmes, it succeeded almost despite the objectives of the original designers. It grew out of a USAID-sponsored renewable energy project with Kenya's Ministry of Energy, the sole aim of which was a reduction in the use of fuelwood.[9] Traditionally, Kenyan city dwellers cooked on a small, charcoal-fired metal stove, usually made in the informal sector from old oil drums. With assistance from ITDG, a similar stove with a ceramic liner was found in Thailand. Various adaptations were tested, and it was found that the ceramic lining helped diffuse and retain heat, lowered carbon monoxide emissions, reduced cooking time and cut down on burns. In a laboratory setting it achieved fuel savings of 50 per cent, and in home use savings ranged upwards from 25 per cent. Training, extension and demonstration work were carried out to a large extent by a Kenyan NGO, KENGO, with support from ATI. And like many other successful projects, the Kenyan *jiko* had a particular *champion*, a Kenyan named Max Kinyanjui, who added heart and soul, as well as blood, sweat and tears to the anodyne planning, research and marketing with which most reports are concerned.

Within the first four years of its introduction, 180 000 *jikos* were produced and sold, and by 1987 when the counting stopped, it was estimated that 84 000 were being made every year. There were several reasons for the success of the *jiko*. First, although its developers had 'gone technology-shopping' in Thailand and then seemingly 'transferred' a technology, the new stove had, in fact, evolved through several prototype designs and had been rigorously tested before release. It helped that the new stove was similar in appearance to the one already in use. But it also helped that it looked as though it had been improved. When a genuinely improved version was introduced in Thailand, it didn't sell because it didn't look any different from the traditional bucket stove. The 'new improved' Kenyan ceramic *jiko* had a bell-bottom shape and was painted, two visible but technologically useless 'improvements'. The new stove, however, was appreciably better in performance. The ceramic liner could be made by local potters, not far from where informal sector metal-workers produced the casing. Although, or perhaps because the stove is now manufactured in the formal as well as the informal sector, the price has gradually fallen, and because of the competition, quality has been maintained.

Like the Zimbabwean *Tso Tso*, the success of the ceramic two-pot Sri Lankan stove came about through an unforseen but fortuitous combination of objectives and institutional arrangements.[10] In 1979, Sarvodaya, Sri Lanka's largest NGO, made a copy of the *Lorena* stove. Unlike most stove producers, Sarvodaya's primary objective focused on the person who actually used the stove. The aim was first to improve the quality of women's lives by reducing the amount of time required to gather fuel and cook, and to add to their health by improving the smokey environment in which they worked. A second objective related to more hygienic food preparation. Although a part of it, forests came last.

The *Lorena* stove was not a success in Sri Lanka. Because it took longer to light, it took longer to cook a meal. It had four cooking holes, two of which were unnecessary in the average Sri Lankan kitchen, and it cost significantly more than the traditional stove. Visitors from the Indonesian NGO, Dian Desa, introduced Sarvodaya to a ceramic stove they had developed, but its design was too complex for Sri Lankan potters. It was, however, simplified into a three-part model which could be assembled in the home by a mason using straw, mud and dung to hold the components in place.

Because Sarvodaya worked in five thousand different villages, it could test hundreds of stoves under real-life conditions; the results were positive. There were problems of quality control, as some potters were better at making stoves than others, but the main difficulty related to cost. The traditional mud stove used in rural areas, being made at home, was free. Firewood was not a problem; it was relatively easy to obtain and it was usually free. The trade-off, therefore, was not between the price of the stove and the price of wood. It was between having a child or a woman go in search of wood on the one hand, and purchasing a stove on the other. Even at a low price, the choice – for the average male – was obvious. Dissemination in the countryside, therefore, became a problem of *selling* the stove, almost regardless of price.

It was once again concern about trees that moved the stove to the next stage. In 1984, Sri Lanka's Ministry of Power and Energy did some calculations. It estimated that the average annual household consumption of firewood was 2.5 tons. If the Sarvodaya stove saved 20 per cent, and was placed in half a million homes, it could save 250 000 tons or 2.5 per cent of the annual energy consumption of the country.[11] Although the amount was not great, the government decided to take action, and created – as part of a national fuelwood conservation programme, an Alternative Energy Unit under the Ceylon Electricity Board. A key to the eventual success of the Sri Lankan stoves programme was the appointment by the Ceylon Electricity Board of a man with rare drive and commitment to the project, R.M. Amarasekera.

With financial assistance from the Netherlands Government and technical assistance from ITDG, the initial emphasis was placed on rural areas, and a quarter of a million Sarvodaya stoves were distributed. Because fuel in the rural areas had little cash value, however, it was necessary to subsidize the stove, making the programme non-sustainable in a strictly financial sense. In 1987 an urban programme was launched, with financial support from British ODA and technical assistance from ITDG. Here the situation was very different, because the urban areas depended on firewood trucked in from the countryside. ITDG first made a detailed study of the potential market and concluded that if the stove was to be sold in any volume, the price would have to be directly related to the cost of fuel, and that there would have to be a payback period of less than a month.[12] In other words the stove would have to sell for less than the cost of a month's supply of wood if it was to find its way into the hands of the poor. Because the project aimed to become self-financing, the selling price, in turn, determined the upper limits on the cost of production.

In test situations, it had been found that poor workmanship and use of incorrect clay resulted in too many breakages – at a cost to reputation and sales. It was decided, therefore, that if quality control was to be assured, production had to be placed into a limited number of semi-skilled hands: tile- and brick-makers in urban areas and potters elsewhere. A solution was found near the town of Negombo, north of Colombo, where there are dozens, if not hundreds of tile- and brick-makers, all with kilns and most using simple, labour-intensive technology.

Protracted and sometimes painful negotiations with tile makers continued for two years. Experiments were undertaken to find the best clay, and to develop a process to keep the cost of the stove within the limits determined by the market survey. Finally, an arrangement was made with interested firms, on four conditions: the firm had to have an existing relationship with potters, had to be willing to invest and to provide space and equipment, had to have storage space and excess capacity, and had to have adequate access to clay. The arrangement was similar to a franchise operation, for in return, the project would provide the potters with training, follow-up, and quality control. The project would also identify wholesalers, would mount a promotional campaign with potential retailers, and would conduct a general publicity and advertising campaign.

Despite intensive planning, the evolution of the project took its own course, demonstrating the limitations of a blueprint approach. The relationship between an international NGO, the Ceylon Electricity Board and Negombo tile makers was not exactly a marriage made in heaven, nor was it one that might have been imagined when the first *Lorena* stove was produced in 1979. Nevertheless, there were remarkable achievements in a relatively short period. In July 1987, one factory with four employees working on stove production turned out 480 stoves. By December 1988, seven factories were in production, employing 55 workers and producing almost 9000 stoves each month.[13]

At that rate, the annual production and sales target of 100 000 seemed more than achievable. But in 1989, sales began to fall off, settling at something between two and four thousand a month. There were several probable reasons. The market may have been saturated once the first hundred thousand were sold, and further sales reflected only replacements and a smaller number of new buyers. Quality control on early stoves was not as rigid as it should have been and complaints found their way into the market place. This problem was compounded by a weak wholesaling arrangement and by potters outside the programme producing look-alike copies at a lower price. Imitation may be the sincerest form of flattery, but when the clay is wrong, stoves crack and sales drop.

Nevertheless, in a field that had seen dozens, if not hundreds of failures, the Sri Lanka stoves achievement is impressive. In addition to demonstrating that it was essential to get the technology right, it showed the importance of planning. *Before* going into major production, a detailed, *professional* costing exercise was carried out, and the production scale and process were then determined on the basis of an appropriate selling price. Although this is a standard business technique, it is largely unknown among development agencies. As a result, many a 'good' stove has either been subsidized or has failed in the market place. Or, as in the case of the Zimbabwean *Tso Tso*, it is purchased by those who can afford it, rather than the poorest for whom it was intended. There were two other factors which made these three stoves programmes successful. The first was that they all succeeded in urban markets, bearing out the observation that fuel – for good reasons or bad – is not a problem for individual families in the rural areas. For this reason greater efforts in many countries are being placed on commercial, rather than domestic fuel efficient stoves – for village baking, brewing and fish smoking. Secondly, each of the successful stoves had a *champion*; David Hancock, Max Kinyanjui and R.M. Amarasekera were all individuals for whom the stove – its design, its manufacture, its dissemination – was a genuine labour of love.

Living better electrically

There is nothing experimental about conventional electricity systems. Electricity is a 'mature' technology, one that is well known and well understood in most countries. The cost of electrification is high, however, especially in rural areas. The result is that only 27 per cent of those in the rural areas of Latin America have electricity, an increase of just 4 per cent in two decades. Asia and North Africa, with approximately 20 per cent rural electrification, have had similar rates of growth, but the rest of Africa, at 4 per cent, has remained unchanged.[14]

Although the strongest initial demand is usually for lighting, electricity is an important infrastructural investment, especially in increasing the diffusion of development options away from urban centres. It is essential to the establishment of garages, repair shops and small-scale industries. It can be used to improve the milling of grain or the pressing of oil seeds; for crop drying, cane crushing and other food-processing equipment; for sawmills, mechanical workshops and for irrigation pumps. Electric pumps in India and Bangladesh, for example, offer a considerable saving in operation over diesel pumps. Decisions about rural electrification, therefore, reflect some of today's most critical development questions: the balance between rural and urban investment; the role of the private and public sectors; the choice of technology, and the growing gap between the rich and the poor.

Oil-fired generating plants were built in huge numbers in the 1960s, but with the oil crises, attention turned to hydro-electric power generation. Choosing between hydro, where the potential exists, and coal or diesel-generation is not always straightforward, however. Diesel incurs fewer capital costs, but has higher running costs. Some of today's Third World hydro projects, on the other hand, are among the most expensive and ambitious anywhere, and their environmental impact has become a major consideration in cost projections. Nuclear power, once seen as a salvation, is high in capital cost, and most Third World projects have run into a myriad of technical, financial and political problems.

Rural electrification in the South is often a self-conscious attempt to accelerate what has happened elsewhere at a totally different pace and, understandably, in a different way. Modern technology is more sophisticated and costly, and Third World countries start with fewer technical and economic resources, and with lower levels of rural development. As Gerald Foley observes, 'For many utilities, and the international agencies which lend or grant them money, the prospect of a major expansion of their rural electrification programme is an operational and financial nightmare.'[15]

Options

The Pavlovian donor rush to renewable sources of energy for power generation has been both short-sighted and inadequate. There is nothing especially sacrosanct about renewable energy unless it can out-perform the more mature approaches, technically and economically over time. That said, there *are* alternatives to more coal, diesel and monster hydro-electric dams. The cost of photovoltaic electricity dropped between 1970 and 1990 from $30 per kilowatt-hour to only 30 cents, and it is expected to drop to one third of that by the turn of the century. This will offer real energy alternatives to many countries in the South.

One of the most elementary of appropriate technologies relates to the effective and efficient management of existing systems. Because of frequent power shutdowns, many Indian farmers keep spare diesel systems, at an estimated investment of $370 million.[16] Power cuts and trippings accounted for a third to a half of the loss of productive capacity in the Indian cement industry in the mid-1980s.[17] During the same period, losses to Pakistan's power system through daily blackouts was as high as 38 per cent. In Brazil it has been estimated that projected power demand could be reduced by 30 per cent by the turn of the century through simple efficiency measures such as improvements in industrial and commercial electric motors and changes in the approach to domestic, commercial and street lighting.[18]

Windmills are not a new or experimental technology. They become experimental when attempts are made to have them do new things in places where there are weak wind regimes. In Argentina, which has 60 000 operational windmills and which accounts for 20 per cent of total world production of windmills, successful diffusion was the result of four things. The first was adequate wind for the purpose envisaged. The second was an *appropriate* purpose – to fill water tanks for cattle. Where more ambitious purposes have been sought, such as crop irrigation or electricity generation, success has been much more elusive. The third was the existence of a light engineering industry which permitted the manufacture and repair of windmills on a widespread basis. And a fourth was the investment of a private American firm in local production. Using designs that were already eighty years old, Aeromotor's main objective in the 1960s was to produce for export to the United States. But with production costs half of what they were in the US, the result benefitted both countries.[19]

Let there be light

'Micro-hydro' refers to a power generating plant with output of less than 100 kilowatts; 'mini-hydro' conventionally refers to plants generating between 100 kW and 500 kW, and 'small hydro' covers the range between 500 kW and 1000 kW. In industrialized countries a 100 megawatt power plant is considered small; nevertheless, micro-power units can be a cheap and well-tested technology for remote areas with appropriate water resources. Small hydro was a common means of power generation in the early years of the twentieth century, and only began to lose favour when the technology for high-voltage transmission lines were developed. In 1914, for example, there were an estimated 7000 small hydro plants in Switzerland,[20] and before the advent of national grids they were a common means of power generation in many other countries. In Sri Lanka an estimated 600 micro-power plants were installed before 1956.

With the development of national grids, however, and ever-increasing amounts of cheap fossil fuels, interest in micro-hydro diminished and existing plants fell into disrepair. Renewed interest in the technology began in China. In the fifteen years after 1970, it is estimated that China established a phenomenal 76 000 small hydro plants, generating 9500 megawatts of power as part of what the World Bank terms 'the most massive rural electrification effort ever attempted in the developing world.'[21] The total worldwide potential for stand-alone small hydro power plants may be as high as 100 000 megawatts, of which only a fraction has so far been tapped.[22] In Peru, for example, the small hydro potential is estimated at 12 000 megawatts against a total installed 1982 capacity of only 3300. Potential of a similar magnitude exists in Thailand, Indonesia, Pakistan, Sri Lanka and Jamaica, while lesser but not insignificant potential exists in India, the Philippines, Bolivia, and a number of African countries.[23]

In Nepal there has been considerable success in introducing the technology.[24] The story began in the 1960s when two independent bodies, the United Missions to Nepal (UMN) and BYS, a Swiss-Nepali engineering firm, began to produce non-electric turbines for rural milling projects. In 1975, with a small grant from the Mennonite Central Committee and CIDA, the UMN began to develop a pilot hydro-electric project, followed not long afterwards by BYS. As the technology was being refined and the pilot phase ended, a need for credit arose: because of the cost, farmers and entrepreneurs would need help in establishing plants. The Agricultural Development Bank of Nepal (ADBN), which had an appropriate technology unit of its own, stepped in and provided five to ten year loans for up to 80 per cent of the cost of an approved installation. Training and extension, key elements of the programme, were provided by the manufacturers and the ADBN.

In the early 1980s the Asian Development Bank also became involved, extending a loan to the Government of Nepal in order to expand credit operations. By 1987, the number of manufacturers had risen to seven. Over 650 turbines had been installed by 1990, and 500 more potential sites had been identified. Although the benefits of the schemes are difficult to quantify precisely, some general observations are possible. The micro-hydro schemes are significantly cheaper than large-scale hydro-electric power generation. There are major savings in time, and sometimes of money, over traditional techniques in the milling of wheat, maize and rice. And with some crops, such as mustard, yields have increased by as much as 30 per cent.[25]

The ITDG effort in Sri Lanka provides an interesting case for comparison.[26] Grid electricity prices increased rapidly during the 1970s, and there was renewed interest in old micro-hydro schemes that had been installed during the first half of the century. Although much of the electrical equipment was irreparable, the civil works – weirs, canals and penstocks (the pipes through which the water falls to the turbine) were in reasonably good condition.

Most Sri Lankan tea estates had such schemes, and because each had several trained engineers and a ready demand for electricity, it was thought that they would provide a good testing ground for a renewal of the technology. For the tea estates, the project was of interest because locally generated power promised to reduce costs, and because power cuts from the grid had enormous consequences. A power failure of less than four hours will lower the quality (and therefore the price) of the tea in production. Cuts of eight hours or more can result in the complete loss of the tea in process at a cost of several million rupees.

In the early 1980s, ITDG worked on the rehabilitation of several schemes in the tea estates, one of which had originally been installed in 1898. Working relationships were established with a small British firm, Evans Engineering, for the production of new turbines, and with a Sri Lankan firm, Brown and Company, on their installation. One of the most important technological developments was an electronic load controller. It is essential that the frequency of electricity remain constant. But fluctuations in demand require a governor which can alter the water flow. This presents a problem which, in the past, was controlled mechanically with centrifugal governors linked to the water valves. Oil hydraulic systems are used on most modern turbines, but for small schemes they have serious drawbacks: they are expensive, difficult to repair, and they require a relatively sophisticated degree of on-going care and maintenance.

Various experimental electronic load controllers (ELC) were under development in Europe at the time, but none suited the Sri Lankan requirements. With ITDG funding and technical involvement from Evans Engineering, however, a suitable prototype was produced by another small British firm, GP Electronics, and by the late 1980s, over 100 units had been exported and successfully installed in China, Thailand, Malaysia and other countries. The ELC made a significant difference to the cost of renovating the Sri Lankan micro-hydro plants, to other ITDG micro-hydro projects in Colombia and Peru, and to some of the Nepal projects.

By 1983, ITDG had refined the technology to the point where, with good training and follow-up, it was replicable and sustainable. But there were worries within the organization that simply rehabilitating micro-hydro projects on nationalized tea estates did little for the poor. Reducing the cost of tea production would add to the country's foreign exchange earnings and might improve the balance of trade, but the workers on the estates themselves – descendants of low-caste Tamils who had migrated from India in the nineteenth century – remained among the poorest in the country. A unique scheme was therefore developed in conjunction with a Dutch-funded

Integrated Rural Development Programme. The IRDP would fund 30 new schemes on the condition that the net surplus produced through the reduction in use of grid electricity was paid into a development fund for estate workers.

Dances with wolves

Having demonstrated the effectiveness of the technology and gained the confidence of the government and the tea estates, ITDG expected other donor agencies to come forward to support the rehabilitation of some of the hundreds of schemes that remained untouched. They did, but not in the way that might have been anticipated: the perceived opportunity was for sales, not power generation. The first to arrive, in 1983, were the Chinese. Engaged by the World Bank to write specifications for ten pilot schemes, Chinese engineers not surprisingly drew up specifications that could be met only by Chinese equipment. Although several international firms tendered for the contract, the bulk of it went to China. The results were not good. The Chinese equipment looked impressive, but without follow-up and spares, without sufficient training for the operators, without a Sri Lankan agent and local technicians to provide technical assistance, one by one the systems failed, mainly because of problems with their complex hydraulic governors.

Then came the Canadians. Under CIDA auspices, a consulting firm produced an extensive report which, among other things, projected an internal rate of return that was so high (and so wrong), that an overnight fortune seemed possible in micro-hydro. The report, which cost almost as much as ITDG had spent on micro-hydro in Sri Lanka altogether, was quietly buried. Then, in 1985, the British Overseas Development Administration began to take an interest. Extrapolating from the ITDG experience and projecting a possible budget in the neighbourhood of £10 million, ODA thought it might be possible to renovate 140 or more schemes.

A British consulting firm was engaged to prepare feasibility studies, but things gradually turned sour. The ODA objectives had little to do with appropriate technology, local production or cost minimization. Knowing this, the consulting firm designed systems that maximized British content: high-cost turbines rather than the basic versions used by ITDG; British switchboards rather than the perfectly adequate varieties that have been made in Sri Lanka for half a century; concrete-lined ductile iron penstocks – the Rolls Royce of penstocks. Apart from the effort to maximize British content, there was no particular reason for the firm to specify anything less than the very best, for if the project went ahead, they would have minimized

145

risk and confusion (and possible damage to their reputation) by avoiding unknown products, small firms and Sri Lankan manufacturers.

Sri Lankan engineers, unimpressed with the technical quality of the reports, were shocked to discover that British engineers with no direct experience of micro-hydro, were to be charged at *more than one hundred times the salary of a Sri Lankan engineer*. Negotiations became more strained when it was proposed that ODA would supply the equipment and consultancies (the consultancies alone would take up 25 per cent of the budget) and Sri Lanka would cover the cost of the civil works. Half of the £10 million, therefore, would be provided by the Government of Sri Lanka, but the entire amount would be charged to the tea estates as a *loan*.

This made it imperative to the tea estates that the project be as cost-effective as possible, which it clearly was not. From a minimum of 140 schemes, the proposal now called for a maximum of 60. Suddenly an appropriate technology no longer looked appropriate or even feasible. Worse, in anticipation of new schemes, some of the estates had run down their spare parts supplies and had neglected preventive maintenance, leading to costly damage and closure of some existing plants.

By 1989, the ODA scheme had dissolved into a modest, face-saving proposal for two pilot schemes. Meanwhile, a Japanese team began a survey of the potential for micro-hydro, and by 1991 were putting the finishing touches on plans to upgrade three existing systems, and refurbish a fourth. Relying heavily on imported Japanese equipment, the project anticipated raising the rated capacity of the four systems from an existing total of 133 kW to 390 kW, at a cost of 915 million Japanese Yen. This worked out to approximately US $6.6 million, or a staggering $26 000 per kW, more than ten times what ITDG had spent on its most recent schemes, and anywhere from eight to twenty times higher than accepted international costs *for entirely new schemes*.

Lessons

If there is a single lesson to be drawn out of energy projects, it is the importance of setting clear and reasonable objectives. Success comes from dealing with people's immediate needs rather than with vague concerns about the environment. (Einstein once defined environment as 'everything that isn't me.') As important, perhaps, using poor people and poor countries as guinea pigs for underdeveloped technologies is likely to result in failures which simply reduce future options. In terms of reaching the poor, the most successful examples in this chapter are the Sri Lankan and Kenyan stoves, both of which were similar to known, traditional stoves, both of which were cheap and which provided clear, short payback periods.

Several of the projects were advanced by the existence of a local manufacturing base which could produce and repair components. And the successful projects all benefited from systematic monitoring and evaluation. Gradual evolution and adaptation were the rule in most cases, and this required time. Short, unrealistic time-frames are the cause of many failures that are often unfairly ascribed to the technology. One of the reasons for the 'success' of the Chinese biogas and micro-hydro programmes, for example, has been the huge government investment in research, training, dissemination and follow-up over a twenty-year period. This was accompanied by a willingness to tolerate failure and to learn from it. An estimated 85 per cent of the Chinese biogas plants installed between 1973 and 1978 – more than have ever been produced in all other countries combined – failed not long after installation. Andrew Barnett correctly warns about concepts of success and failure: 'In industrialized countries it is common to think of technologies taking more than 30 years from the initial innovation to total *saturation* of the market. In many cases, the investment in energy technologies in the rural Third World has been so modest and so recent that questions of success are premature.'[27]

In virtually all of the cases described, the commercial or semi-commercial sectors played a vital role in the ultimate dissemination of the technology – providing credit in the case of Nepal's micro-hydro; investment in the case of the Argentine windmills; technical expertise in the case of Sri Lanka micro-hydro; manufacturing know-how and marketing expertise in the case of the Zimbabwean *Tso Tso* and the Sri Lankan stove. The role of government was also important in most cases, in recognizing – whether in connection with Sri Lankan stoves or Nepalese micro-hydro – that alternatives to simply 'extending the grid' are essential if the rural poor are to be reached within the lifetime of those already born.

And in each of the cases discussed, development agencies played a key role. NGOs and individuals with a basic interest in appropriate or alternative forms of energy were often important to a success. Interestingly, most of the cases also involved one or more bilateral agencies. In most instances, except that of micro-hydro in Sri Lanka, where things went badly wrong, this involvement was constructive and supportive.

CHAPTER X

The house that Jack built: construction materials

I tell this tale, which is strictly true,
Just by way of convincing you
How very little, since things were made,
Things have altered in the building trade.
Rudyard Kipling, *A Truthful Song*

MORE THAN A billion people in today's world lack adequate shelter and live in unsanitary, unsafe conditions which provide little protection from the elements. There is no lack of good ideas and practical solutions for the problem. It is the *availability* of affordable, durable construction materials that determines how much and what type of construction will take place in a given country. Expenditure on building materials in the Third World absorbs between three and five per cent of GDP and represents an immense drain on foreign exchange. For example, the total Third World import bill for construction material rose from $3.3 billion in 1970 to $35 billion in 1982. Much of the bill was charged to Africa, where in some countries over 90 per cent of the value of commercial building materials is imported.[1] The real challenge, therefore, is to ensure that affordable, durable materials are widely enough produced and in sufficient quantities that they can reach the poor and, where possible, create jobs in the process.

Much of what is known about building construction has been known for centuries, and in many countries of the South, the old ways remain the best available for most people. But with increasing populations and growing energy costs, the old ways are no longer always efficient. In some cases they have been superceded by modern technologies which produce the same materials – bricks, mortar, roofing materials – at a high cost in capital equipment, and at a loss in employment opportunities.

This chapter examines four intermediate technologies in construction materials: lime production in Malawi, cement making in India, the production of bricks in Botswana, and the development of a new building product that looks like an old one – fibre-reinforced concrete roofing tiles. In addition to the lessons these cases have to teach about construction materials, they also carry messages about diffusion, and about the thorny question of profit: what it is, how it is calculated, and what happens when it is suppressed.

148

The Balaka lime project

Malawi, a beautiful and sometimes forgotten central African country, is also one of the poorest in the world. Only four others – Mozambique, Ethiopia, Chad and Tanzania – have a lower per capita GNP; at $170 in 1988, Malawi's was the same as that of Bangladesh. Roughly 3.7 million Malawians, out of a total population of 8 million, are of working age. Population growth is expected to push this number up to 5 million by 1996, but jobs for job-seekers are in short supply. It is estimated that the shortfall in job creation during the 1990s will be between 92 000 and 120 000 annually.[2]

Starting around 1980, several institutions and programmes were established in Malawi to assist small- and medium-scale enterprises, with an emphasis on rural, off-farm job creation and import substitution. One of these institutions, Indefund, was established in 1981 to provide medium-sized loans (between $11 000 and $125 000), mainly for non-agricultural projects. In Chichewa, *Inde* means 'yes', and by 1989, Indefund had said yes to 86 projects, making loans at 18.5 per cent interest for periods of two to twelve years, and leading to the creation of an estimated 1500 jobs.[3]

One of the projects was a pilot scheme for the production of hydrated lime. Lime production for construction purposes dates back to ancient Egypt, and lime producers using old techniques can still be found throughout Latin America, Asia and Africa. Limestone, plentiful in the Chenkumbi Hills of south-central Malawi, is mined by traditional lime producers, but their yield is low and the quality of their product has limited value to end users. As a result, Malawi imports almost half its annual requirement – 3000 tons, at a cost of approximately $325 000.[4] Roughly half the lime goes to the construction industry and the rest is used as a reagent in the production of sugar. An ITDG feasibility study, conducted in 1987 on behalf of the government, found that by upgrading traditional production techniques, better quality lime could be produced locally, reducing dependence on imports and creating jobs for Malawians. Given a projected rise in the demand for lime, the investment proposal met the criteria established by Indefund.

The project that emerged, for the establishment of a pilot plant to produce consistent, high-quality, chemical grade lime for the sugar and construction industries, had a secondary goal. By integrating parties with different interests and skills in the project, it was hoped that a model for further collaborative efforts might be developed. The project was co-ordinated by a USAID-supported body, READI (Rural Enterprise and Agro-Business Development Institutions Project). It involved credit from Indefund, technical assistance from ITDG, and the production of kiln and factory equipment by a local engineering firm. The borrowers were four Malawian entrepreneurs, operating a small company called United Mining Company Ltd. Sited near limestone quarries at Balaka, the project involved the manufacture of a steel-encased vertical shaft kiln in which the lime would be fired. It was a continuous-feed process that required the development of a number of pieces of moderately sophisticated equipment, including a motor-driven hydrator which mixed quicklime with water after the firing process.

As with many, if not most, projects of this sort, things went wrong throughout the trials. Some of the specifications had been drawn up incorrectly, and some of the manufacturing was sub-standard. A decision to switch the fuel source from charcoal to coal led to damage on the first firing, and this caused delays until the kiln could be repaired and the process corrected. ITDG withdrew from the project before completion, mainly for financial reasons, and the technical work on an improved Mark II hydrator was completed by the local engineering firm. By 1991, however, the project had been commissioned and was producing chemical grade lime of a consistent quality. The Malawian entrepreneurs were in business, 50 jobs had been created, and a rare partnership in terms of government bodies, donors and entrepreneurs had proven workable.

Among the key lessons contained in a 1991 evaluation were the need for good co-ordination and leadership, the importance of adequate time for the project to mature, and an ability to tolerate and learn from failure – all consistent with other successful projects focusing on new technology. But the involvement of different parties with different skills and interest was also judged critical to the success. Each of the parties specialized in what it new best – ITDG consultants in lime technology; a local manufacturer in producing the kiln and other equipment; Indefund in credit. The four Malawian entrepreneurs – whose personal savings were at risk – were, of course, central to the project, as they provided a framework on which the project could be constructed.

Mini-cement in India

In nineteenth century Europe, cement was manufactured in vertical shaft kilns (VSK) very similar to the lime kiln developed in Malawi. Gradually, however, production shifted to a rotary kiln process which allowed continual operation and which, along with greater fuel efficiency, produced better, more uniform cement. Although it was revived and widely used in Germany during the Second World War, the VSK process has now all but disappeared from Europe. It can still be found in Australia, however, and in the 1960s began to find favour in China. By 1975, 28.3 million tons of cement, 60 per cent of the total Chinese production, was being manufactured in VSK mini-cement plants, each with a daily capacity of under 200 tons. By 1983, 81 million tons, which represented 75 per cent of the entire Chinese output was being produced in mini-cement plants.[5]

In India, various experiments with the VSK began after the Second World War. There were basically three strands to the research. The first had a military purpose. Following India's brief war with China in 1962, the Indian Army sought the means to produce small batches of cement where and when it was needed, instead of relying on transportation from distant factories. The second research stream was commercial, inspired in part by a fit of pique. A Jodhpur flour and rice miller, D.P. Saboo, required cement for alterations to his factory, but his application for an allocation – cement being heavily rationed in the 1970s – was refused. Annoyed, Saboo decided to make his own cement. His first effort, in his own garden, was successful enough to encourage him to continue with the experiment.

The third research strand had more conventional origins. The Cement Research Institute of India, using the military research as a starting point, began VSK experiments in the late 1960s. In addition, under the auspices of the Uttar Pradesh Government, a researcher named M.K. Garg undertook several vertical shaft kiln experiments based on efforts that the military had by then abandonded. When the government lost interest in 1972, Garg took his passion with him to the newly formed Appropriate Technology Development Association (ATDA) in Lucknow, where the experiments continued – with funding and technical support from ITDG and Appropriate Technology International.

The first impetus for Indian research into the viability of mini-cement plants may have been military in origin or simply pique on the part of D.P. Saboo. But there were good developmental and economic reasons to undertake the research. Unlike large plants, the smaller units could be established where there were limited deposits of suitable raw material. The smaller plants could also be set up in areas where limited demand would not justify a larger plant. By producing close to the market, costs could be reduced because of shorter transportation distances.

Between 1981 when the first mini-cement plant (MCP) went into operation and 1986, some 60 commercial plants were commissioned. The mini-cement plants were, therefore, a modest success but, as with so many things in India, for a complex web of reasons that were not entirely planned at the outset. Part of the impetus for research had been the great shortage of cement through the 1960s and 1970s, and the strict pricing and rationing control on large plants. This climate of control may actually have discouraged production and expansion in the modern sector and thus boosted the attractiveness of small-scale production. Although cement was partially 'decontrolled' in 1982, mini-cement plants remained totally exempted, which meant that they could sell at whatever price the market would bear. Where there were shortages, this gave mini-cement a modest price advantage of perhaps 5 or 10 per cent over the larger producers.[6]

When a mini-cement plant is compared with the more standard large-scale variety, the actual cost of producing a ton of cement is almost the same.[7] But when average market prices are compared, the advantage enjoyed by the smaller plant being located closer to its customers gives it a further advantage. As a percentage of total price, transportation accounts for 16 per cent in the case of large-scale production, and only 10 to 11 per cent in the case of mini-cement. Beyond the price advantage, in a market where adulteration is common, local production has the advantage of more intimate customer-client relationship; trust, therefore, is also a factor.

The major limitation of the MCP is its less efficient use of energy. A mini-cement plant uses between 11 and 22 per cent more power per unit of production than the larger plants. Despite this drawback, the MCP has several advantages besides its ability to produce a price-competitive, high quality product. On average, the MCP requires 25 per cent less capital investment per unit of output than the large plants. And unlike the rotary kiln plants, which have a foreign exchange component of as much as 15 per cent, the VSK has none.

The job creation factor is also important. In addition to being more labour-intensive, an MCP requires fewer highly skilled workers than a large plant. A 100 ton/day MCP produces annually at the rate of roughly 250 tons per worker, whereas large-scale plants produce 600 tons per worker. By 1986, the result was that large-scale firms employed approximately 110 000 people, while the mini-cement plants employed 60 000.

In his studies of the economics of mini-cement plants, Sanjay Sinha warns that research and development must continue if the MCP technology is to keep pace with the continuous research and development efforts in the large-scale industry. He observes that although mini-cement should not be expected to replace large-scale production, it has a very solid place in the technology of cement production and represents an economically beneficial alternative. 'In countries with a lower reserve of technical and managerial skills as well as in India, in the short- to medium-term, the industrial dispersion effects of mini-plants will undoubtedly have a positive developmental effect.'[8]

It is worth noting that the mini-cement plants and the costings used in this chapter all relate to standard Portland cement of the same quality as produced in the large-scale plants. Portland cement is the minimum standard which can be sold in India, but in China there are six permissable grades. While Portland cement is specified for bridges and multi-storey buildings, lower grades suffice for single-storey dwellings and other less-demanding uses.[9] The Chinese policy has had a major and positive effect on the diffusion of mini-cement plants in that country, many of which do not have to produce to the high specifications demanded of their Indian counterparts. Indian mini-cement plants thus came into being *despite* the lack of an appropriate government policy on cement grades.

The policy issue is one strand of research on a different approach to cement being undertaken by the International Development Research Centre (IDRC). Going back to basics, in the 1980s IDRC began to study the properties of the cement used in Egyptian pyramids, and in Roman construction. Known as 'pozzolan' or 'pozzolana' cement, it was named after Pozzuoli, a town in a volcanic part of south-western Italy. Early builders had discovered that pozzolan, basically a volcanic ash with a high silica content, when ground together with lime and mixed with water, formed a durable cement. A similar mortar produced from lime and crushed brick has been produced in India for centuries, and it has been found in the ruins of Mohenjodaro in Pakistan, dating back to the third millennium B.C. The modern relevance of pozzolana cement is that unlike Portland cement, the production process does not require energy for heat. And it is based on a raw material – volcanic ash – that is widespread in many developing countries. Studies in Bolivia and Guatemala, for example, have shown that pozzolana cement could be produced at half the cost of Portland cement. IDRC research in the early 1990s identified, *inter alia*, two key issues related to the material's potential in Latin America: the need for a reliable, speedy test to evaluate the potential of pozzolan deposits, and the establishment of appropriate specifications for different types of construction.[10]

Although the economics of pozzolana cement seem straightforward, the question of attitudes is critical. As with many traditional technologies, pozzolana cement did not enjoy the benefits of modern research and marketing that were applied to Portland cement during the twentieth century, and so it remained a 'second class' technology in most of the places where it survived. In their day, the Stanley Steamer and the Studebaker Electric Automobile were highly competitive with cars powered by internal combustion engines. But, in part because of cheap oil, research, development and marketing went one way, and they went the other. This is one of the key lessons in the Indian mini-cement story: the economics of manufacturing – in almost any sphere – are situational and can change. Mini-cement production in India may have flourished despite a lack of government policy on differing cement qualities, but it was made competitive, in part, because of government restrictions on large-scale manufacturers. Had these restrictions not been present, the economic advantages accruing to large-scale producers in access to credit, subsidized power and other inputs might very well have made the small-scale effort less possible and less attractive, despite its obvious employment-creation advantage.

Botswana: a few bricks short of a load

With a population roughly one-tenth of one per cent of India's and a completely different resource base, Botswana's approach to development necessarily differs greatly from India's. Nevertheless, there are parallels, or potential parallels in the introduction and diffusion of new technologies.

In Botswana in the late 1980s, all cement had to be imported, and because local brick production was of a low quality, bricks had also to be imported.[11] Trucking bricks in from South Africa was an expensive and arduous proposition, and so most building was done with cement blocks. Although building with cement blocks was 60 per cent more expensive than with bricks, the simple non-availability of good bricks gave the advantage to cement. It also provided an opportunity for local brick production.

Brickmaking can be an entirely manual operation – from the digging of the clay to the mixing, moulding and firing of the bricks. Being an old technology, various levels of mechanization are available, depending on scale and the desired level of investment. Machinery includes mechanized mixers, various kinds of mechanical or automatic presses and extruders, and different types of kiln. Using data from existing small-scale pressing plants and figures from a feasibility study for a large-scale plant, Raphael Kaplinsky observed much greater potential economies in small-scale Botswana brickmaking than existed in the case of Indian cement. A small-scale plant, for example, employing 29 people and turning out a million bricks annually, compares favourably in job creation with a large-scale plant employing only 4.5 times the number of workers but with 24 times the production. When capital costs are factored in, the comparison is more striking: 'Botswana's annual consumption of bricks ... could either be met by a single plant costing P5.33 million, employing 131 people and operating at about 40 per cent of a single-shift capacity ... or with 11 small-scale pressing plants employing 319 workers and costing P1.57 million.'[12]

The more striking economy of the small-scale plant can be seen in the selling price of bricks required to break even over 20 years. The small-scale brick press with a purpose-built kiln could sell bricks at 43 per cent of the large-scale plant's selling price, and 20 per cent of the imported brick price at the time the studies were done.

For a potential investor with a calculator, such observations in the mid-1980s made brickmaking an appealing investment opportunity. In addition to traditional brickmakers, there were two such investors. The first was a Motswana who had worked in a Zimbabwean brick factory. In 1982 he had purchased used brickmaking equipment in Zimbabwe and set up a factory in Francistown. The machinery had the capacity to produce half of Botswana's annual demand at the time, but in addition to unanticipated problems with the local clay, the plant proved to be technically and managerially beyond the owner's capacity. Eventually he sold it, and in the first two years of operation, the new owners produced to less than four per cent of capacity.

The second investor was an NGO, the Southern Rural Development Association, which grouped some of its building materials and mining operations into a subsidiary called the Minerals and Holding Trust (MHT). With assistance from several donor agencies, MHT began a small-scale brickmaking operation in the south of the country, with manually operated brick presses and a two-chamber stationary kiln. Assistance was provided by ATI and others in developing, adapting and testing brick presses from Belgium and Britain. The factory ran consistently at a loss because, Kaplinsky says, 'they were not aware of their production costs'. They sold their bricks at about 30 per cent less than actual cost, and at only 23 per cent of the cost of the imported bricks against which they were competing. Understandably, the bricks sold well but the operation required frequent injections of donor support to stay in operation, while MHT sought ways to reduce costs, rather than increase prices.

One innovation, the provision of an output incentive to workers, did bring the cost down by 13 per cent, but because one of the sponsoring international NGOs deemed this to be 'ideologically unsound', the practice was halted.

Unlike the Balaka Lime Kiln, the partnership between those with a possible interest in bricks in Botswana was limited. The private investors received no technical or managerial assistance, while the NGOs observed none of the financial discipline inherent in a market-based operation. The level of expertise and management skill available among potential investors was insufficient to kick-start a brick-making industry despite its very real profit-making potential. This left the field to NGOs which could offset continued losses with injections of cash for new 'phases' of the 'project'. Worse, it can be argued that by selling below cost, MHT may actually have discouraged other potential investors, thereby actually holding back diffusion of the technology.

Fibre concrete roofing: lessons from the Black Country

The story of fibre concrete roofing (FCR) is fascinating in both its simplicity and its complexity.[13] The technology seems simple and straightforward. Natural fibres such as coir, sisal or jute, are mixed with concrete and formed into sheets with a thickness of about a centimetre. In the early stages of development, corrugated roofing sheets were the main product, although these gradually gave way to the production of smaller pantiles, S-shaped roofing tiles that can be laid so the downward curve of one tile overlaps with the upward curve of the next.

Because the technology was relatively simple; because the capital investment required to set up a small plant was low; and because there is an almost insatiable demand in the Third World for inexpensive, durable roofing material, the FCR technology, once adequately tested and developed, began to take off at great speed. By the early 1990s, FCR roofing equipment could be found in 60 countries, and as many as 500 new low-cost, labour-intensive manufacturing units were being sold every year. Both the technology and its diffusion were the product of a unique marriage between NGOs and private sector firms in the Third World and Britain. Judged on the basis of Schumacher's criteria – small, simple, cheap and non-violent – the technology is a success. Judged by the more complex criteria of some appropriate technology organizations, it also stands up well. It can meet the roofing needs of a wide majority of the community, and is 'ownable, controllable, operable and maintainable within the community it serves.'

If this book demonstrates anything, however, it is that while an appropriate technology may be small, simple, cheap and non-violent, its development is often the opposite. The efforts involved in the development of FCR were not small. Getting the technology right was far from simple, and although the research and development investments were perhaps small by the standards of construction materials giants, they were large for the players involved. And if non-violence suggests harmony among colleagues, FCR was anything but non-violent. More than any other technology described in this book, FCR somehow succeeded in a climate of ideological acrimony, and amidst varying degrees of stubbornness, myopia and confusion.

The story began during the early 1970s when a British building materials consultant named John Parry visited Ghana to look into brickmaking potential. Parry realized that there were easier ways of making bricks in Ghana than those favoured by his employers and, gradually falling under the influence of Fritz Schumacher, he eventually set up his own consulting firm to advise clients on more appropriate building technologies. Serving on the Board of Directors of ITDG, he became involved in various building materials projects, experimenting first with brick-moulding equipment and then with roofing material.

By 1982, some of the new techniques and machinery had been widely tested, but Parry was frustrated that much of the equipment sent to Africa and Asia lay idle. He was especially concerned about fibre cement roofing sheets and tiles. Prototype equipment was not replicated, materials were not being produced in any significant volume, and much of what was being produced was not being properly used. Roofing sheets cracked and broke, tiles did not fit together properly, and roofs leaked. In short, it was beginning to look like one of those not-quite appropriate technologies – a good idea that did not really work, except under tightly controlled experimental conditions.

Believing that the technology *could* work, and frustrated at 'too much running around' and not enough emphasis on the production of 'damned good equipment', Parry decided to alter the nature of his consulting firm, and go into the production of low-cost, appropriate construction-materials equipment.[14] His company, J.P.M. Parry and Associates, established a small manufacturing operation at Cradley Heath, in the Black Country near Birmingham, and Parry called it 'Intermediate Technology Workshops'.

Up to that point, several NGO attempts to programme the sheet and tile-making equipment through small groups of women or unemployed youth had only limited success. NGOs with school building programmes, for example, would buy the equipment so that parents could make the tiles themselves and then reap the benefits of a productive enterprise afterwards. Where training was good and production was adequately controlled, high quality school roofs followed. But few viable enterprises continued after the initial impetus. In Kenya, for example, Action Aid established several such organizations, but most survived only because Action Aid continued to purchase their output for ongoing projects elsewhere. Of ten groups in Kenya established by ITDG in the mid-1980s, only four survived by 1990, none of them thriving.

Quality control was sometimes a problem and this led to marketing difficulties. But there were other marketing problems. Selling a new tile in a climate of economic and attitudinal competition among corrugated aluminium and galvanized iron sheets, as well as concrete and burned clay tiles was not an easy matter for tiny entrepreneurs without experience in marketing. Some of the enterprises had been established in rural areas where markets were limited. Corruption was an additional problem in some cases. Inexperienced in bribery, some found it inexplicable that a builder would deliberately choose an inferior, more expensive product over theirs.

John Parry was undaunted. By 1985 he was focusing most of his roofing business on the equipment for making tiles. Originally an entirely manual operation, Parry developed a simple vibrating tray that produced a tile 25cm wide and 50cm long. The vibrator consolidated the mixture of sand, cement and fibre on a plastic sheet, de-aired the mixture, and produced a uniform thickness of either 6 or 8 millimetres. The cement, formed on a plastic sheet, was then laid on a mould in the shape of the desired tile. After drying and curing, the tile was ready for transfer to the building site.

In travelling to meet customers, Parry and his staff learned several important things that helped improve the technology. The first was that quality control in the tile making was essential. Poor mixing, poor curing, or carelessness in the vibration process could all lead to tile breakage and failure. Reducing such failures to a minimum was essential in getting the product into the market, and good training and follow-up were therefore essential. The tile requires a different roofing structure than that used with other materials; it requires more timber than galvanized iron sheet, but less than concrete or clay tiles. It was therefore important that roofers also be properly trained in installation.

The original tilemaking machines were electric and could be operated from a car battery or from a mains supply. But many of the building sites where FCR might be used had neither, so a hand-crank model was developed. This was a useful alternative where labour was cheap and plentiful, but in some cases this additional cost could reduce the economic viability of the tile. So in 1990, a gyro-drive vibrator was developed which enabled one worker to handle the entire process. Basically the operator cranks a flywheel and then flicks a switch to engage the vibration. Like a child's toy car, the momentum in the flywheel continues to supply power while the operator prepares the tile. Because Parry had developed other products that used the vibration technique, including floor tiles, hollow concrete blocks and pipes, the next innovation was a detachable electric vibrator which could be used with the form-making equipment in tiles as well as in other products. And for countries where fibre was either unavailable or added significantly to the cost, such as Ghana, an alternative was found in chipped stone.

158

Although much of his equipment was still sold to or through development organizations, Parry had no difficulty in finding small entrepreneurs who could turn it into a successful business. The company established agents in a dozen countries and provided them with training. They in turn provided training to their customers, and in some cases sent them to Cradley Heath. Because there is generally a greater mark-up in roofing than in tile production, Parry found that some of his most successful customers were those already in the roofing business. The tile gave them a product that was both superior to what they had been buying, and was in many countries significantly cheaper.

In 1985 the company sold about 50 sets of tilemaking equipment, and by 1990, output had risen to 500. By then the company had exported equipment to 60 countries, and had steady orders from about 20, from Vietnam to Uganda to Nicaragua. By the mid-1980s, however, Parry and the NGOs with whom he had once formed a mutual admiration society had parted company in acrimony and accusation. Parry had grown increasingly disenchanted with what he saw as the amateurish NGO approach to production and marketing. Establishing producers drawn from villages and the ranks of un-employed youth had not worked, and the blame was being placed unfairly on the technology.

In refining and extending the definition of 'appropriate', on the other hand, some NGOs believed that the manufacture of tile-making equipment should be transferred to the Third World. ITDG's support for the development of the technology in the 1980s was thought by many to have been predicated on its eventual manufacture in Africa and Asia, not in Cradley Heath. If there were profits to be made in the sale of tile-making equipment, they should be generated in the South, not the North. A set of Parry tilemaking equipment could be made for significantly less in Third World countries than in Britain, and some set out to prove it. Action Aid, for example, assisted a Kenyan NGO in establishing a workshop where copies of the basic equipment were made at half the Parry price and without sizeable foreign exchange considerations. In response to the obvious criticism that the Kenyan machine and other copies did not reflect the cost of research and development invested by Parry, the NGOs said that much of Parry's initial investment and travel were subsidized by development agencies. They also argued that a large proportion of his customers were still development organizations.

Parry's reaction was a broadside against shortsightedness. Indeed, the selling price of cheap imitations does not reflect the cost of research and development, and when supported by NGOs, probably does not reflect the real capital cost of manufacturing the machinery either. As in the case of brick manufacture in Botswana, tile sales themselves may not even cover the cost of production. He is less acerbic about private sector copies and cites a case in Accra. The private sector copier there has as much an interest in seeing the product function properly as Parry does; future sales depend on it. But NGOs which move in a subsidized world without a bottom line, Parry believes, going from fad to fad, have no vested interest in the success of the technology, or of the enterprises they purport to 'establish'. Often they fail to provide adequate technical advice, follow-up and repair services. Many do not know the first thing about business. They tend to be hostile towards Parry because he is creating a dependence on British goods and services without realizing that he is equally dependent on his customers in the South: dependence, he argues, is a two-way street.

Although there is much cant on both sides of the debate, the scales tip in Parry's favour. A small enterprise named 'Shelter Works' in Nairobi exemplifies some of the challenges that face the small tilemaker. Shelter Works was founded in 1988 on a plot of rented land without electricity or water. The proprietor started in a shed with one battery-powered tilemaking machine and 100 moulds, but was uncertain about his prospects and did not leave his full-time employment until early 1990. In the intervening period, business was touch and go. Realizing that his output was insufficient to cover even the most basic costs, he sold his car and invested in three more machines and another 750 moulds. He arranged for electricity and a water connection, and because marketing rather than production emerged as the main problem, he had a telephone installed. He also realized that potential customers for roofing tiles often needed other construction materials, so he began to diversify into concrete and stabilized soil blocks. Without allied construction materials, potential customers would sometimes visit and then go elsewhere; they wanted a one-stop dealer. By 1990, Shelter Works was a going concern with nine employees – a number that fluctuated with orders – and the proprietor was spending most of his time on marketing.

Shelter Works works because the proprietor produces good tiles. This is perhaps in part because of his own background in mechanical engineering and because he has a foreman and workers he can rely upon while he is doing the all-important selling job. Under-capitalized at the outset, he had enough savings, in the form of his car, to expand and diversify when the need became apparent. His sales improved with the publicity attached to a large housing project that began at about the same time he went into production. The first phase of the Koma Rock Housing project used FCR tiles on 1700 middle-income houses, giving a major fillip to the product. A further benefit arose from its being certified by the Kenya Bureau of Standards. Although NGOs had sought this approval for several years, it came as much because two employees of the Bureau – listening to the sales pitch from the NGOs – bought tilemaking equipment for themselves and had a vested interest in seeing it approved.

As in the case of the Tinytech oil press in Zimbabwe, the drive and skill necessary to operate a productive enterprise profitably are not things that can be plucked out of a catalogue as easily as a tilemaking machine. It makes little difference where the machine is made if it does not produce, but Parry has been able to do something that NGOs have had difficulty with. He has been able to get the machines into the hands of genuine entrepreneurs. Some may be well off, but most are not. Like the proprietor of Shelter Works or the Ghana Airways stewardess who took time between flights to go to Cradley Heath for training before buying Parry equipment, many are entrepreneurs on their first outing, individuals who want to augment their income or be their own boss and who, in the process, will create jobs and products for others.

At £1000 for a basic starter set of tilemaking equipment, the price charged by J.P.M. Parry and Associates is far from exorbitant. No matter what the mark-up, it is not producing massive profits for the company. In fact the Parry workshop at Cradley Heath is much more reminiscent of an NGO operation than a modern manufacturing plant. It is less well equipped than the GRATIS Workshop in Ghana or the Rural Industries Innovation Centre in Botswana, and is half the size. Because it is located in an industrial area similar to the 'Third Italy', much of the manufacture of components and test items can be farmed out to small firms in the immediate area. So a large work force and plant are not necessary. Some of its staff are former VSO volunteers, and most of its Board of Directors have international experience, several with NGOs. One, David Astor, an early supporter of Schumacher, was central to the foundation of ITDG in the 1960s.

The company produces an occasional newsletter that is reminiscent of NGO newsletters, and it has a ten-point description of what it takes to be a good agent for Parry equipment. The major points could well serve as a guide for development agencies involved in small-scale enterprise development. According to Parry, a good agent must:

o be well regarded in the business community and by the public sector; known to be honest, reliable and thorough;
o have good financial standing, with sufficient funds to put some equipment and spares on the shelf and to stand the cash drain

involved in the start of a business, and during periods when sales are slow;
- have premises which are fairly central, accessible and easily found by customers, with facilities on the same site or closely adjacent, to demonstrate equipment and give basic training in its use;
- have a flair for business promotion;
- be familiar with the construction industry and procedures by which building materials are chosen for projects, and have a good perception of what ingredients are necessary for customers to do well in *their* business;
- have the technical ability to understand the operation of Parry equipment and the application of the products in order to give advice and service to customers.[15]

European and American firms with Parry's interest in genuinely appropriate technology can probably be counted on the fingers of one hand. Even if its profit margin was 50 per cent, the company would not be making a fortune for anybody. It lives on sales, but it thrives on innovation. It manages because it watches the bottom line and produces saleable products, but it grows because its employees genuinely enjoy what they are doing. They have produced a viable technology and the machinery to make it, but they continue to innovate, develop and improve the machinery, which – as Sanjay Sinha notes in the case of the mini-cement plants – is an important part of the business of staying in business. Rather than seeking ways to undercut Parry, those genuinely interested in appropriate and intermediate technology might be more productive in seeking ways to support such firms. Rather than criticism, Parry and those like him need and deserve solid encouragement from the development community.

On leading the blind

The projects described in this chapter are only samples of the building materials and construction technologies that have been developed in response to Third World needs. Much work has been done, for example, on introducing adobe construction to countries where it is not known, and improving it where it is. A wide variety of equipment to produce stabilized soil blocks – a compressed mixture of soil, sand and cement – is available, and many improved construction techniques for inexpensive housing have been devised using untrained labour and local materials.

Because low-cost building materials are intended to find their way into use among the poor, new techniques and technologies must be especially well tested. As with other products, some of the best successes have come about through the involvement of craftsmen and entrepreneurs for whom the technology is a next-step from what is already known. Parry's best customers are those already in the roofing business, and people familiar with similar materials. For some, a new material will be an addition to a product line, while others, such as Shelter Works in Nairobi may discover that alone, one product is not enough to sustain a new enterprise. Thorough economic analysis of costs is necessary, as the fine pricing line between the products of mini- and large-scale cement production demonstrate. But alone, a clear profit potential is not enough. Without good management and financial discipline, even sure-fire investments – like brickmaking in Botswana – will fail.

The most successful projects in this chapter and throughout the book have usually flowed from some form of collaboration between researchers, government, NGOs and the private sector. In some cases, as with the Balaka Lime Project, the collaboration was planned from the outset. In others it was sequential. The Indian military research on mini-cement plants was taken over by formal research institutions, and dissemination fell largely to the private sector.

Government policies had an explicit role in the success of mini-cement plant development in China, but they have an important implicit role in the development or failure of other technologies. A roofing technology like FCR has shown itself to be cheaper than many of the alternatives. In Ghana, for example, it is 44 per cent cheaper than aluminium sheets.[16] In Kenya, its installed cost is 40 per cent cheaper than concrete tiles.[17] But because its installed cost is the same as that of galvanized iron, there might not seem to be much in the way of economic choice between the two. The production of galvanized sheets, however, is high in capital costs, creates one fifth as many jobs as cement tiles and requires three times the foreign exchange for every square metre produced.[18]

As with mini-cement plants in India, this suggests the need for a more pro-active policy stance in favour of the intermediate technology if job-creation and import substitution are serious government objectives. Such policies might include:

o the purchase by government of FCR tiles instead of galvanized sheets wherever possible. (The same applies to aid agencies. If NGOs simply bought their tiles from existing micro-entrepreneurs instead of setting up fragile new producers, the older ones would quickly become more successful producers and employers);
o the changing of building codes in appropriate cases to allow and encourage the use of FCR tiles where they are not at present permitted;

o the banning of inappropriate roofing materials. For example 32 gauge (19 mm) corrugated galvanized roofing sheets are so thin that they rust out within three or four years, at significant cost to users and – in the form of foreign exchange – to the country.

Other policies might include reductions in sales tax, the provision of business promotion services, and preferential interest rates for tile producers over those producing other less appropriate roofing materials.

The roofing tile case demonstrates two other lessons. The first is that entrepreneurs are not created overnight, and that great caution must be exercised in mixing micro-enterprise creation and new technologies. More important, people without experience in business should avoid the temptation to advise others without experience. In traversing an obstacle course, the sighted generally make better guides than the blind. To use another metaphor, fragile vehicles can carry only so much freight. A project that is overloaded with too many objectives is much more likely to fail than one with limited objectives. Cheap, durable roofing tiles produced locally are one thing. No matter who owns the production equipment, jobs will be created. To expect, however, that a new technology with an uphill battle into a competitive market can also be owned and successfully operated by poor people without business experience and skills, may be asking too much of them and of the technology.

CHAPTER XI

Light engineering and the very late starters

Mighty things from small beginnings grow. John Dryden

MASS PRODUCTION AND industrialization as we know them today were neither inevitable, nor were they the only way to structure industrial development. Modern alternatives or variations include the Japanese approach, using a wide range of flexible suppliers, and the example of Emilia-Romagna's 'Third Italy', with its thousands of small-scale entrepreneurs. This chapter will address another aspect of industrialization that receives too little attention in the literature on appropriate technology, and in thinking about manufacturing and industrial development – the role of light engineering.

Writers have characterized Germany, Italy and Russia as 'late' industrial developers, and Albert Hirschman refers to Latin American countries as 'late late' developers, a title that could also be used to encompass what are now more generally referred to as 'Newly Industrialized Countries' (NICs). John Ohiorhenuan suggests a further industrial category, the 'very late starters', those which, by the early 1990s, had achieved little in the way of self-sustaining industrialization, and which, because of the advancement of NICs, start (or start over again) from a position of even greater relative disadvantage than was the case in the early years of independence.[1]

Most 'very late starters' are in sub-Saharan Africa, and unlike countries in Asia and Latin America, most have an extremely weak light engineering sector. Before it became clear that they were *very* late starters, many of these countries accepted the trickle-down approach to growth, and unquestioningly equated industrialization with development. Eager to transfer the reins of their economies from European to African hands, and recognizing the limited ability of local entrepreneurs to finance industrialization at the pace or levels desired, many governments became directly involved in the process themselves, aiming to promote import substitution, create jobs, diversify the export base and diversify production away from the urban centres where it had been located in colonial times.

Given the thinking in the 1950s and 1960s about growth, development and the transferability of technology, there was no particular reason to think the approach would not work. Economic euphoria in

165

the post-independence era was almost as heady as political euphoria. Riding the wave of a world boom that began during the Second World War, many African economies were expanding at an unprecedented rate of growth. In 1956, British Africa as a whole imported four times what it had in 1920 (at constant prices), while British African exports were ten times what they had been in 1937.[2]

Many countries embarked on extremely ambitious industrialization schemes. For political and ideological reasons, some, like Tanzania and Ghana, emphasized state ownership, while others, such as Ivory Coast and Kenya welcomed foreign investors. Still others, like Nigeria, took a mixed approach. Although predominantly capitalist in outlook, they sought to keep certain industries in African hands, or aimed for levels of investment that were beyond what was available internally – much as Japan had a century earlier.

Report from the Institute for Advanced Studies in Hindsight

With hindsight, it is not difficult to see what went wrong and why. Many investments were unwise from the outset, but many others did make sense under the prevailing economic situation – before the 1973 oil shock, and before the long downward price slide for tropical primary commodities. Part of the problem from the beginning, however, was that investment decisions were often made for political rather than economic reasons. Sometimes corruption was involved. Decisions were made without a full understanding of the economics of production, while still others were made on the basis of incorrect predictions about market growth or export potential.

A classic case of this was the establishment in Ghana of a mango canning factory whose operating capacity exceeded the entire world trade in canned mango products at the time. Bad decision-making in another case resulted in a Ghanaian trade delegation returning from a mission to purchase bottle-making equipment, having signed a contract for a plant that could manufacture bottles *and* plate glass. The minister responsible wanted the best glass-making plant available and thought plate glass might make a good export. The plant never produced plate glass and in later years was often unable to produce bottles.[3] The Zambian Government purchased the world's second nitrogenous fertilizer plant with a special delicate electrolytic reduction process based on coal; the factory quickly became a perennial and heavy loss-maker. A tyre-manufacturing company, established on the clear understanding that it would operate with Zambian latex, was still importing rubber 15 years later.[4]

Perhaps the grossest case of bad planning was the establishment of a steel industry in Nigeria. The plan, initiated in 1975, called for a blast furnace and two direct reduction plants, based on domestic iron and coal. The first reduction plant was commissioned in 1981, and by 1985 there were 16 rolling mills in operation. A confidential government report in 1984 stated, however, that the project was uneconomic and would suffer large recurrent losses to the end of the century. By 1989 the project had cost $3 billion, and a further billion dollars was required for the completion of the first phase. Meanwhile the first reduction plant operated at one fifth of capacity because of power cuts and shortages of *imported* iron ore.[5]

The state-owned Zimbabwe Iron and Steel Corporation, the largest manufacturing concern in the country, operated at a loss which contributed Z$493 million or 16 per cent to the country's budget deficit between 1980 and 1987, and was projected to run at a continuing loss through the 1990s.[6] In both Zimbabwe and Nigeria, the high cost of locally produced steel was passed on into the economy through other manufacturers who used their product.

These spectacular cases have their counterparts in hundreds of smaller investments. The backward and forward linkages of many of the industries were weak, and large plants stood in grand isolation from the rest of the economy. A sparkling new petro-chemical complex could turn out sophisticated products from a high-technology plant, and never purchase a single nut or bolt from the local economy.

Inevitably, much of the manufacturing plant installed in Africa during the 1960s and 1970s was highly dependent on imports for its functioning. These imports included foreign technical assistance and management, spare parts, and raw materials. The domestic content of Nigerian cement production fell from 80 per cent in the mid 1960s to 40 per cent in 1975.[7] A heavy proportion of manufacturing was in consumer goods, and the import component was often especially high. Nigeria was self-sufficient in beer production in 1968, but by 1977, 41 per cent of production costs were accounted for by imports. Throughout Africa, few manufactured goods were exported, and as the prices of African primary exports declined, the cost of local manufactures increased in relative terms. For countries such as Ghana and Zambia, heavily dependent on a single export, the effect was catastrophic. Some plants closed, while in many others capacity utilization plummeted. Inefficiencies piled on one another; preventive maintenance declined, products deteriorated and prices continued to increase.

The result was disastrous in both real and relative terms. Investments had been squandered, often with the very best of intentions; jobs were not created, few imports were actually substituted in any significant measure and the cost of manufactures usually did not fall, it rose. In 1986, manufactured exports from all of sub-Saharan Africa totalled $3.2 billion, less than what was exported in the same year by Malaysia alone.

One cause of the disaster was a poor fit between small domestic markets and the enchantment with mass production. A further contributing factor was (and remains) a lack of choice in technology. Some industries operate at a fraction of capacity, not because of mismanagement or market miscalculations, but because the smallest plants available are far larger than the situation warrants. Added to this is the problem of supplier control of patents, and limited sources of supply. In the particleboard industry, for example, machine suppliers will sell only complete, integrated packages. Some choices, however, were simply bad: the large and capital-intensive often won out over known, smaller, more appropriate technologies. Aid agencies were sometimes to blame, providing inappropriate advice or aid tied to inappropriate equipment. In some cases, corruption played a role.

But there are other historical reasons for inappropriate choices in manufacturing technology. One is that pre-independence industry in Africa, owned and operated by expatriates, focused to a large extent on industries with an immediate return rather than on the development of a long-term manufacturing capacity. Commercial capital was similarly dominated by foreign banks, which followed the pre-set industrial mix. Add these limitations to a more or less monopolistic pre-independence manufacturing structure and the *normal* development of a market economy is subverted from the outset. In Zimbabwe, for example, it is estimated that in 1982, half of all manufactures were produced under monopoly conditions, and a further 30 per cent under oligopoly conditions. Over half of all manufacturing output was produced by firms employing more than 500 workers.[8]

The tin men

There were two other cards in a deck stacked against African manufacturing industries. The first, the education system, will be discussed in Chapter XIV. The second was the virtual absence throughout much of the continent of a light engineering capacity. There was, and in many countries remains, a very limited scope for repair and maintenance beyond the modern factory gate. There is little capacity to manufacture spare parts locally, no machine tool industry, and virtually no engineering innovation beyond the most rudimentary. Each large-scale plant must either import its own repair facility, stock an excessive amount of spares, or hope for the best. By the late 1980s, the rule in many countries was to hope for the best, with the result that plants, or sections of plants closed until a single spare part could be flown out from the manufacturer.

For the development of appropriate technology, this presents a special problem: in countries with a constricted capacity to produce and maintain even simple machines, and no serious innovative engineering capacity, the production and dissemination of many of the basic technologies described in this book are badly constrained.

Zimbabwean industry is far from typical of the African condition, partly because of its historically large white settler population and partly because of its three decades of import substitution and protection. Its relatively large formal manufacturing sector, although starved of new equipment and some raw materials after the mid-1960s, in 1990 resembled a somewhat threadbare European economy more than it did an African economy. Zimbabweans take pride in telling visitors that over 7000 different products are manufactured in their country. But with jobs in the formal sector costing US$26 000 each and running US$100 000, or even US$200 000 behind demand each year, and with 20 000 job losses predicted with the 1991 structural adjustment, it makes sense to look at microenterprise development and informal manufacturing for possible salvation.

The Confederation of Zimbabwean Industries (CZI) suggests that the layoffs, along with microenterprises already operating in the informal sector will form the nucleus of 'a large number of small new companies'.[9] One has only to visit a place called Magaba on the outskirts of Harare, however, to find out how likely this is to happen, and to glimpse a part of Zimbabwe that is very much like other African countries. Magaba is a crowded, fenced-off area into which a large number of Harare's informal sector producers were forcibly moved in 1989. The area has about 300 stalls and shops, most without electricity. There are sign makers, painters, welders, carpenters, vehicle repair shops and used parts dealers. A few shops produce wrought iron stoves, and some make chain-link fence with a simple device developed some years ago at the Rural Industries Innovation Centre in Botswana. There is a section where tinsmiths produce buckets, pans and implements from tin sheets. But beyond a single bench saw and a crude wood-turning lathe, there are no machine tools.

Although there are ostensibly a number of organizations that might assist these micro-entrepreneurs to develop their products, skills and markets, they are, in fact, left almost entirely to themselves. The CZI deals with large industries. The Zimbabwe Entrepreneurs Association deals with small entrepreneurs, but not this small. The Indigenous Business Development Centre regards them as a lost cause – people who have been turned into 'monsters' because of their struggle to survive: 'cheating, stealing and producing inferior goods'. SEDCO, the Small Enterprise Development Corporation, defines 'small' as having fewer than 50 employees and fixed assets of less than US$170 000. By that definition, everyone in Magaba qualifies, but SEDCO loans are only available to businesses with a three year track record, and most in Magaba have no records at all. In any case, to be classified as a manufacturer, a firm must be registered, and to be registered, it must have an initial capital outlay of Z$30 000 (US$10 000), far beyond the capacity of any of the Magaba producers.

Thanks to a particular donor interest, a study of Malawi's informal metalworkers, conducted on behalf of USAID in 1989, resulted in a better understanding of the importance of metalworkers, and led to clearer opportunities for action. The study[10] concentrated on enterprises which had a direct investment of less than US$500 and gross annual sales under US$4000. It found that, 'in terms of product value, the aggregate output of the informal metalwork enterprises probably leads all other producing informal subsectors except tailoring.' Forward linkages to agriculture, food-processing, transportation and consumption were particularly strong. There was also an important but undervalued backward linkage to Malawi's metal imports which eventually become scrap. Because the informal sector recycles scrap, each product is, in effect, an import substitute.

Tinsmiths produce watering cans, buckets, oil lamps, toys, stoves, pots and pans. Blacksmiths produce hoes, axes, trowels, crowbars and other tools, while metal fabricators produce hand trucks, window and door frames, wheelbarrows and ox carts. The most common metalworkers are tinsmiths, who often work in clusters in a market area. Although each tinsmith is independent, working in the same area with others has several advantages. Tinsmiths and their apprentices can learn new designs and techniques from others – soldering, the use of a hand tool for knurling edges in order to provide strength and design qualities to the finished product. Buyers patronize areas where there is a good selection of products, and in a competitive setting, new producers learn quickly about costing, pricing, quality control and customer preference.

Nevertheless, the products of Malawian metalworkers are simple and the output is crude. In the Lilongwe Town Council Market, where some of the products are made and sold, there is no electricity, and metalworkers produce their goods in the open, seated on the ground. The Biwi Triangle, an area of shops built for small entrepreneurs by the International Labour Organization, has a more organized appearance, and is equipped with water and electricity. Here, among three or four dozen vehicle-repair shops, metal fabricators and carpenters, is a man who has been experimenting with the casting of aluminium. Frank Soko's tiny foundry is almost unrecognizable as such; his raw material is undifferentiated scrap, and his products are crude. But his is the first and only small commercial aluminium foundry in Lilongwe. Frank Soko's skills and output are extremely limited, but within months of startup he was able to obtain an order from the Lilongwe brewery for a spare part that would otherwise have been imported. The brewery wanted 50 of the parts, but Soko was so encouraged by the order that he produced 150.

While there is much discussion among development planners and economists about the idea of 'graduating' from the informal to the formal sector, it should not be forgotten that a great deal of the 'graduation' in Africa has actually been in the other direction. As happened in Ghana, when the formal manufacturing sector contracts and becomes less relevant, mechanics and technicians move into the informal sector. With a view to having some of Malawi's metalworkers 'graduate' to the formal sector, to greater value added and to more employment creation, the USAID study observed several areas where they could be assisted: through improved but appropriate production technology; through the introduction of a wider selection of better tools; through improved workshop layout and production flow-through; business management awareness and comprehension; and through various forms of organization which would improve skill dissemination, increase access to credit, and give metalworkers a voice in the policy-making arena.

'Doc' Powell and the Technology Consultancy Centre[11]

So far, except by way of quotation, only a few individuals have found their way into this story. This is more a problem of space than of design, for the real story of technology in history is the story of individuals – 'dirty fingernail people' like Frank Soko. Some of them are *champions* – zealots, idea thieves, pragmatists, innovators, inventors. The best known have names like Fulton, Hargreaves, Edison, and Faraday, but behind them is an army of individuals like D.P. Saboo, relentlessly producing cement among his marigolds; or John Parry, making better and better tile-making vibrators in Cradley Heath; or Veljibhai Desai producing his Tinytech oil expellers in Rajkot. One of the most unlikely of these champions is a laconic British engineer with a background in air-lubricated bearings, who went to Africa on a contract in 1970. Twenty years later, still in Ghana, John Powell was surprised to be awarded the Order of the British Empire. But his Ghanaian friends were not. In fact many fully concurred with the mistaken upgrading of the award by the *Ghanaian Times*, which reported that Doctor Powell had been knighted.

Powell had gone to the University of Science and Technology to teach, but to his surprise, in 1971 was appointed Director of the University's newly established Technology Consultancy Centre. TCC grew out of recommendations in an ITDG report prepared by George McRobie and Sir John Palmer, and in its early years it resembled many of the other appropriate technology institutions in the South. With assistance from ITDG and other non-governmental organizations, it experimented with a wide variety of appropriate technologies. After much trial and error – with technologies, techniques and implementing partners – some of its efforts were successful: glue, soap, textile weaving and honey.

But because Powell was a mechanical engineer, he was drawn to steel and iron, and to the machines that cut and shape metal. The Kumasi of 1971 was already much further advanced in its informal metalwork sector than today's Harare or Lilongwe. Erroneously called 'The Garden City', Kumasi – located 250 kilometers north of Accra – is a traditional axis for north-south and east-west trade, and lies at the heart of Ghana's cocoa-growing country. It was a logical staging point for traffic, and a thriving vehicle repair business grew up on the site of an old military magazine. When the town council moved the repair shops away from the centre of Kumasi, they took the name – Suame Magazine – with them. By 1971, Suame Magazine was a chaotic, sprawling place with 1600 separate owner-operated businesses, including 1100 workshops. Five hundred were involved in vehicle repair or modification and 300 were speciality shops offering welding, carpentry or blacksmithing.

Suame Magazine was a logical place for TCC to start, and an early survey homed in on a shortage of coach bolts used in the production of wooden truck bodies. Descending into a long nightmare of economic disaster, Ghana was already suffering from a perennial shortage of virtually everything imported. As a result, a few black-smiths were making coach bolts to special order. But they were expensive and not very good. Powell had seen half a dozen centre lathes in the Magazine, used mainly for machining brake drums, and he assumed that if a process could be developed, higher quality nuts and bolts could be produced.

As these things go, it did not take very long. Within 18 months of opening, TCC had developed a process using mild steel rod which was produced from recycled scrap at the Tema Steelworks. The rod was converted into a hexagonal bar on a horizontal milling machine, then turned on a lathe to produce a shaft of the required length. Then it was cut with a small piece of the hexagon remaining to form the head. The thread was produced in a secondary lathe operation, and nuts were made by simply drilling and threading the same hexagonal bar. TCC had the technology, and the nuts and bolts it produced in its own shop sold without any difficulty. It was to take eight full years, however, for the technology to 'transfer'.

There were three basic reasons. The first was machines. Although there were some lathe operators in Suame, there were no milling machines. This was an obvious drawback that would – in a carefully planned situation – have halted the project before it started. When TCC overcame that hurdle through an arrangement with ITDG to import used British machines and sell them to potential entrepreneurs, it discovered that most of the existing lathe operators were lathe operators, not entrepreneurs. Machining brake drums was the limit of their willingness to take technical and economic risks. Finding genuine entrepreneurs, therefore, became the second hurdle. And the third was the process. The first genuine entrepreneur, Solomon Adjorlolo, abandoned nuts and bolts very quickly when he found that the process, developed in the campus workshop where he was trained, did not work in his shop. His workers' productivity (and therefore his profits) were considerably lower than had been anticipated.

The Adjorlolo brothers

It is worth following the story of this particular entrepreneur and the milieu in which he operated, not only because of his eventual success but because of what he represents for the development of a genuine African industrial base. Solomon Adjorlolo was a technician in Kumasi University's Physics Department when it began to produce standard resistance-plug boxes for secondary school laboratories. Seeing an opportunity in other teaching aids, Adjorlolo decided to set up his own business and in 1972 established a small workshop in Anloga, a part of Kumasi where other tiny carpentry industries were located. The two-person partnership was grandly named 'School Science Import Substitution Enterprises', or SIS for short.

With two wood-turning lathes, a small electric drill and a universal woodworking machine, Solomon and his brother Ben were producing 36 different items a year later, among them T-squares, tripods, ammeters, voltmeters, rulers and drawing tables. But as the bottom began to fall out of the Ghanaian economy, the market for cheap, locally made substitutes for imported educational items dried up. Desperate, the Adjorlolos took orders from TCC for benches and tables used in other projects. They manufactured a few broadlooms until cotton yarn disappeared, taking the weaving business with it. Finally, in 1974, in an effort to stave off collapse, they purchased a used metalworking production lathe, hoping to make metal jigs and cutters for other woodworking shops in Anloga. That too proved only a partial solution, and knowing that TCC was looking for an off-campus nut and bolt producer, they took a capstan lathe on loan and early in 1976 went into the nut and bolt business.

SIS productivity was lower than TCC's, and the Adjorlolos gradually realized that they could make a better profit using the machines for other things. Having done some repairs for neighbouring saw-bench operators, they now saw an opportunity to produce spindles and bearing housings, and with a newly acquired welding set, they began to produce complete saw-benches. Not long afterwards, they produced their first wood-turning lathe, and within months, a dozen were in operation in Anloga.

The circular saw bench and the wood turning lathe were to the woodworkers in Anloga what the Spinning Jenny was to the eighteenth-century British textile industry. Within five years the area had been transformed from a place where carpenters and sawyers produced very basic furniture, into an area half a mile long where lathes whirled and saws screamed from dawn until well after dark. Products which had once been exclusive to large-scale formal sector producers were now being made by micro-entrepreneurs. And offcuts from the big sawmills – formerly a waste product – could now be put to productive use.

In the late 1970s, SIS began to turn its attention to corn milling, attempting to replicate imported machines which had become unaffordable. Import shortages proved the mother of invention, and eventually, with assistance from TCC, a corn-milling machine was developed which was in some ways better than the import. Used ball bearings replaced the brass bushings of the original, and broken half-shafts from trucks, made of better steel than the imported model, prolonged the life of the replica. In 1978, the SIS corn mill sold for half the price of the imported model. By 1985, with Ghanaian currency all but worthless, the price of the local mill had increased eight-fold, but was still half the price of a smuggled model. And in 1991, under the full weight of structural adjustment, a fully convertible currency and totally liberalized imports, SIS was still competitive. A British corn milling machine cost $2100 in Ghana; an Indian machine cost $515, and the SIS model cost $400. In the 1980s, SIS diversified into corn hullers, palm kernel crackers and presses, cassava graters, potters wheels, block presses, and a combination circular saw-bench and planing machine. In 1991 they were experimenting with the development of a large clay-mixing machine and an extruder for the Department of Rural Housing which hoped to foster a brickmaking industry. Now employing almost 30 workers, SIS engineering, as the company was now known, had crossed the line from informal to formal; from micro, to small to medium-scale

174

enterprise. The Adjorlolo brothers had become an appropriate technology centre in their own right.

Although SIS was a spectacular example, perhaps because the two brothers had the right combination of technical and business skills, TCC has had many other successes with small engineering workshops, some of which became significant producers of nuts and bolts. These individuals, along with Solomon and Ben Adjorlolo, were genuine entrepreneurs; people who stayed with their endeavour, who adapted, who enjoyed what they were doing and who were able to roll with the punches and with the body blows that the turbulent Ghanaian economy threw at them. Some of their products were developed with the help of TCC. But in later years the tables were reversed, when Solomon became an occasional consultant to TCC, assisting it in the development of machines and techniques for other clients. He also acted as a consultant to government on small enterprise development. And his brother, Ben, produced a 40–page handbook on how to start and manage a small-scale industry.[12] Something of a philosopher, Ben urged patience, saying that those who run fastest fall most heavily. 'A journey of a thousand miles,' he wrote, 'begins with the first step.'

John Powell identified four stages of technology. The first and most primitive stage is characterized by hand tools that are not designed according to scientific principles. The fourth involves the use and development of scientifically designed automatic machinery. Much of Africa, including the tinsmiths of Malawi and the informal metalworkers of Zimbabwe, remains in the first stage, while governments and multinational investors have concentrated on leapfrogging into stage four. But it is only a parody of stage four; automatic machinery may be *used* in the formal sector, but it is often not used well, and it is certainly not developed indigenously.

Between the first and fourth steps, the second is actually the preliminary stage of development in mechanical terms; it involves hand or human-powered machines designed in accordance with scientific principles. The next stage, Powell's third, relies on scientifically designed machines, powered mechanically. By the mid-1980s, with SIS Engineering actually producing such equipment, and with hundreds of machine tools at work in Suame Magazine, Ghana had clearly moved from a position somewhere between stages one and two, to stage three.

Pumping iron

The importance of these developments to the genuine transfer of technology and the ability of a people to develop their own

175

technologies cannot be overestimated. But in 1985, there remained a gaping hole in Ghana's metalwork story. Bronze casting had been known for centuries in West Africa and, unlike Malawi, small-scale aluminium casting was reasonably well developed. But there were no iron foundries. As a result, metal fabricators like the Adjorlolo brothers often used scrap steel where iron would have been adequate. But as scrap steel became more expensive, the need for an alternative grew. In addition, some things, such as grinding plates for corn milling machines, had to be made from iron, and still had to be imported – legally or otherwise.

The irony was that scrap iron was plentiful, littering roadsides, workshops and farms where expensive imported tractors and heavy equipment lay rusting. Engine blocks were being used in Suame Magazine to fill giant potholes in the muddy tracks between shops. Almost a backyard technology in Asia, in Ghana iron casting was still *terra incognita*. TCC took up the challenge. Resurrecting a small crucible imported several years before, fueling it with the palm kernel charcoal used by local blacksmiths, and using a blower made from a knapsack sprayer engine, TCC melted its first charge of scrap iron in May 1985.

By then, TCC had learned that technology development and transfer were not going to take place on a university campus and had established what it called an 'intermediate technology transfer unit' (ITTU) in the centre of Suame Magazine, which by 1985 had expanded to some 40 000 workshops. There clients could make regular contact with TCC engineers for consultations on simple problems, for design assistance or business advice. There, potential clients of a new technology, such as nut and bolt manufacturers, or potential buyers of a machine tool, could be trained in a production setting, sometimes for a year or more before going out on their own. And there, metalworkers saw for the first time what was possible with a ferrous metal foundry. By 1991, there were six small foundries in operation.

GRATIS

That TCC survived the 1980s is something of a miracle, given the chaos and total unpredictability of Ghana's economy. But these were not the only problems. The University of Science and Technology had from the outset maintained an ambivalent attitude towards the idea of appropriate technology. Many academics felt that a university should be on the cutting edge of technology development, not wasting its time in a dirty place like Suame Magazine, developing second-rate technology for second-rate industry. Donor support was important to TCC's development, but it was often completely unpredictable. Early support from ITDG, Scottish War on Want, Oxfam, Oxfam Quebec and the EEC had been essential to several key projects. CIDA provided important technical and financial support, but there were long periods of famine while Canadian evaluators and consultants tried to figure out what to do between phases. USAID's brief fling with appropriate technology in Ghana resulted in a building and equipment for a second ITTU in northern Ghana, although an impenetrable wall of red tape caused the commissioning of the building to be delayed for six full years after the project agreement was signed. The ITTU did not actually become operational for another three years, making the nine year total something of a record in project protraction.[13]

But it was government support that was most important, both for sustaining grants and – through some of Ghana's darkest days – for the morale and protection it provided. In 1987 this support manifested itself in a very important way. The government approved a new idea proposed by John Powell: the establishment of intermediate technology transfer units in several Ghanaian cities and towns, linked together by a central co-ordinating unit. The project, under the Ministry of Industries, Science and Technology, would be called GRATIS – the Ghana Regional Appropriate Technology Industrial Service.

With funding from the EEC, CIDA, GTZ and British ODA, the project began in 1987. The ITTU in Tamale, originally funded by USAID, was handed over to GRATIS, and the government contributed a large workshop at Tema originally constructed with Indian Government assistance. By the end of 1990, three more regional ITTUs had opened. And through consultancies and the sale of products from their own shops, the first three ITTUs covered a remarkable 75 per cent of their costs that year. Although their efforts extended beyond engineering into agriculture, beekeeping, spinning, weaving, dyeing and food production, metalwork continued to be a major part of their operations.

Lessons from the metal trade

History shows that in industrialized countries, machine design, fabrication and adaptation have played a crucial role in the industrialization process. It was the development of the turret lathe around 1840, the universal milling machine in 1861 and the automatic lathe in 1870, that turned haphazard mechanical operations into a science, fuelling a second industrial revolution in Britain. Moreover, close links between small and large engineering firms have been critical to

177

the process of innovation and development. Without a local industry capable of testing and adapting technology to local needs, a country remains totally beholden to outside interests and influences.

Science is an important element of technological development. Many of the early inventions of the British industrial revolution worked *despite* a lack of scientific knowledge. Mechanically talented innovators succeeded as much through luck as through knowledge. In the second half of the eighteenth century, however, this changed, and most serious technical advances were essentially scientific.[14] Many of the successes of the informal sector in the South are similarly lucky, based perhaps on good mechanical knowledge, but without scientific foundation. In 1990, GRATIS began to deal with this problem by engaging a mining and mineral engineer to study small-scale aluminium foundries. As a student at the University in Kumasi, the engineer had done her final year project in Suame Magazine, and had found, predictably, that aluminium casters there had no scientific knowledge of their trade. As a result, any aluminium scrap was used; pouring temperatures were usually too high; gating and venting – the way the aluminium is poured and how gasses escape during the pouring process – were crude. Rejects were consequently high, and quality was poor.

With assistance from Valco, the giant aluminium smelter, GRATIS was able to obtain a pyrometer for measuring temperature, simple testing equipment, and samples of pure aluminium and silicon against which local products could be tested. Gradually some simple rules of thumb were developed for a training programme. For example roofing sheets and drink cans, produced by extrusion or rolling, have a low silicon content and are therefore inappropriate for casting. More scientific approaches to gating and venting were developed, and simple techniques for testing the fineness, and the moisture and silicon content of the moulding sand were also developed.

As with the casting of iron, what may seem at first glance a very simple advancement was, in fact, a major step forward into a new type of industrial era. It bears out the importance of Schumacher's general view on the importance of *intermediate* technology – moving from the known to the next most appropriate level before making a mad dash for high technology.

The forward and backward linkages of Ghana's light engineering capacity are enormous. For agriculture, small machine shops are producing ploughs, planters and seed drills as well as more traditional agricultural implements. Forward linkages include the wide range of textile, wood and food processing equipment being produced by SIS Engineering and other clients of TCC and GRATIS. Light engineering has important urban as well as rural implications.

Linkages with the formal sector are only beginning to demonstrate their potential. As is the case with the Malawi tinsmiths, many Ghanaian producers use scrap metal, and therefore have at least that much import substitution effect. But when they can produce good machines that are cheaper than imports in a liberalized, unprotected market, the import substitution effect is much more important. More crucial than that, however, items such as nuts and bolts, produced by the tens of thousands during the 1980s, were essential to the building of fishing boats and trucks and, in the form of wheel bolts, to keeping trucks and cars on the road when no imports were available.

When imports did become available, most producers were well enough trained to move into speciality production for hard-to-get or very expensive items. The ITTUs and clients of TCC and GRATIS are actually producing parts for large, formal sector enterprises. One produces sprockets for a motorcycle assembly plant. Others have made special replacement parts for equipment in sugar mills and gold mines. Although the structural adjustment programmes have killed some small-scale enterprises, they have been unexpectedly beneficial to others. With funds available for rehabilitation of existing plant, large-scale manufacturers have discovered that a local production capacity exists for specialized spare parts. In 1991, for example, the main GRATIS ITTU at Tema produced ten heavy cast-iron sprocket wheels with one-inch teeth for the chocolate factory, thus contributing to exports. The oil refinery, harbour facilities and ships in port have all ordered spares. The Ghana Water and Sewerage Corporation had funds to rehabilitate water systems throughout the country, many of which had been inoperable for years for want of spares. A key problem was brass pump impellers, which differ from pump to pump, depending on the head, the flow of water and the speed of the pump. Because the Tema ITTU had developed a pattern-making capacity, it was able to respond to a wide range of orders, and saw this as a first step to introducing more complex types of metal-casting to other ITTUs and clients.

It might be useful to ask where the small-scale production machine shops and foundries might have come from, had there not been a TCC and a GRATIS. It is highly unlikely that they would have developed by themselves in twice the time, regardless of any special interest by government or donors in small-scale enterprise. In fact, had they not developed *before* the liberalization programme, liberalization might well have killed the opportunity instead of supporting what had developed. Credit was an important element in getting TCC clients off the ground, but it was one of the least important. The long and careful development, by specialists, of appropriate techniques and technologies was an essential part of the mix. It took eight years before the nut and bolt technology was adequately developed for transfer. Establishing six foundries took five years of thinking, and five more years of experimenting.

There are two other elements in the story of Ghana's success in light engineering. The first was the development of informal industrial areas like Suame Magazine. Smaller versions exist in most Ghanaian towns, and in other West African countries. Magaba, Lilongwe's Biwi Triangle and Town Council Market are very small, very pale versions of the same thing. The growth that comes from such clustering is not confined to engineering. It was equally true of seventeenth-century Dutch painting and eighteenth-century Austrian music. The African industrial areas recall the experience of the British Midlands, the Connecticut Valley and the Third Italy, and suggest that such clusters are not only an important element of learning and marketing, they may form an important building block on which diversification and greater sophistication can, with care, be constructed. This was certainly true of Anloga, with the advent of locally made saw benches and wood turning lathes.

This bears out the concept of collective efficiency in 'industrial districts', advanced by Piore and Sabel in their book about industrial societies, *The Second Industrial Divide: Possibilities for Prosperity*. The key to prosperity in Japan, the Third Italy and elsewhere, has been the ability to move away from what the authors regard as the mindlessness of mass production towards a 'flexible specialization' in which skilled workers in small companies, or small units within companies, are able to respond to changing economic conditions, markets and tastes. There are, of course, more advanced examples of Third World industrial districts which have gone on to become major exporters: the cotton knitting industry of Trippur in South India and shoe production in Novo Hamburgo in South Brazil.[15]

But in Ghana, the change in a place like Suame – from chaotic and cut-throat competition (in machining brake drums) to the beginnings of flexible specialization – would not have happened in only twenty years without catalysts like TCC and GRATIS. The catalyst within the catalyst, however, is the second fundamental element in the Ghana story: the presence, throughout the country's worst years, of a *champion* of intermediate technology and microenterprise development. John Powell's first twenty years in Ghana were enormously productive despite what seems, in retrospect, a long series of uphill battles with government, academics, donors and a perverse economy. He certainly did not create TCC or GRATIS alone; many excellent, dedicated Ghanaian engineers, social scientists and entrepreneurs worked with him over the years and supported key efforts when they seemed most likely to fail. And despite the problems with different

180

institutions, there were many within government, the university and donor agencies who recognized what was happening, and who provided invaluable support at the right time. Without them it would not have happened. Equally, much of it, and perhaps all, would not have happened without Powell.

A reason justifying more discussion of 'champions' in development literature is that by leaving them out, the ultimate reason for a project's success or failure is often ignored. The counterpoint to this, however, is that apparently successful projects can be the product of one individual's enthusiasm, passion, or obsession. This 'Lawrence of Arabia Syndrome' can show immense promise while the Great Unifier is there, but things often fall apart once he or she leaves. This has not happened at TCC. After Powell left in 1986, there was an unfortunate slump in donor funding, but the sky did not fall; the institution continued in the capable hands of several Ghanaians who had been there with Powell for years. In addition to continuing with older activities, TCC went on to develop new and innovative projects in other fields.

The ultimate test of sustainability for GRATIS is time, and the support which it will continue to require from government and donors. Regardless of the future role of TCC and GRATIS, however, the seeds sown in Suame Magazine and other Ghanaian towns are already bearing fruit. In bringing together good people with diverse interests and attitudes, sound engineering skills and money, John Powell only proved what was already known by those who understood Ghana and knew something of the history of technology: that Ghana could make it.

PART THREE

An enabling environment

Since we've been overtaken by events, at least let's try and organize them.

Jean Cocteau

CHAPTER XII
Perspectives on women and technology

Home is the girl's prison and the woman's workhouse.
George Bernard Shaw

HISTORICALLY, WOMEN APPEAR not to have been intimately involved in either technology or science. The degree of truth in this observation, however, depends to a large extent on one's definition of technology and science, and on who is observing and writing the history. It is not difficult to identify durable historical artefacts developed by men – from the pyramids to iron and steel – and the steam and internal combustion engines these technologies made possible. Because women have traditionally cultivated crops and preserved the harvest, woven and sewed clothing or tanned leather, much of their culture-bearing technological legacy cannot be put on display in museums.

By excluding women from academic and later from scientific education, by disenfranchising them politically and constraining them from the legal ownership of property, most societies have, until recent years, maintained powerful barriers to women's entry into enterprise, industry and technological development. Those women whose accomplishments actually found their way into the market-place and into the historical records are, therefore, very special individuals: Catherine Green, who allowed her employer, Eli Whitney, to take full credit for her part in the development of the cotton gin; Mary Somerville, the nineteenth-century mathematician; Ada Lovelace, to whom the computer industry owes a great debt for concepts of programming developed one hundred and fifty years ago.

In recent years it has been increasingly recognized that women are more than Adam's rib, more than an adjunct to productive society, more than simply mothers, cooks and drawers of water. They, along with men and children, *are* society. Legal and social changes in the status of women over the past century in the North has had an effect in more recent times on the behaviour of development agencies. In the 1970s and more so in the 1980s, the approach towards women moved beyond projects which aimed to make them better mothers and cooks. Projects no longer focused exclusively on health, handicrafts and sewing machines. Greater attention is now paid to the traditional knowledge of women, and to the need for new approaches

185

which reduce their workload and reduce the amount of time required to carry it out. But the simple recognition of problems and past short-comings, recognition that women's employment need not be stereo-typed, that a woman *can* be a blacksmith, a welder or a lathe operator, does not solve the problems or create many genuine opportunities in such fields. There are still enormous social, technological and educational constraints involved in making even the smallest step forward.

In many ways, therefore, the role of technology in development is more critical to women than it is to men. Because while small technological changes can improve the lives of women, they can also unduly exacerbate the weakness of their position in society, and damage what fragile advantages they may already have.

This chapter is *not* about the disparities in status, labour, income or access to services that women suffer. Nor does it belabour the fundamental truth that although women are major contributors to any nation's production of goods and services, a high percentage of their work is not reflected in national accounts. The important role played by women in agriculture, food production, family income, and child and family health has been well documented over the past two decades. Neither does the chapter attempt to provide a comprehensive overview of technologies and techniques which have proved successful in improving the economic status of poor women. These are covered elsewhere.

The chapter discusses and illustrates *strategies* (rather than projects) which are aimed at advancing women into more productive lives as part of the development mainstream.

Options for women

The irony in attempting to discern alternatives for women in the development process is that many potential options are closed off in the very early years of a woman's life. In many countries girls receive less care and attention than boys. Their food intake is lower and their health is poorer. In large parts of India, for example, the under-five mortality rate for girls is 50 per cent higher than it is for boys.[1] Female education is notoriously poor, with low entrant and high dropout rates. UNDP estimates the 1985 literacy rate of women in 44 'low human development' countries at 52 per cent of what it is for men. While great achievements have been made over the past twenty years in increasing the primary and secondary enrollment of girls, female primary enrollment in the South is 71 per cent of what it is for boys, and secondary enrollment is only 53 per cent.[2]

For those women who do obtain an education, gender stereotyping is no less prevalent in the South than it has been in the North. In

Ghana, for example, by the end of secondary school, 12 per cent of girls have opted for physics, chemistry and biology courses, and only 5 per cent are enrolled in mathematics. At university the imbalance continues: female enrollment in science faculties ranges from a low of one to a high of only 22 per cent. Mid-level Ghanaian technical schools have a one per cent female enrollment.[3] The upshot is that women, whose needs are often greater than those of men, face the development challenge with fewer skills, less education and little spare time. And they often do so pregnant and in poor health.

In considering strategic approaches to women and technology, a methodology has been suggested by two writers. In 1987 Judith Tendler reviewed a number of 'better performing' Ford Foundation grantees, with a view to identifying why some were successful and others were not.[4] Her approach, using 'measures of significance' and applied to women's livelihood issues by Katherine McKee,[5] provides a useful means of focusing on the narrower issue of women and technology.

Tendler posits four measures of significance, the first of which is influencing government policies and market forces. The second has to do with genuine and sustainable improvements in income. Following from this is the extent to which such improvements contribute to more general growth of employment and an expanded economic base, and whether or not beneficiaries have in some way been 'empowered' by the change. 'Empowerment of the poor,' Tendler argues, 'is central to their ability to increase their incomes.'

McKee breaks Tendler's measures of significance into three broad strategic approaches. The first, programming strategies based on a geographic area, usually encompasses a range of activities such as credit, marketing assistance, basic education, skill development and health programmes. The second – sector-focused strategies – deal with a particular industry or occupational area. The third, function-based strategies, can also be called the 'missing piece' approach, because it focuses on a particular constraint which, when removed, is expected to allow beneficiaries to advance. The most common 'missing piece' strategy today relates to credit, although there are others such as health or specialized approaches to education – improved and expanded primary education, or basic management training. Lack of credit, however, especially for the poorest, is increasingly seen as the major stumbling block to genuine, sustained income-enhancement.

The function-based strategy: too soon eureka

Within the function-based credit strategy, there is a growing school of purists who would limit external involvement to the barest minimum. This 'minimalist' approach suggests that credit *alone* is the missing piece in the development puzzle, and that little else should be offered. Stripped-down credit offers very limited training, no extension services, and no investment advice. This is essentially how the Working Women's Forum (WWF) of Madras, the Grameen Bank in Bangladesh and the Self-Employed Women's Association (SEWA) of Ahmedabad began, and preliminary evidence is beginning to show that the approach works, especially for women. Four of Tendler's six 'better performing' organizations were focused mainly or exclusively on poor women, and started with minimalist credit programmes. Three of them – WWF, SEWA and Grameen Bank – growing to significant scales of operation.*

A new and relatively small minimalist project may help to illustrate the approach better than the older, more established organizations. Throughout the 1980s in Kenya, CARE operated a comprehensive, area-based approach to income generation for women in one of the country's poorest districts.[6] The programme began with a goat-rearing project and gradually expanded into training and the provision of grants for the promotion of agro-business, horticulture, beekeeping and other small enterprises. But an internal review in 1988 confirmed what CARE already knew: most of the efforts were both unprofitable and patently unsustainable. Searching for a solution, CARE turned to the stripped-down credit model, adding only training in basic bookkeeping.

The approach is simple. Basically a women's group approaches CARE for assistance. After careful scrutiny and basic training for five elected group members, CARE provides the group with a two-year loan, not exceeding KSh20 000 ($800). Interest is set at 12 per cent. The fund is then managed by the group, usually on a consensus basis, making loans to individual members at rates of interest that are established by the group itself, ranging between 5 and 20 per cent a month. Loans may not exceed KSh2000 ($80) and each borrower must have three guarantors.

Although still new and relatively small, by 1990 the CARE programme found itself with the same sort of results as larger organizations like SEWA and Grameen Bank. Despite the high rates of interest charged by the groups to their members, on-time repayment rates were in the neighbourhood of 95 per cent. Perhaps more important was the discovery that most borrowers were making healthy profits on their loans, and many groups were likely to replace

---

* By 1987, SEWA had 15 000 members and WWF had 38 000. By the end of 1990, Grameen Bank had 800 000 borrower-members.

or exceed the amount of the original CARE fund within the two-year framework. Apart from such obvious successes, the minimalist approach proved to be inexpensive, easily replicable, and required little in the way of technical assistance. Moreover, it was capable of reaching large numbers of poor women.

A superficial glance, therefore, seems to demonstrate that the CARE programme and others bear out minimalist claims. They seem to support McKee's observation that, 'Contrary to the predictions of many, the availability of credit has enabled self-employed people and micro-enterprises to stabilize and modestly increase their incomes, move into newer and more profitable lines of work, and build up a savings cushion'.[7]

Unfortunately, a more rigorous examination of the CARE programme and other frequently cited success stories reveals that this is only partially true. Tendler notes that many income-generation projects fail because they are too ambitious. 'They represent unrealistic assessments of what organizations can do and of how people can improve their incomes.'[8] The pendulum, swinging from the complex integrated programmes of the late 1970s, now reaches the other extreme in its arc, and in the non-interventionist strategy finds answers which may not be there.

As with other organizations, like SEWA in India, virtually all the CARE loans are for trading. The women, many of whom are already petty traders, simply take their loan, go down the road to the next town where they purchase maize, sorghum, soap or clothes, return home and sell at whatever mark-up the traffic will bear. This is particularly successful in a district where village market economies are weak and where the availability of capital is stunted. The project has proved that poor women can be good credit risks. They *are* increasing their incomes and building a savings cushion. But there is little or no value added in what they do, no increase in productivity, no reduced dependence on external sources of supply. And to assume that there are many opportunities where poor women can quickly repay a loan which costs between 5 and 20 per cent *per month*, and make a profit, is to live in dreamland.

Women borrowers assuredly make the best of their loans, but their endeavours are limited to the narrow confines of the world to which they are generally restricted. This is why so many never get beyond traditional handicrafts, food processing and petty trade. It would be a very unusual individual who could create a job or even a meaningful increase in income for herself with a $50 loan. This is confirmed in the limited statistics available from Grameen Bank. Over 90 per cent of the Bank's 1990 loans were made to women, yet more than half were for three traditional activities: milk cows, paddy husking and cattle fattening. As for moving on to higher value-added activities, there is no evidence that the Grameen approach has had much success. Less than one per cent of its loan portfolio in 1989 was devoted to joint activities, and most of the women who borrowed from Grameen in 1983 were still taking tiny loans eight years later.[9]

Without tried investment opportunities based on sound technical information and *knowledge* (there is a distinction), minimalist credit programmes for women will result in minimal improvements. When applied to technology, the functional approach has similar limitations. As examples in previous chapters have demonstrated, the development and display of an apparently 'good' technology seldom results in widespread uptake. Credit is certainly a missing bridge on the road to development, and technology is another. But alone they provide only part of the solution.

The sectoral approach

Genuine *productive* female job creation and meaningful income generation remains an extremely difficult proposition. The BRAC poultry project in Bangladesh is a case in point. Going well beyond the minimalist and functional approaches, and actively seeking productive investments for poor women, BRAC devised and tested its approach to poultry rearing, and then built in training, supply and extension services. Before going ahead, BRAC workers learned as much as they possibly could about poultry. Essentially it was BRAC, not the borrowers, that created the productive income opportunity – for 80 000 poor women.

There are three preconditions for a successful sectoral approach. First, a targeted sector should have large numbers of poor women already in it. In the BRAC example, one reason for success was that chickens were not new to women. Secondly, there should be a strong market for the product. And third, there should be government recognition of the sector's importance in order to promote supportive policy measures.

From a technology perspective, the approach may be further subdivided. Marilyn Carr suggests four distinctions.[10] The first is increased productivity of known or existing work through improved technologies, techniques and supporting services. A second is increased access to previously unavailable opportunities – through co-operatives, credit or technological change. A third approach involves the development of existing skills to produce new products or modified traditional products. And finally, a fourth involves new skills for new products or modified traditional products. Each sub-

190

division suggests different complexities in training, institutional development and technological assistance.

The BRAC poultry project cuts across several of Carr's categories. It provides skills that modify a 'traditional product'. It includes new technologies (better chicks, vaccine), substantial organization, new support services and access to credit. And there is a strong demand for a product (chickens and eggs) that women already know.

Marty Chen offers a similar example from India, where traditionally women have responsibility for the care and feeding of milk animals, and for the processing of milk products.[11] In the 1970s and 1980s, aiming to integrate women into the national dairy programme, a number of NGOs and parastatals in Andhra Pradesh began to develop all-women dairy co-operatives, training female extension workers and technical staff, and providing credit. By 1988, there were 23 000 active members in 400 women's dairy co-operatives and a further 73 000 in mixed co-operatives. In addition to improved income levels, the programmes gave women recognition and leverage (i.e. *empowerment*) at a policy level. And although these numbers are small in relation to the estimated 74 million Indian women engaged in dairying, the Andhra Pradesh success shows other organizations and other states what the potential may be.

Organization: smooth as silk

Food and post-harvest production are obvious areas that meet Marty Chen's criteria – large numbers of women are already involved, and there is a strong demand for the products. Another is the area of textiles and clothing. There can be very few organizations dealing with women that have not supported a spinning, weaving or sewing project. On a small scale, such projects can be highly successful. But replication – 'scaling up' to 'measures of significance' – has proven much more difficult.

A classic case of the scaling-up problem can be found in Botswana, where dozens of NGOs, vocational schools and Brigades have, since the 1970s, organized women into weaving, knitting and sewing projects. School uniforms were often the primary output and there have been some striking successes. Bothakga Handknits, for example, which started in 1974, grew to 30 employees within ten years.[12] Starting with only two workers in 1973, Mopipi (Pty) Ltd. had grown by 1990 into a company with 65 employees and an annual turnover of $300 000.[13] The Lobatse-based Designer Stitches, founded in 1985, grew into an enterprise with 21 workers within only four years. Established by local women, these companies and many smaller ones were formed in part as the result of a minimalist government policy, aimed at encouraging local enterprise with a generous package of grants and concessional loans.

As with other positive examples, these briefly-described success stories in Botswana conceal a number of problems. Raphael Kaplinsky, referring to one of the cases cited above, says that 'the provision of finance alone has proved disastrous, since the owner lacked the experience and technological capabilities to manage such a relatively large enterprise efficiently.'[14] Debt has grown, and bankruptcy was at one point staved off only by direct assistance from the Swedish International Development Agency. For many other producers, the situation was worse. According to Kaplinsky,

> the effective freeing of the capital constraint on small-scale industry unleashed a flood of enterprises, more than half of which were in knitting and sewing, mostly providing school uniforms. Yet in the absence of effective marketing surveys, overcapacity was rapidly reached... Moreover, despite the relatively simple tasks involved in these small-scale sectors, the technological and managerial capability of most of these small entrepreneurs was pathetically inadequate for the task at hand. Their rate of failure has thus been significant.[15]

Sometimes production bottlenecks are the barrier to scaling up. Silk and sericulture – the growing of silkworms – is an ancient village art in Asia. High in employment creation and low in capital cost, it has the potential in many countries to generate regular income for large numbers of village women. A bottleneck in Indian silk production was identified in the reeling process, in which silk is spun from the cocoon onto a reel, or *charaka*.* New, improved *charakas*, developed by the Central Silk Technological Research Institute in Bangalore, and the Central Sericulture Research and Training Institute in Mysore, were placed in dozens of homes for testing. In 1988, SAMUHA, an Indian NGO involved in sericulture, sought to evaluate the new *charakas*, and with assistance from ITDG made some surprising discoveries.[16]

In a laboratory setting, the new *charakas* had demonstrated superior characteristics over the centuries old village technology. In the field, however, it was found that the new model produced silk thread at half the rate of the traditional *charaka*. Further, the new model could only be used with the best cocoons – of the sort that had been used in the lab tests. As these represented only 35 per cent of the average home's supply, the new *charaka* was either abandoned or

---

* The Indian *charaka*, also spelled *charkha*, was the technology on which Eli Whitney (or rather, Catherine Green) based his cotton gin in 1793.

modified by the user. It was also discovered that the 'centuries old' village technology had, in fact, been continuously adapted by users. Some *charakas* had ball bearings, chain drives, metal shafts, and a few even had small electric motors.

In Bangladesh, BRAC began to look into sericulture in the late 1970s, but rather than focusing on a single aspect of the process, took a more holistic approach. Working closely with the government's Sericulture Board, BRAC employees learned everything they could about silk, silkworms and the mulberry tree on which the worm feeds. They experimented with the raising of silkworms and the growing of mulberry trees. They experimented with spinning, weaving and dyeing, and with different field approaches, providing poor village women with silkworms and guaranteeing the price of silk. Land for mulberry trees being limited, government permission was obtained to plant them along the verge of rural roads controlled by the Forest Department. By 1989, with almost 9000 mulberry growers and silkworm rearers, the programme had proven itself on a pilot basis and was ready for wider diffusion.

The expansion called for the planting of 7.6 million mulberry saplings within three years. With a 70 per cent survival rate and 100 trees per grower, approximately 53 000 women were expected to benefit from mulberry trees alone. In 1990, Mulberry yields produced on average, approximately Tk22 per day, an amount higher than the minimum wage, in return for light, part-time work, usually not far from home. In all, some 60 000 jobs were expected to be created in trees, egg rearing and silk reeling, at a total cost of Tk37 million.

At roughly a million dollars, this seems like a lot of money, but it translates into Tk620 or $16 *for the creation of a single, self-sustaining job*.[17] Essentially, BRAC had taken an old, known technology, and applied modern work-flow techniques to it, learning everything it could about sericulture and ironing out the bottlenecks during the development phase. Although not strictly a traditional activity involving large numbers of women in Bangladesh, the raising of silkworms was neither capital-intensive nor time consuming. Trees, on the other hand, were well known to women for whom they have always been a source of income and fuelwood.

Many of the hurdles faced by women in attempting to escape poverty and improve incomes are the same as they are for any self-employed individual. Access to raw materials is essential. Credit may be an important factor. Government policies regarding prices, marketing boards or agricultural inputs such as seeds and fertilizer are critical issues. In the Bangladesh case, the access provided by BRAC to credit, silkworms, mulberry seedlings and training, as well as access to a stable market, were essential to success. Education, attitudes, choice of technology and luck all play a role. But for women, there is an additional element that plays a critical role: time.

Reducing the time required for food preparation or fuel gathering may allow a woman to devote greater efforts to income-generation activities, or possibly just a few hours less each week working. The palm oil press in Ghana did neither until improvements to other parts of the production process were made. The most attractive feature of many fuel-efficient stove programmes for women – who do the cooking – is the amount of time, rather than money, they save. Any new activity must, therefore, be time-conscious. Women whose time is already filled with work will not be able to take advantage of a new idea unless additional time requirements are minimal. The 'improved' Indian *charaka* may have produced a better silk, but it took twice as much time to do so. The low amounts of time involved in Bangladesh mulberry tree planting, on the other hand, made it especially attractive to village women.

Strong cultural taboos

Socio-cultural constraints can be an important factor in the success or failure of new approaches for women. For example among the Ashanti in Ghana, the weaving of brilliantly coloured *kente* cloth is normally done by men and boys on narrow looms. Attempts over the years to introduce weaving projects for women failed because of a strong cultural taboo. Outsiders thought the taboo had to do with weaving, but in fact it had to do with the traditional loom, and when it was discovered that the restriction did not apply to broad looms, the uptake on weaving projects for women improved significantly.

Although it may be unwise, particularly for outsiders, to push too hard against apparently firm cultural constraints, it is perhaps worth remembering that in Europe and North America there were, at various stages in the first half of the twentieth century, 'strong cultural taboos' against women driving automobiles, voting and smoking cigarettes in public. (When asked if she thought women should be allowed to smoke in public, Gertrude Stein asked, 'By whom?') Until recent years in Bangladesh there were 'strong cultural taboos' against virtually every aspect of women's participation in meaningful income generation. Women could not ride bicycles or motorcycles, and were therefore excluded from the field management of development projects. Women could not work in factories except as sweepers. And with the exception of a tiny, urban elite, women could not work in public at anything.

Many of these cultural biases – apparently not so strong after all –

have fallen away without significant opposition in a very short period of time. It has been discovered, mostly through large-scale rural NGO projects, that women, although nervous at first, are quite able to ride bicycles and motorcycles to villages and (surprise), actually prefer it to remaining on the sidelines. Men may grumble, but the world does not end. Bangladeshi NGOs and private sector firms have also discovered that women can work alongside men in textile factories, pharmaceutical plants and even in metal fabrication shops without the sky falling. The CIDA-funded CARE Rural Maintenance Project has, since 1985, employed 60 000 destitute women in the maintenance of 96 000 kilometres of rural farm-to-market roads. The project has demonstrated that poor women can and will do such work, that the quality of their labour is good, and that this form of road maintenance is significantly more cost-effective than the way it had previously been handled.[18]

A Sarvodaya project in Sri Lanka, funded by the International Development Research Centre, trains women to produce handpumps in a machine shop. This non-traditional female activity may seem to over-stretch a point about avoiding gender stereotypes, until it is remembered who in the family is responsible for fetching water. Too many pump maintenance projects have been placed under the control of men, often far away from the pump site. When pumps fail, as they often do, water must be found from an alternative source – usually the same distant, unhygienic source that the pump was supposed to re-place. Many pump repairs require neither genius nor men, and could easily be handled by the women for whom the pump is an important part of daily life. The aim of the Sarvodaya project is to establish rural workshops where women can go one step beyond simple repairs and actually *produce* some of the basic handpump components.

Beginnings

Although there are many things women 'should not do', there are very few constraints on men. Marilyn Carr observes that 'the only rule appears to be that when a new technology which brings upgraded skills and higher returns is introduced, the men take over.'[19] Worse, in some cases it is taken over by the government. 'Empowerment' is therefore an important part of increasing the ability of poor women to earn better incomes. The formation of groups, co-operatives and other institutions which can speak on behalf of women and be heard, in a village or nationally, is a key part of changing the poverty-aid-technology matrix. Empowerment also flows from the social and behavioural skills, the creativity and the motivation that accompany group formation.

The question of empowerment is a complex one. Katharine McKee asks, 'is it more empowering to achieve modest, tangible gains through an incremental strategy, or to pursue a potentially higher reward, risking failure? And second, do the potential sociocultural gains justify the economic risks, especially for very poor women?'[20] Difficult as it may be to find the right answer, it is worse when new strategies offer no improvement of any kind; when they simply disempower. Paddy husking in Bangladesh, once exclusive to women and one of the few ways a poor woman could earn cash income, has been taken over by mechanical and automatic mills in much of the country. In the 1980s, the new technology displaced women at the rate of more than 100 000 annually, and in the process, ownership, control and employment went to men. It is estimated that by 1987, 27 000 mills had displaced almost 35 million days of women's work annually.[21] The new technology was made economically attractive in part through the availability of subsidized electricity and cheap credit, most of it derived from donor agencies. Too often the choice of technology and the means of obtaining it is made by those least implicated in the outcome.

A chapter on women and technology should perhaps end without firm conclusions, as so much is still being learned. Credit programmes, for example, have become a popular tool for the advancement of women. Alone, credit may help, but alone it is not enough. The same can be said about technology. Because technology, which can increase women's productivity and the price they charge for their labour, can also do the opposite.

Although there are areas of great promise, there are no simple prescriptions and there are none on the horizon. Successful interventions require sensitivity to the complexity of each situation. And if they are to succeed, they require professionalism of a high order – professionalism in research and organization, and professionalism in learning, listening and above all, *remembering*. And they require professionalism in applying what has been learned.

One of the key measures of a successful development strategy for women has to do with genuine and sustainable improvements in income. But the extent to which such improvements contribute to more general growth of employment for women and a wider economic base, is perhaps as important in the long run. Interventions which succeed in increasing a woman's earning capacity may well reduce poverty and even social inequality. But micro-level short-term increases in income and productivity can be wiped out by overnight policy changes. Institutional development, advocacy and policy reform – all ingredients of *empowerment* – are therefore legitimate and important objectives for any intervention aimed at improving the lives of women.

CHAPTER XIII

Employment and the informal sector: the economists lose control

That the developing countries cannot do without a modern sector ... is hardly open to doubt. What needs to be questioned is the implicit assumption that the modern sector can be expanded to absorb virtually the entire population, and that this can be done fairly quickly.
                                                                E.F. Schumacher

IN 1973, RICHARD Jolly observed that 'Unemployment is increasingly emerging as the most striking symptom of inadequate development in most countries of the Third World'.[1] When he wrote that sentence, three quarters of those who would be unemployed two decades later were not born. By the early 1990s the situation was appreciably worse, and worsening. In the North, unemployment is largely a result of what economists call 'a deficiency of aggregate demand'. In the South the causes are often considerably more complex, involving not only inadequate demand, but inadequate supply, mismatches between opportunities, expectations and education, inadequate institutional mechanisms, and market distortions, both local and international.

Unemployment and underemployment have three prominent causes. The first, in rural areas, is land: land ownership and the employment it generates; security of tenure and the willingness to take risks and to adopt new technologies; size of land holding, which may create or reduce labour requirements. The second cause is a deficiency in human resources – in some countries both quantitative and qualitative. The third cause of unemployment – technology – is a mixed blessing. The introduction of modern technology has increased agricultural and industrial production, but in most cases it has done the reverse for employment. The negative employment impact of large-scale, capital-intensive technology, designed for industrialized economies and industrial work forces, has been a powerful contributor to underemployment in the South. Added to this problem is the widespread technology-related shift to synthetics in industrialized countries. This has dramatically cut into the demand for many basic Third World exports such as jute, sisal, rubber and cotton, lowering both foreign exchange earnings and the returns to agriculture.

The absolute poor in the Third World devote over three-quarters of their income – which is derived mostly from labour – to food. The low-paying, part-time, daily-wage, and seasonal work to which they have access, is negatively influenced by a variety of factors. The poorest are more prone than the average to illness and disability, which in turn affects their ability to work. Child mortality among the poor is higher, resulting in more replacement births, which both increases dependency and removes mothers from the work force.

Unemployment and underemployment are usually understated, especially for the poorest. The closer a person is to desperation, the more likely she or he is to work for whatever meagre wages or food are available. Also, because the poorest generally have the lowest levels of education, they tend to be the least employable. During seasonal fluctuations or periods of general economic hardship – bad seasons, bad years, drought, flood – these people become the most desperate.

Rural unemployment rates are generally lower than those in cities because of access to seasonal labour in the countryside, because of extended family networks and the availability of other productive assets such as a family homestead. Poor urban women are less likely to work than men, because more of them are married than their rural counterparts, and are less likely to head a household. Those who do work earn less than men, although not so much from wage-discrimination in the workplace, as from a gender bias in health, mobility and job-entry, and especially in education. This results in women being less well educated than men, and therefore less able to compete for urban jobs.

The employment prognosis for the future is bleak. During the 1990s, 40 million new jobs must be generated in the South *every year*, simply in order to absorb those already born. In India, there are 10 million new entrants to the job market every year. In Indonesia there are 1.2 million and in Mexico there are a million, more than double the number of jobs created in those countries during the best years of the 1980s.[2] In China it is estimated that there are 110 million people severely under-employed. Unemployment in the South will continue to rise, and it will be increasingly concentrated among the poor. The average annual growth of the labour force in the South is 2.1 per cent, and in some African countries it is closer to 4 per cent.[3] Yet labour demand has been increasing at the rate of only one-third to a half of one per cent each year. Urbanization and industrialization are reducing labour intensity, while both are raising the number of those seeking employment. The concentration of workers in large firms and in unionized public sectors reduces employment opportunities among new, poor, uncertified entrants. And inappropriate technological changes in the South and in the North only add to the problem.

The combination of poverty on the land and in rapidly expanding cities has led to the development of a vast unorganized 'informal' sector. The pathos of this 'teeming, motley circus' is summed up well by Paul Harrison:

> ... hawkers, tailors, whores, rickshawmen, market mammies, fortune tellers, watch-repairers, bush garages, one-man engineering workshops. Enterprises of this kind employ as much as half the work force in the typical developing city. They require little capital, so anyone can set up in business. Their technology is labour intensive, often using improvised or second-hand equipment, creating the maximum employment. The raw materials they use are cheap and locally available, often recycled waste. Their products and services are low-cost, within the budget of the urban poor who for the most part cannot afford modern sector goods.
>
> Yet this great reservoir of savings, enterprise and inventivity has been, in the vast majority of countries, ignored or neglected... It gets little or no official credit. Most of its capital is raised from family savings – the rest from moneylenders at exorbitant rates. It bumbles on, with inefficient management and ad hoc marketing. Indeed, it is often discriminated against or harassed. Official specification and standards rule its products out of many markets. City zoning and licensing arrangements make much of it illegal... Informal enterprises often have to work in shantytowns, without light, power or water, sometimes even without a roof over their heads. Slum clearance programmes bulldoze away as many workplaces as homes.[4]

The 'informal economy' – disorganized, usually illegal, neglected by planners and aid agencies, denigrated by economists and harassed by officialdom, represents as much as half the work force in Third World cities, and a growing proportion of the rural work force. Enrique Iglesias, President of the American Development Bank has acknowledged that the informal sector in the Caribbean and Latin America represents 30 million individuals, or one third of the work force, and that between 1980 and 1985, while the modern formal sector grew by only 2 per cent, the urban informal sector grew by 6.8 per cent *annually*.[5]

National development strategies in most Third World countries concentrate on agricultural production at one end of the development spectrum, and urban-based industrialization at the other. Between these poles lie the small-scale informal-sector 'entrepreneurs'. Village-based or urban, often alone, in many cases individual women or groups of women, these unsubsidized people have contributed significantly to keeping national economies afloat while subsidized industry and the formal sector stagnate, and in some cases collapse around them. Carpenters, metal fabricators, bakers, soapmakers, weavers, tinkers, tailors and candle stick makers, they are the backbone of the 'underground economy' or 'black market'.

Definitions of 'small-', 'medium-' and 'large-scale industry' vary. Sometimes they include measures of capital investment as well as numbers of employees. In this book, 'large' means an enterprise with more than 50 employees. Micro-enterprises have three or fewer workers, and many are single-person operations. 'Small', therefore, indicates enterprises with more than three and less than 50 employees.

Much of the informal sector, especially that part engaged in off-farm rural activities, is made up of women. In Bangladesh, for example, women represent 34 per cent of the work force in rural industries; in Honduras women own 61 per cent of all small enterprise, and in rural Guatemala, women contribute 50 per cent of the work-force in textiles, 47 per cent in food processing and baking, and 65 per cent in commercial services.[6] In Lima, almost half a million people are directly or indirectly dependent for their living on street traders; 274 of the city's 331 markets have been constructed by the informal sector, and 95 per cent of all public transport is operated by 'informals'. Between 1960 and 1984, it is estimated that the municipal government of Lima spent US$174 million on urban low-cost housing; during the same period, the informal sector built housing valued at more than US$8300 million, 47 times more than government.[7] In Ghana, studies have shown that the value added for microenterprises employing fewer than ten people was three to five times higher than in large-scale industry, and that the capital required to create jobs was one twelfth of large-scale industrial requirements. The return on capital in small workshops was 73 per cent, while in large-scale manufacturing during the 1970s the figure was only 4 per cent.[8]

Operating beyond the control of administrators and out of sight of the statisticians, the informal sector exposes the irrelevance of much economic planning. It also underscores the need for greater recognition of the fundamental right to economic initiative. Maria Nowak makes the case succinctly and passionately:

> Despite considerable rhetoric about satisfying basic needs, fighting poverty and, more recently, growth with equity, in many Third World nations, misery is still on the rise, fuelled by high rates of population growth and structural adjustment policies, which do not always have a human face. This rise in misery, which also reflects a major failure of foreign aid, cannot be checked through assistance and charity. However it would certainly be attacked more effectively if, apart from an environment more conducive to self-help and microenterprise development, socialist and market-oriented governments alike would recognize the individual's right to economic initiative by providing access to capital, training and technology.[9]

Capital

Despite its size and its significance to the economies of most countries, the record of domestic and international assistance to the informal sector is poor. Many countries have established specialized organizations designed to offer a range of support services to small enterprise, but their output is generally low, and the focus is usually on credit, combined with a limited approach to training. Success is often measured in loan repayment rates rather than in productive job creation. Between 1978 and 1983, one such body in Tanzania established only one surviving small industrial enterprise each year for every two staff members. In Zimbabwe, several bodies have been established which might assist the informal sector, including the Small Enterprise Development Corporation, the Zimbabwe Entrepreneurs Association and the Indigenous Business Development Centre. None, in fact, do. Ghana's Entrepreneur Development Programme – under the National Board for Small-Scale Industries – has a mandate to assist microenterprises, but activities seem to consist mainly of raising false expectations, with credit applications in some cases taking more than a year to process. Most of these organizations do not reach the poorest elements; they are often prohibited from working with unregistered, 'informal' enterprises; and few have the mandate or the capacity to deal with the broader macro-economic and legal climate which make such enterprises both possible and necessary. In Peru, only one third of one per cent of all credit was channelled to the informal sector in the late 1980s.[10]

Subsidized interest rates, introduced to assist the poor, have often attracted the better-off who are more familiar with the value of money. Rather than assisting the poor, who are used to paying very high interest rates, subsidies have often done the opposite, putting low-interest programmes into the hands of the wealthy. A further problem is that small enterprise-oriented credit operations are invariably biased towards trading operations rather than producers, because petty traders are more likely to be profitable, and can start making repayments quickly. Productive enterprises, must therefore resort to the family for financial assistance. A recent study shows that in Nigeria, 98 per cent of financing for *productive* enterprises is family-based. In Tanzania the figure is 93 per cent, and in Bangladesh it is 75 per cent.[11]

Education

The relevance of education to the development of local technological capacity, to national economic growth, to improved equity and to poverty reduction has been incontrovertibly demonstrated. A detailed 1989 study[12] concluded that education contributes significantly to growth, and that returns on education are comparable with, or more than returns on physical capital. It found that education is significant in reducing poverty and improving income distribution, and that the contribution of *primary education* to growth and income distribution is much more significant than for most other levels.

Four years of education can be directly correlated with better agricultural output – an average of 8.7 per cent in 31 countries surveyed, and over 20 per cent in Nepal alone.[13] Primary education means better health and nutrition, improved child survival and lower fertility. On average, every additional year a mother spends in school is associated with a fall in infant mortality of approximately 9 per 1000.[14] For micro and small-scale enterprises, primary education means an ability to follow written instructions, to measure accurately, and to understand some of the basics of science and organization. But these facts, known and widely reported for years, have not resulted in any appreciable shift in official development spending: approximately 10 per cent or $2.5 billion is spent annually on education, but less than one per cent of it goes to the primary level.[15]

While great improvements in enrollment and literacy rates have been achieved over the past three decades, there has been a slippage of resolve, and a concomitant deterioration in recent years. India spent 3 per cent of GNP on education in 1987, or about $10 per capita. Thailand spent 8.5 per cent, or $156 per capita. In Pakistan, the female primary enrollment ratio rose from 13 per cent to 22 per cent between 1960 and 1970, but in the period 1976 to 1986, it rose only 2 per cent, leaving Pakistan with the lowest female to male enrolment ratio in Asia, and the fifth lowest in the world.[16] The overall enrolment ratio in Bangladesh is falling, and in India there is an increasing tilt in educational spending towards secondary and tertiary levels – at the expense of the stated objective of universal primary education and literacy.[17]

In some countries the quality of education and the availability of books and supplies is also worsening. Perhaps the greatest loss in investment, however – for children, parents and society – is in high drop-out rates. In Pakistan, for example, the percentage of grade one enrollment completing primary school in 1987 was 49 per cent; it was 28 per cent in Nepal and only 20 per cent in Bangladesh. These figures compare unfavourably with countries such as Indonesia, Sri Lanka and Malaysia, where the rates were 80 per cent, 97 per cent and 88 per cent respectively. Restraint on government spending is likely to make the situation worse, validating a 1989 warning from the Director-General of UNESCO:

If adjustment policies are to be carried out without regard to the poor and vulnerable ... over the necessary investment in the social sectors including education, then current disequilibria and economic tensions in North-South relations are likely to turn into a dangerous erosion of human resources that risks undoing the educational progress achieved, and might set back the countries of the South by a whole generation or even more. What is so preoccupying is that the greatest damage seems to have been done at the very foundation of the educational pyramid, that is in primary education and in basic literacy for adults and out-of-school youth.[18]

The level and type of employment associated with a secondary school education has changed dramatically, especially in Africa since the 1960s and 1970s. Because of the inability of the formal job market to keep pace with the number of school leavers, the education system has actually been turning out more and more graduates for *self-employment*, without explicitly recognizing the fact, and without adjusting the curriculum to better arm students for the inevitable.

Vast sums have been spent on vocational training, although much of it is impractical, and for many students (and employers) it is regarded as a second-class means of obtaining a diploma, rather than as a key to employment. Many of those in the productive informal sector learn their skills through apprenticeship rather than in school. A detailed study of micro and small engineering enterprises in Ghana's Suame Magazine, for example, found that 84 per cent of the proprietors had received their training through apprenticeships and that only 16 per cent had any formal technical education.[19] While apprenticeship has a long and honourable history as an educational tool (witness Peter the Great's experience as a carpenter in a Dutch shipyard), it has severe limitations in today's world. Analysis, experimentation, knowledge of basic science and measurement are more important to the development and adaptation of technology than ever before.

But in much of the Third World, technical education is regarded as it was in Victorian England – something for the lower orders. An Englishman returning from the Paris Exhibition of 1867 noted that 'France, Prussia, Austria, Belgium and Switzerland possess good systems of industrial education ... and England possesses none.'[20] Somehow this Third World throwback to Victorian England has to change; a *premium* must be placed on technical education, as it was in European countries eager to catch up with and surpass Britain's industrial revolution.

There have been many experimental efforts to do this. Mapfure College for ex-combatants in Zimbabwe provides technical and business training to young adult would-be entrepreneurs, and then works with them in the establishment of co-operative business enterprises in carpentry, construction and metal fabrication. The Botswana Brigades, village-based youth polytechnics in Kenya and the 'education with production' experiments in Zimbabwe and Botswana are efforts to equip students with genuine skills for employment. The Malawi Entrepreneur Development Institute (MEDI) has added a strong entrepreneurial element to an institution that started basically as a vocational training institute. And in Nigeria, the National Directorate of Employment has instituted a number of self-employment programmes.

In the past, many of these programmes or projects were small in scale, were tied to the enthusiasm of a single individual, or were crudely designed to keep people in the rural areas rather than to enhance the scope for enterprise, income or human fulfilment. A newer generation of programmes, however, is more national in scope – as in the case of Kenya, where the problem of microenterprise development and job creation in the informal sector is being addressed at the highest political level. The most successful projects, such as the Technology Consultancy Centre in Ghana and GRATIS, work with people already in the labour market, and provide a larger package of inputs, including access to credit, raw materials, machinery and follow-up business advice. Selecting individuals from those already in the market has the advantage of reducing technical training costs and it increases the likelihood of assisting people who are genuine entrepreneurs. GRATIS and TCC in Ghana, and MEDI in Malawi each have rigorous tests in order to ensure that their 'students' have the right mix of motivation, analytical skills and problem-solving ability.

Kenneth King argues that this approach, replicated and vastly expanded, must be the educational approach of the future:

> Explicit promotion of the enterprise culture may help at the margins, but ... if enterprise and self-employment is only promoted through education and training institutions, there will be little effect. A really major set of changes in the enabling environment and in the financial support of microenterprise will be necessary to alter the dominance of education and training for employment towards some significant measure of education and training for *self*-employment.[21]

Writing about the American educational system, which he believes is mired in outdated form and content, Robert Reich might be describing the most urgent educational requirements of the Third World. In order to increase the stock of problem-solvers, innovators and entrepreneurs, he argues that the formal education system must concentrate on the creation of four basic skills.[22] The first is a capacity for abstraction, an ability for individuals to interpret and rearrange for themselves the chaos of information that surrounds them. The second is a capacity for 'system thinking'. Reich describes system thinking as an ability to see reality as a system of causes and consequences, as discovery of opportunities that lie in the relationships between cause and effect. The third is a capacity for experimentation, a willingness and an ability to forego some of the stultifying security that is engendered by textbook-bound educational systems, and to act on the newfound capacities for abstraction and system thinking. And finally, if it is to equip individuals for innovation, problem-solving and leadership, an educational system must be able to foster in people an ability to collaborate, to work in teams, to share problems and information.

Technology

While minimalist credit can be an important entry point into the informal sector, it has serious limitations for the longer-term growth and development of both individuals and industry. But credit alone, whether minimalist or otherwise, is often as far as small enterprise development programmes go, partly because it is an obvious need, and can be easily 'evaluated' by examining loan repayment rates. One reason for the limitations of such programmes is that tested investment opportunities for the micro-level borrower simply do not exist in many countries. Often it is incorrectly assumed that credit, having provided the wherewithal to obtain a welding set or a cassava grater, has solved the job-creation problem. But as examples in this book have shown, working with new tools, new materials, and new production techniques creates new problems, and is not something that should be left to chance, especially where an impact on the poor is anticipated.

Although the need for integration between credit and creditworthy opportunities is widely acknowledged, there is an unfortunate and widespread programming mismatch between credit and technology: most established credit institutions have little interest in technology, while many NGOs and technology institutions have no interest in the micro-entrepreneur. The Technology Consultancy Centre and GRATIS in Ghana are two exceptions, although finding donors who would contemplate a marriage between credit and technology was not a simple matter for them. TCC approached the problem by importing reconditioned British machine tools and selling them at cost to its clients. GRATIS started a hire-purchase scheme which gave its clients access to machinery which existing credit institutions would not finance.

Policy

Few enterprise development organizations, especially those interested in the informal sector, take a strong interest in policy development. Some economists suggest that informal sector enterprises do not graduate into the formal sector, do not grow, and are not a source of economic dynamism. In some cases – perhaps a large percentage – this is true. Many individuals in the informal sector are not there from choice or because they are 'entrepreneurs'. They are there because they are desperate.

This does not diminish the importance of the sector, however, nor does it detract from the need to take it far more seriously. Nor does it deny the fact that many informal sector industries, like SIS Engineering in Ghana, do 'graduate'. Many more would enter the formal sector if they could – in order to gain greater legal and economic security, and to take advantage of official credit markets. But Hernando de Soto demonstrates the high cost of crossing the barrier. His researchers in Peru established a fictional, nine-worker garment factory and applied for registration: the exercise required 11 permits, consumed 289 days and cost the equivalent in cash and time of 32 times the monthly minimum living wage. Permission to occupy land and build a house on state property required 207 bureaucratic steps and the involvement of 48 different government offices. At a week for each step, the process would have consumed almost seven years.[23] The same exercise carried out in Tampa Florida took 3.5 hours, and in New York, 4 hours.[24] Unable to afford the cost of entering the formal system, informals therefore remain outside, reluctant to invest in new technology or expensive equipment, unable to gain access to mainstream markets for their sales, borrowing from informal credit sources at exorbitant rates, often producing poor quality goods, while evading taxes, building codes, and labour regulations.

In the late 1980s, interest in the informal sector and microenterprise development began to achieve a degree of prominence in Latin America, in part because of the pioneering activities of individuals like Hernando de Soto, NGOs such as ACCION International and the Carvajal Foundation in Colombia, and the work of the Inter American Development Bank and USAID. The Government of Colombia has had an active programme of support for the informal sector and microenterprise development since 1984. The Government of Ecuador, NGOs and a formal sector financial institution – the Banco del Pacifico – have worked together on microenterprise development since the early 1980s. In Guatemala, the Urban Microenterprise Multiplier System, an unusual coalition between government agencies, 15 NGOs, local banks and multilateral development agencies, was in the late 1980s making more than 5500 loans a year to micro-entrepreneurs.[25] Although this programme and many others are still in the early stages of development, the progress is both positive and encouraging.

The cost of informality

The costs to people, to governments and to society of an un-supported, unregulated, anonymous informal sector are enormous. Among those identified by Hernando de Soto are:

o declining national productivity: formal sector industries spend undue amounts of time, energy and money complying with official regulations. In an effort to avoid costly labour regulations, they use inappropriate technologies which require more capital and fewer workers. The informals – undercapitalized, dependant on high rates of interest, devoid of legal facilitating instruments, and usually suffering from an excessive ratio of labour to capital – are also inefficient;

o reduced investment: the insecurity of the informal sector and heavy regulation of the formal sector weigh heavily against investments in both;

o an inefficient tax system which overburdens the formal sector;

o increased power and water costs for the formal sector (the use of half of Lima's water and electricity, for example, is unaccounted for);

o stunted technological progress: in the absence of property rights, protection for technological innovation and access to cheap credit, a major part of the productive sector remains technologically retarded;

o difficulties in formulating macroeconomic policy: the absence of accurate data on the scope and size of the underground economy introduces a considerable degree of uncertainty into the design of macroeconomic policy.

Although small-scale enterprise has gained popularity among donor agencies in recent years, attention outside Latin America generally remains focused on small industry development corporations, often ineffective in their stated objectives and in reaching the poorest of the micro-entrepreneurs. The conventional approach still compartmentalizes support into credit, technical assistance, and vocational and business training. Important as these are, integrating, legalizing and promoting the informal sector, and providing it with access to the formal marketplace is more critical. For this to happen, an appropriate official climate for micro-enterprise development is necessary. This includes simple legal and bureaucratic requirements for registration and reporting, and a democratization of access to services such as credit, water and electricity. And it requires decentralization. Decision-making authority for approvals, loans and other services must be in the hands of officials in direct contact with the problems that a policy or funding mechanism seeks to address. Better local policy analysis on the informal sector is also urgently needed. The formal business and banking communities must be drawn into the challenge, and NGOs could become more involved in policy analysis as well as in actual programme implementation.

Marilyn Carr notes that, 'while donors express a theoretical preference for the macro-policy approach, external assistance rarely takes the form of policy assistance, and support for small enterprise is rarely a consideration in policy leverage situations.'[26] The challenge, therefore, for governments, NGOs, donor agencies and the formal private sector – if there is to be encouragement of enterprise, meaningful development of local technological capabilities, and a reduction in unemployment – is enormous.

CHAPTER XIV

Technology: the policy factor

A price has to be paid for anything worthwhile: to redirect technology so that it serves man instead of destroying him requires primarily an effort of the imagination and an abandonment of fear. E.F. Schumacher

MOST APPROACHES TO appropriate and intermediate technology start at the bottom, with projects. This book has attempted to demonstrate the importance of *context* to the efficacy of such projects, and to show that a country's policy framework is critical to the success or failure of an intervention. If anything is clear from history and from the cases described in this book, it is that the development and application of appropriate technology must be approached from the top as well as from the bottom if it is to succeed.

A period of adjustment

The 1980s, sometimes called a 'lost decade' for the South, was a time of adjustment that overflowed like a tidal wave into the 1990s. More than 'adjustment', it was a wholesale retreat from the failed and often mismanaged governmental *dirigisme* that characterized the 1960s and 1970s. The retreat was a forced march, a new kind of *dirigisme*, stage-managed by multilateral and bilateral donors and sometimes innocently referred to as 'policy dialogue'.

Adjustment was a logical accompaniment to a period of deregulation and privatization in western Europe and North America, and to the collapse of communism in eastern Europe. In the parlance of international financial institutions, structural adjustment means the comprehensive reform of macro- and micro-policies that hamper economic performance. Adjustment is required as a response to various 'shocks' (oil crises, collapsing commodity prices) which work against standard development objectives such as employment, economic growth, poverty reduction and improvements in the balance of payments.

The term 'inappropriate policies' can be a euphemism for many things. In general, however, it refers to excessive state intervention in the economy: investment in huge, flawed state enterprises, misguided price controls, and high levels of protection in support of inefficient import-substituting industry. It includes overvalued currencies which favour the import of capital goods over local manufacture, while reducing traditional exports.

The prescriptions, usually in the form of policy conditions set out in the adjustment lending programmes of the World Bank and the IMF, and widely supported by bilateral donors, include varying degrees of currency devaluation, reductions in government expenditure to better reflect real resources, and the bringing of domestic prices of key products, such as petrol and fertilizer, into line with world prices. Adjustment involves trade and exchange liberalization as well as liberalization of domestic prices, and a variety of 'institutional reforms' such as the closure of inefficient government enterprises, or their sale to the private sector. By reducing the role of the state, it is believed, inefficiencies will be reduced. Likewise, 'rent-seeking' activity will be curtailed. 'Rent seeking' is an anodyne economic term which refers in large part to the corruption that flows from excessive control. In return for access to foreign exchange, scarce raw materials or products, or simple permissions, government employees extract 'concessions' or non-productive 'rents' from producers and consumers.

It is believed that by reducing opportunities for rent-seeking – through trade, price and exchange liberalization – and by replacing state inefficiencies with private entrepreneurship and the market-place, the disastrous effects of decades of control and mismanagement will be swept away. Devaluation and trade liberalization will further improve efficiency and reduce poverty by 'tilting incentives back in favour of food and export agriculture, and by promoting labour-intensive industrialization.'[1]

When adjustment programmes were introduced in the early 1980s, they were seen as reasonably short-term undertakings; short term pain for long term gain. Although adjustment would involve hardship, it was like chemotherapy. The cure would kill some healthy cells, but in the end the cancer would be gone. It is still perhaps too early to say how many good cells have gone, and how many bad cells remain, although the subject is one of great debate. In his entertaining book, *The Rhetoric of Reaction*, Albert Hirschman surveys two hundred years of reactionary argument. He discusses three generic methods of attacking and ridiculing one's opponent. The 'perversity thesis' argues that the proposed action will have the opposite effect of what it seeks to achieve. The 'futility thesis' claims that it simply won't work. And the 'jeopardy thesis' argues that the change will threaten some other hard-won achievement, and is therefore not worth the cost.

The jeopardy and perversity theses feature prominently in the debate over structural adjustment. The pro-adjustment jeopardy argument says that without adjustment, all the development gains of previous years are endangered. Anti-adjustment rhetoric argues that it places all the gains of previous years in danger. The pro-adjustment perversity argument states that protectionism and state intervention – which sought to develop local capacity, protect infant industry and increase employment – created instead, a false, uncompetitive economy that led instead to fewer and fewer state options and greater poverty for more and more people. The anti-adjustment position argues that attempting to alleviate poverty by cutting government expenditure and throwing economies open to the market place does precisely the opposite, by inducing massive layoffs and forcing cutbacks in health and educational services.

Of babies and bathwater

Despite the passage of a decade of adjustment programmes, during which substantive empirical evidence should have become available, the arguments are still used to mask strong ideological views on the role of state and market, making 'truth' difficult to discern. Hard-line Northern theorists of different persuasions, unable to prevail at home, often find the South a more congenial place in which to do battle. There are a few observable facts, however. The first is that although adjustment programmes have not worked as quickly as was once thought possible, there is some evidence, in some countries, that they have had some success in curbing inflation, improving the balance of payments and rejuvenating the economy. There is also some evidence in some countries that they have had no success.[2] There have been special hardships for those most directly affected by job losses, and less quantifiable but real costs to the poorest who bear the brunt of reduced subsidies and increasing food prices. Longer term effects in reduced infrastructure, such as health programmes and education – one of the few avenues of escape from poverty – have also been large.

Modest success (and the futility of returning to what prevailed before) has reinforced the international financial institutions in their cause. However for the South, continued acceptance will depend very much on clear, demonstrated, positive results. Unfortunately, it is often the harsh negatives that become apparent most quickly, with political instability and riots following in their wake. The negative effects, and criticism coming from such non-ideological places as UNICEF,[3] caused some rethinking in the late 1980s, and adjustment programmes were subsequently adjusted themselves, to include welfare elements, targeted subsidies, job creation and retraining efforts.

The purpose here is not to debate the necessity of adjustment, but to suggest that infatuation with the notion of 'getting the prices right', to the exclusion of all else, including social and political objectives, equity, poverty alleviation and environmental issues is naively simplistic. It is especially simplistic in its view that more labour-intensive production and an increase in manufacturing exports will naturally flow from 'right prices'. The theory is that after clearing out all the cobwebs that distort factor prices (labour, raw materials, capital equipment), real prices – competitive internationally – will prevail. By allowing the market place, rather than governments to set prices, profit-maximizing behaviour will determine the best allocation of resources and the choice of technology. In countries where labour is abundant and wages are low, labour-intensive 'appropriate' technologies will prevail. Market forces will thus promote full employment and efficient use of all resources.

This is all very well in theory, but even the strongest Northern advocates of liberalization and getting the prices right in the South do not practice what they preach. Many donor agencies are blatant in their use of aid funds, for example, to promote or prop up home industries. Examples cited in previous chapters have included Canadian locomotives, and British, Chinese and Japanese hydroelectric equipment. Northern government rescues of ailing or moribund domestic businesses – such as Chrysler in the United States in 1979, or the Savings and Loan fiasco of 1989 – are legion. In 1991, it was reported that the government-owned Hydro Quebec, one of the world's largest producers of electricity, was selling power to 13 multinational corporations at one third of the price to other consumers, and at almost 40 per cent less than what it cost to produce.[4] It is estimated that by the end of the 1980s, one third of all standard American manufactures enjoyed some protection against foreign competition.[5] These Northern countries were doing precisely what their governments and the World Bank were attempting to halt in the South.

At the other end of the spectrum, one of the effects of unbounded liberalization in Ghana, achieved through 'policy dialogue' with lenders and donors, was the wholesale importation of used clothing from Europe and the United States.[6] 'Obruni Wawu' people call it, meaning 'the white man is dead' and his clothes have been sold. The irrepressible Ghanaian humour is found in another name for the phenomenon – 'Bend Down Boutique' – a description of open-air markets where the used clothing is spread on the ground for inspection. But good humour does not conceal the madness in what is happening: street urchins wearing cast-off Hard Rock Cafe T-shirts, while hundreds of Ghanaian tailors and textile workers lose their livelihoods. Courtesy of the Multi-Fibre Arrangement, Southern textiles enjoy no such liberalization in the North. In Ghana's textile sector, commerce has been liberalized; but production has been stifled.

Unfettered market forces may promote employment and efficiency in general, over long periods of time in advanced market economies, but they don't work as well in climates where markets fail, where inappropriate industries – often monopolistic – are already in place, and where the short run is what counts for human survival. What is so odd about the confident donor macroeconomic prescriptions is that in the view of many economists, macroeconomic theory is in a state of near anarchy, and neoclassical theory, apart from its distance from important political realities, has serious drawbacks as a basis for policy recommendations in the Third World.[7] Economist Tony Killick argues that conditionality – using aid to force policy change – is a tricky and labour-intensive business, and that donors should exercise both caution and humility in their approach.

> Beware the temptation of exaggerating the appropriateness of policy prescriptions derived from mainstream theory, and the over-confident advocacy of those prescriptions ... Avoid simplistic and single-solution responses to complex problems and economic systems. Serious economic problems are usually complicated and so too are the ways in which specific interventions work their way through an economy. In similar vein, beware the temptation to apply similar prescriptions across countries ... By the act of laying down policy conditions, donors willy-nilly become active players in the domestic politics of the recipient country. As such, however, their power to bring about major change is usually very circumscribed and they operate at many disadvantages ... The danger is that donors will use their muscle in ways which have political consequences which they are not in a position to anticipate, and whose risks will have to be borne by others.[8]

The point is made more strongly in a 1991 study on democratic development, which asks whether Northern donor agency efforts to foster democracy in the South are compatible with the pressures they apply for specific economic policy changes. 'Questions are increasingly being asked about the extent to which the actions of large international institutions are subject to democratic scrutiny and accountability, particularly when such interventions can dramatically affect the lives of millions of people. Can governments maintain democratic legitimacy in the eyes of their own people if they are seen to be too much driven by outside forces and pressures?'[9]

In the South, spending on arms averages about four per cent of gross domestic product. In some countries it is considerably higher. Rather than forcing simplistic and often theoretical solutions on complex economic, social and political situations, the 'policy dialogue' might

213

be more constructively applied to the elementary question of military spending. Donor agencies could simply insist, for a start, that countries which spend more than say, two per cent of gross domestic product on arms will be ineligible for aid.

On the more complex question of economics, however, planners must recognize that Third World economies suffer from a number of severe non-market 'distortions' that affect the supply and demand of goods, services, and especially technology in perverse and negative ways. Economists should not, therefore, be allowed to get away with the idea that the advancement of technology has only to do with economics. It has also to do with attitudes, ideas, individuals and institutions. Getting the prices right is necessary, but alone, it is not enough to promote optimum technological change. Prices, after all, are only a means to an end; getting the priorities right is also essential.

Socio-economic distortions

If the problems which adjustment programmes address – price fixing, subsidies, overvalued exchange rates and inflation – are set aside (i.e. cured), there remain a number of socio-economic distortions which strongly affect the choice of technology. Different social groups, for example, have different access to technological change, to markets and to skill development, as other chapters in this book have demonstrated. Land tenure patterns can have a serious effect on the adoption of new technologies because of the need for economies of scale required to justify even simple scaling up from manual techniques to animal traction, or the introduction of a tube-well.

Distortions caused by attitudes are a particular problem, especially in Africa and Latin America. Large-scale production is often equated with modernity and development, while locally produced goods, the informal sector and small-scale labour-intensive technologies are regarded as inferior, or even as tools in a plot by the North to continue its subjugation of the South. Two examples from Ghana illustrate the problem. During the 1970s, the Technology Consultancy Centre developed locally made equipment for soap production. The only large-scale soap manufacturer, Lever Brothers – heavily dependent on imports for its production, had all but ceased operations by the mid-1980s, encouraging many small entrepreneurs to invest in the new technology. The trade liberalization that came with structural adjustment, however, allowed Lever Brothers to resume operations, and within months, the small soap manufacturers were out of business, their savings and livelihoods gone.

The cause was not price or quality; the local soap was cheaper and the quality was identical to that of the more popular Lux. The cause was attitudes, shaped by massive advertising campaigns, attractive packaging, perfume, and a pathological belief that foreign is better. The pervasiveness of this attitude can be seen in Ghanaian prices of the ultimate consumer icon, Coca Cola. If there is a single international product whose manufacturer prides itself on the uniformity of its quality, it is Coca Cola. In the 1970s, the company left India in a much-publicized high-level squabble rather than compromise the quality of its product. Yet in Ghana in 1991, locally produced Coca Cola sold for 150 cedis a bottle, while imported tins (made not in the United States, but in Ireland!) sold briskly alongside the bottled variety, for 250 cedis – a 66 per cent premium for 'foreign'.

Another example of the inability of markets to deal with technological choice is demonstrated in the world's electricity supplies, divided between 110 volt and 220 volt systems. Part of the world drives on the right, part on the left. There are broad gauge and narrow gauge railways, often in the same country. Steam and electricity were abandoned in the development of automobiles before the technologies that might have made them profitable had been properly developed, but railways are still powered by diesel and electricity, and in some cases by steam.

Further attitudinal problems are posed by the phenomena several writers have referred to as 'engineering man', 'economic man' and 'bureaucratic man'.[10] Engineering consultants, whether they work for government, donor agencies or the private sector, generally favour the most modern, technically efficient equipment which, in the international marketplace, is usually capital- rather than labour-intensive, is frequently urban-biased and of an inappropriate scale. Economists, unfamiliar with the technical aspects of a proposed solution to a problem, are understandably prone to accepting the 'best' engineering advice.

By the time a proposal reaches 'bureaucratic man' – an individual who is usually technologically conservative and traditionally averse to altering the status quo – the options have been substantially reduced and the decision is all but made. What influence he* retains, will normally be biased in favour of reducing the workload, especially in a situation where human resources are scarce and demands on time are severe. This places a premium on economies of scale rather than smaller projects which are more complex and require more time, more judgement, and greater risk. Risk avoidance, in fact, common to engineers, economists and bureaucrats alike, results from low tolerance in government for deviation, non-conformism and failure.

* Gender-specific references reflect the fact that most technological decision-making is still heavily male-dominated.

(Hirschman's 'perversity thesis' comes into play here: risk avoidance unfortunately encourages inappropriate and, in the final analysis, inherently more risky investments.) That engineers, economists and bureaucrats all veer naturally towards large-scale, inappropriate technologies has been demonstrated by Jeffrey James, who compared the very different development strategies of Tanzania and Kenya, and found much more similarity than difference in their technological choices.[11]

A final socio-economic distortion is worth mentioning again: corruption. Corruption is not unique to any particular time or place, as those who followed the Recruit scandal in Japan or the Savings and Loan collapse in the United States know. But it has a particularly pervasive influence on the choice of technology in the South, especially where purchases from the North are concerned. Third World officials are often insecure and badly paid. Decision-making is slow, files are lost and forms are unavailable. Procedures are interminable and simple transactions become impossible. In Brazil, obtaining an export license in one documented case required 1470 separate legal actions, and involved 13 government ministries and 50 agencies.[12] Hernando de Soto's example of registering a fictional small garment factory in Peru is similar. The pointlessness of the lengthy and costly exercise was demonstrated by the fact that none of the authorities involved ever realized they were dealing with a simulation.[13] Poverty, insecurity, rigid adherence to rules combined with a reluctance or an inability to delegate, weak rule of law, and an obsession with status, all lead to obvious temptation and predictable results. The Westinghouse nuclear plant scandal in the Philippines, the Bofors uproar in India, the Nigerian cement scandal of the 1970s, or the leasing by the German rocket corporation, OTRAG, of a part of Zaire larger than West Germany itself are all large, public examples of what can happen when unscrupulous salesmen come to town.[14]

Institutional distortions

Institutional distortions introduced by foreign equipment sellers are one thing. Foreign investors introduce another kind of technological distortion. As interested in reducing risk as the individual bureaucrat, corporate investors – usually in the form of multinational corporations – will, in the absence of pressure to do otherwise, import a known technical package, rather than attempt to develop something more appropriate locally. The known, usually made for applications in the North, is inevitably high in capital investment and low in labour intensity. It is big, not small; it is complex rather than simple.

216

And the linkages it will make within a Third World economy are likely to be limited. The trade-off between profit maximization and risk aversion is subjective, but it is very real for investors going into an uncertain situation, and it thus has very real technological implications.

Research and development provide an element of technology distortion more by their absence than their presence. Investment in agricultural research in the South is, at best, patchy. Heavily dependent on donor funding and adversely affected by economic fluctuations, national research institutions have focused more on export crops than food, and less on food crops grown and consumed by the poor than on those consumed in urban centres. The international agricultural institutions such as the International Rice Research Institute in the Philippines and the International Institute for Tropical Agriculture in Ibadan, have in recent years devoted greater attention to appropriate technologies, such as alley cropping and agroforestry, or small rice threshers. But appropriate technology is not their primary *raison d'être*. Some universities, such as Ghana's University of Science and Technology and the University of Zimbabwe, have opened dedicated technology institutions with a focus on appropriate and intermediate technologies, but in most Southern universities there is a lack of urgency and genuine practicality in research efforts.

Perhaps one of the greatest institutional distortions in the choice of technology can be found in the role played by multilateral and bilateral donor agencies – the very institutions most eager to remove distortions. In 1979, the ILO sponsored a study of donor influence in the choice of technology,[15] and in 1989 ITDG repeated the exercise in a questionnaire and detailed follow-up visits to some of the major donor agencies, including USAID, British ODA, the World Bank, the Inter American Development Bank, DANIDA, NORAD and the Netherlands Foreign Ministry.

The results were profoundly discouraging. It was found that although some agencies have technology advisors and vague technology guidelines, technology is, by and large, a non-issue. Donor agencies are prone to all of the engineering, economic and bureaucratic distortions mentioned above, but within a different context. The first aspect of this context has to do with the broad interests of the donor country. For example the British aid programme bears a distinct relationship to the evolution of the British shipbuilding, iron, steel, fertilizer and telecommunications industries. Canada's heavy assistance to the railway sectors of many Third World countries is closely allied to official support for railway-related industries in Canada. DANIDA's strong support for Third

World fishing and dairy sectors reflects obvious connections to some of the largest Danish industries.

Because donors have been heavily involved in certain sectors for many years, programmes become self-perpetuating. Such bias, while not inherently *wrong*, will push aid in a particular direction. As noted in Chapter III, for example, Canadian support for the transport sector in Bangladesh means railways;[16] for the Japanese it means bridges; for the British it may mean aircraft, while for other donors it means roads. What results is a programme of aid that is heavily skewed towards the mechanized sector, with none to the non-mechanized sector which accounts both for twice the carrying capacity and for 60 per cent of all employment generated in transportation.

The immutability of some types of aid notwithstanding, there is an ebb and flow of fads among donor agencies which can be very costly, especially where technology is concerned. In the mid-1970s, the World Bank, for example, was very keen on appropriate technology. A thick 1976 report on the subject, one of many, stated that 'the Bank recognizes the importance of stimulating appropriate technology and the need to do more in this field ... It is expected that Bank support for appropriate technology will have a significant long-term impact on the choice and effectiveness of technological operations in the developing world.'[17] Over the next fifteen years, the Bank, together with UNDP, did a significant amount of work on the development of appropriate technologies in the water and sanitation sectors. But by 1990, the Bank's Science and Technology unit had been dissolved and appropriate technology was more or less forgotten. As a general rule in Bank projects, and in line with the neo-classical thinking that underlies the issue of 'getting the prices right', technology is chosen according to least-cost criteria.

An indication of how macroeconomic issues have swamped more pointed strategies is provided in a comprehensive study of manufacturing in seven African countries. Although industrial development has always played a prominent role in African development thinking, and has a place in the World Bank's 1989 long-term perspective report, Roger Riddell says that,

> There is, sadly, *no* evidence to suggest that these words will be translated in practice into effective, consistent and reoriented policy recommendations to African governments which the Bank is hoping to influence ... What is more, in its list of six key strategies for African development in the 1990s, the role and place of industry is simply not mentioned. Finally, industrial sector country studies produced by the World Bank in the late 1980s were still dominated by policy advice based on macroeconomic management issues, the overriding importance

of market and price signals and the eclipsing of more interventionist strategies of industrial promotion.[18]

A second donor-created distortion in technology lies in the business of tied aid. Much has been written about tied aid, and efforts have been made by some agencies to untie some amounts. By and large, however, about three quarters of all bilateral assistance remains firmly tied, and a high proportion of the lending of international financial institutions is spent on hardware and services purchased in industrialized countries. Some of the distortions and disasters are well known, and have become public embarrassments. Britain's 1985 sale of 21 Westland W-30 helicopters to India, a deal concluded with great amounts of political arm-twisting, was essentially financed by deducting £65 million from the aid budget to India. A series of major engine malfunctions and one fatal crash led to all the helicopters being grounded within six years. A British ODA-funded jute mill in Indonesia was somehow regarded as a 'technical success' despite a critical shortage of spare parts and a miscalculation of labour availability which kept its utilization at less than one third of capacity. In 1983, an Italian contractor, funded through a $100 million EEC contract, built a road from Mogadishu to the port of Kismaayo. By 1988 the road was already impassable, even though the loan would not be repaid until 2023.[19] Japanese bilateral assistance is managed by four ministries, of which the Ministry of International Trade and Industry predominates. The result is a heavy emphasis on Japanese hardware in aid programmes, and a not uncoincidental subsequent commercial penetration in sectors opened by aid programmes.

A Canadian example, much beloved of Canadian investigative journalists, involved provision of a highly automated, Canadian-made bakery to Tanzania. Poorly designed, grossly overpriced, and purchased without consideration of other smaller, cheaper technologies already available in the region, the bakery became a beacon of inappropriate technology through tied aid. A study of Canadian aid to Tanzania observed that 'the economic costs to Tanzania and the domestic criticism CIDA has faced from media discussions should be sufficient to ensure that CIDA will not finance a similar mistake in Tanzania in the future'.[20]

Maybe not in Tanzania, but the feeble-minded donor approach to technology could be seen littering the floor of one of the GRATIS intermediate technology transfer units in 1991. Canada, long involved in rural development programmes in northern Ghana, required 350 handpumps over a five-year period for one of its projects. CIDA was already involved in supporting the development of a local pump-making capacity in Sri Lanka as well as in Togo, a few miles across the

219

Ghanaian border. It was also, as the main supporter of GRATIS, actively involved in the development of a light engineering capacity in Ghana. In reviewing the types of pump available, CIDA selected a design developed by the Swiss appropriate technology institution, SKAT. It was a model that could be repaired with relative simplicity by villagers, rather than professional technicians. So far, so appropriate. Then it was decided that the pumps had to be imported – from an Alberta firm with no track record in pump manufacture. Over a quarter of the pumps arrived with components that did not fit together. In a kind of 'fitting' irony, the parts had to be sent to GRATIS – for *five* separate machining and strengthening operations.[21]

A further problem for Third World countries in selecting distortion-proof technology is the paucity of information for good decision-making. Weak research institutions, inadequate libraries, small or non-existent travel budgets and limited skill levels mean that decision-makers are often very limited in the choices apparently available, or that they become heavily reliant on consultants and aid agencies, prone to all the problems mentioned above.

And, finally, there is the enormous distortion imposed by a country's power and influence structure. In an effort to maintain its support from key lobby groups within society (few of them representing the poor), a government may promote particular types of modernization, growth, research and development with inherent and strong biases towards the modern formal sector, and away from more appropriate types of investment. It may seem incredible that a bureaucrat or a politician would promote a smaller number of expensive houses, say, over cheaper shelter for more people, but where the poor have no voice, where the media are tame and parliaments weak, such decisions are far from uncommon.

Back to the future: policy options

Given donors' fixation with macroeconomic issues, and given their own prominent involvement in the transfer of inappropriate technologies, suggesting policy options for either donors or Third World governments is a bit like shouting into a hurricane. Perhaps the place to start is with the very idea of policy options. Despite the fashionable loathing for government meddling, much of this book has attempted to show that pragmatic government interventions, developed on a case-by-case approach, are both necessary and possible. This is *not* to suggest that 'getting the prices right' is a bad thing, but that getting the prices right, in itself, is not enough. As Lewis Mumford observed over 50 years ago, 'the gains in technics are

220

never registered automatically in society; they require equally adroit inventions and adaptations in politics.'[22]

Governments have, in fact, always been involved in technological change, from ancient times to modern, from industrialized Western nations to the newly industrialized countries of Asia. They compensate for market failure, they organize trade fairs and exhibitions, they create grant mechanisms, tax havens and research institutions. They create policy and they enforce it, and they also help in establishing society's attitudes towards innovators. The future of technological development in the South, especially in the poorest countries, will be determined to a large extent by the incentives and stimuli of the policy environment in which key players operate.

As noted in other chapters, education and credit can be important engines for poverty reduction, growth and the development of a technological capacity. In many countries these have been skewed, in access, volume and cost, in favour of the better off. They have been standardized for economies that will never be standard, and they have been designed to assist large-scale farmers and large-scale industry. Targeted interventions aimed at removing past distortions, and encouraging the development and adoption of appropriate technologies, are not inconsistent with more general reforms at a macroeconomic level. Nor are they historically inconsistent with the capacity-building technology interventions of governments in industrialized and newly industrialized countries.

Taxation and investment: a level playing field

Governments encourage the establishment of new business ventures, both local and foreign, through a variety of incentives which include special tax holidays, tax reductions and deductions, customs exemptions, guarantees, special permissions and protection from imports. Frances Stewart points out that because governments tend to sweeten the package in accordance with the size of the investment, the playing field is usually tilted in favour of large-scale investors, and concomitantly more inappropriate technologies. Citing studies of industry in the Philippines and Thailand, she notes that firms benefiting from government promotion packages enjoyed a cost reduction factor of between 35 per cent and 39 per cent over non-promoted firms – all local and mostly small – and that semi-advanced technology had a further advantage over intermediate technology among those that were assisted.[23]

Some of the disadvantage suffered by microenterprise has to do with the definition of capital goods and the tax or duty attached to them. A lathe, clearly intended for industrial purposes, may be given

preferential customs treatment, whereas tools used by microenterprises – hammers, planes, saws, sewing machines, bicycles, outboard
motors – may be regarded as consumer items and taxed at a higher
rate. Wittingly or unwittingly, the Philippines, for example, encouraged tractorization in the 1970s, by eliminating all duties on tractors,
but maintaining a 19 per cent duty on power tillers.[24]

Many governments have begun to place greater emphasis on small-
scale enterprise development. Too often, however, this is a piecemeal
effort, a sideline to the main objectives of industrial promotion. In
countries where it is more than a sideline, the impact has been
significant. In Costa Rica, for example, the government made a
conscious decision, within the context of a severe adjustment
programme, to foster and encourage both small-scale industries and
the development of appropriate technologies. A comprehensive plan,
introduced in 1987, was based on the government's view that 'the
market by itself does not assure that social objectives such as equity,
reduction of extreme poverty, and increased social mobility are
achieved'. Because of its job-creation potential and its linkages to
other parts of the economy, small-scale enterprise was therefore
placed on a more equal footing with large-scale enterprise, in part
because of government's intention to 'support ... the process of
adapting and generating appropriate technology to create a broad
scientific base, with which Costa Rica can become a country that
exports goods and services with a high technological content by the
twenty first century.'[25]

Technology assessment

The ability to assess technological alternatives is as important to
government as it is to a corporation, or to a farmer attempting to
decide between one seed and another. All technology leads to
unforseen results and complications; technology assessment is an
attempt to minimize the negative effects of a particular choice.
Technology assessment was transformed from an everyday event into
a formal discipline in the late 1960s, when the United States Congress
passed an act requiring an assessment of the environmental impact of
those technologies and technological activities within the purview of
the federal government.

Ernst Braun defines technology assessment as,

> an attempt to discover all the ramifications and effcts which a
> technology is likely to have when it is in full use. . . . The study must be
> interdisciplinary in nature, requiring knowledge and insights from
> engineering and both the natural and social sciences. Both beneficial
> and harmful effects need to be described and alternative policies for

dealing with this or rival technologies should be elaborated. Groups likely to be benefitted or harmed should be identified and the study must be carried out impartially, both with respect to technologies and to social groups.[26]

This may seem a tall order, and as Braun notes, 'nobody pretends that is possible to foresee all the ramifications of a technology.' But without it, the haphazard hit-and-miss approach of the past is unlikely to change. A 1991 science and technology study of seven countries in Southern Africa found that virtually all production technologies were imported, many of them highly inappropriate to the needs they purported to address. Although all the countries had a variety of sectoral science and technology policies, these were fragmented and inadequate. Only two countries, Tanzania and Zambia, had a ministry of science and technology, and one of these was less than a year old. The minimal efforts at technology assessment in these and many other Third World countries, and within most aid agencies, can only benefit from greater emphasis.

Laws and standards

A wide range of regulations and laws has important bearing on the choice of technology. Genuine interest in microenterprise development and the growth of technological capacity requires an *enabling* regulatory environment; one that establishes reasonable, enforceable standards, but which encourages rather than discourages talent and industry. The fact that the Kenya Standards Bureau approved fibre concrete roofing tiles was one step in the product's advancement as a commercially viable roofing material. The next appropriate step might be the banning of super-thin 19mm corrugated galvanized iron sheets, which absorb great amounts of foreign exchange and which rust within four years.

In China, the official recognition and approval of six different standards of cement made the development of mini-cement plants much easier than it was in India, where only one standard was permitted. The comparative savings in investment, the increase in job creation, and the growth in cement output were enormous. Encouragement is one thing, protection for successful investments is another. James Watt observed that 'an engineer's life without patents is not worthwhile.' Many appropriate technologies cannot be patented, but some can. The Botswana Technology Centre, for example, has developed an inexpensive, battery-powered borehole water level sensor which has high export potential. Although patent protection for the sensor is available internationally, it is not, ironically, available in Botswana.

Many countries have enacted or inherited laws which are directly antagonistic to microenterprise development and appropriate technology. In Zimbabwe, for example, the Factories and Works Act imposes building, water, drainage and sewage regulations that are virtually impossible for small entrepreneurs to meet. Health, hygiene and safety regulations are enforced without adequate reference to the purposes for which they were established. In many countries, such laws are observed in the breach, but remain available as tools to be used against the informal sector when, on occasion, it overflows its geographic, economic or political boundaries.

In short, it is incumbent on governments to cut red tape. This means simplifying procedures, regulations and permissions. It means reconsidering such things as value-added taxes on small transactions, and rethinking labour regulations which, if complied with, would simply put many small businesses out of business. It means revising laws and regulations that impede innovation in new and appropriate technologies; it means using incentives and disincentives to encourage appropriate technological change. And it means support for research and development into appropriate technologies, as well as the use of government procurement to encourage them.

A final note on regulations involves the question of non-tariff barriers to trade. Europe and North America have made a fine art of excluding competitive Third World products from their markets by establishing long lists of quotas, requirements, tests and standards. These present deliberate barriers that most Third World manufactures simply cannot surmount. Non-tariff barriers could perhaps be studied to advantage by Third World countries seeking tools to fend off the inexorable southward flow of mass-produced Northern manufactures.

Attitudes

In attempting to determine why some societies have advanced technologically and others have not, technology historian Joel Mokyr places considerable emphasis on values, and a society's willingness to accept change. He observes that the ancient Greeks valued sports and learning, while the Romans emphasized military and administrative ability. While both societies appreciated wealth, being brave or wise was equally, if not more, important. The exclusion of large parts of society from the development and benefit of these values – slaves, the poor, women – had, and continues to have a major limiting effect on their spread and general acceptance. Historically, the greater the chasm between the values of the educated, literate classes and the working portions of a population, the greater the negative impact on the development and diffusion of technology.[27]

At a more mundane level, it is hard to know what to say about the price of Ghanaian Coca Cola being less desireable than the Irish variety.[28] Regardless of what the World Bank and the IMF say about liberalization, there is a strong case to be made for taxing the advantage out of such a bizarre import. In the long run, however, only education, public awareness (including advertising) and a pride in things Ghanaian will take the place of tariffs. This should not be left to chance. Some very appropriate technologies have failed through inadequate promotion. The disastrous Canadian bakery in Tanzania might never have been built if the makers and promoters of smaller-scale bakeries had their antennae up.

The importance of quality and of taste should not be diminished, however. Toyota, Nissan and Mitsubishi learned this lesson well, much to the chagrin of Chrysler, Ford and General Motors. To deny that the customer is at least sometimes right is to deny history. Too often what is regarded as an 'appropriate technology' is poorly finished or unprofessionally packaged. Some appropriate technology is regarded as second class because it looks second class. And some is labelled third class because it does not work. The Zimbabwean *tso tso* was successful, at least in part because it was attractively designed and painted, and was sold in hardware stores along with other acceptable products rather than in roadside stalls. The 'new, improved' Kenyan ceramic *jiko* also had a certain cachet about it. Had there been time and assistance for Ghana's small-scale soapmakers, they might have been able to add inexpensive perfume and an attractive wrapping to their product before Lever Brothers drove them out of business. Professional finishing and competent marketing are essential ingredients of successful technology development.

Institutions

Institutions have played an important part in the development and transfer of technology throughout history. Because the poor are under-represented in places where decisions are made, however, they are simply not heard, and an appropriate technology that might benefit them often receives little attention. Special efforts are required to ensure that small producers have adequate access to credit, raw materials, agricultural inputs and foreign exchange. In Zimbabwe in 1991, tin shortages were particularly hard on informal sector tin-smiths, for whom tin was the source of their entire livlihood. Because of the political strength of formal sector manufacturers, however, small-scale users were ignored. A similar situation prevailed in Ghana in 1985, with regard to foreign exchange. At the time, an auction system was in use, but there were minimum amounts for which one could bid. Even if small entrepreneurs – in need of something as basic as welding rods, available across the border in Togo – knew how the system operated, their needs were so small that they were simply excluded from the system.

In the South, much modern technology development has been relegated to research institutes which have limited mandates and inadequate resources. Too much emphasis on research and an inappropriate balance of skills often lead to impractical or irrelevant work. Governments and donors need to exert more pressure on these institutions, and particularly on the larger international research bodies to place greater emphasis on issues related to poverty. More research is needed, for example, on tree crops – nuts, fruit, fuel, oil – that can survive on poor land. More work needs to be done on technologies that reduce the need for pesticides and herbicides.

NGOs, which have broader mandates and better resources than many national research institutions, and more practical output, are often less disciplined. They have weaker institutional memories, and are less able (or less willing) to work with governments and the private sector. NGOs may work towards 'empowerment', but most have serious problems of scale. NGOs are favourably disposed towards the concept of appropriate technology, but with notable exceptions, most have very little technology awareness. Somehow this must change.

Co-ordination seems an obvious solution, but 'co-ordination' is another of those words so frequently used in development circles that its meaning has all but evaporated in hot air. To suggest that better co-ordination is required between research organizations, educational institutions, government agencies and departments, donors, NGOs and the private sector is to state something so seemingly obvious, yet so seldom done, that the idea may be a waste of time. Because organizations are so loathe to share and to listen, many genuine attempts at co-ordination wind up placing more emphasis on the process of co-ordinating than on content.

There are, however, glimmers of hope on which interested groups and institutions could build. The GEMINI Project,[29] for example, is funded by USAID to explore micro- and small- scale enterprise development. The project is managed by a Washington-based private sector firm, Development Alternatives Inc., with a core consortium and affiliates drawn from the academic, private and non-governmental sectors. Leaders in the development of small-scale credit, such as ACCION International, work with appropriate technology institutions like Technoserve, ATI and ITDG. Somehow, the natural disinclination of such groups to work together has been overcome, and some of the most advanced thinking and activity in micro- and small-scale enterprise development is the result. The service that GEMINI provides to those interested in such subjects extends well beyond the American development community and will far outlive an individual project's limited time frame.

The United Nations Development Fund for Women, UNIFEM, is a multilateral variation on the same theme. It works in association with other United Nations agencies, but is also closely allied with a wide range of research, bilateral and non-governmental organizations, with a primary programming emphasis on small enterprise and informal sector development, appropriate technology and innovative credit programmes for poor women.

Another example can be found in Botswana, where a 1990 study recognized the inadequacy and costliness of the country's fragmented approach to science and technology, but saw the weakness in other countries' attempts to create formal research or policy institutions.[30] The study acknowledged that Botswana did not yet have 'the capacity to effectively identify, acquire, adapt, develop, service and use science and technology', and that a policy was required which could 'guide national action for technological transformation, and in particular to reduce the country's state of technological dependency'. The study saw needs in several areas: human resource development, economy and production, the need for consistent and appropriate standards and legislation, research and development, information and public awareness, and institutional development. It also recognized that there were greater or lesser degrees of expertise in some or all of these areas, and proposed a short-, medium- and long-range plan. Rather than create yet more institutions, the plan would bring key officials from government, the private and non-governmental sectors, and the educational community together in a variety of co-ordinated fora for the development, co-ordination and control of a thoughtful and genuinely national policy on science and technology.

Without such a policy, a country is left with a loose set of funding programmes, *ad hoc* co-operation between universities, industry and government, and a lot of windy rhetoric. The development of a technological capacity and of technologies appropriate to the needs of any country is dependent upon the institutional, economic and social environment in which they grow. For technology to advance, a government needs good information on the scientific and technological aspects of its economy and infrastructure. Policy makers, administrators and the private sector must be able to recognize and act upon the technological aspects of their work. This requires training, co-ordination, the sharing of information. It means that when opportunities and problems arise, genuine alternatives are considered and weighed openly. It means that there must be good interaction between engineers, economic planners, entrepreneurs and social anthropologists. Such factors are the hallmarks of any society in which technology is effectively harnessed as a tool for development. In countries where technology has not been institutionalized, but where it is nevertheless an essential key to the reduction and elimination of poverty, they are even more critical.

CHAPTER XV

Mastering the machine

These are the days of miracle and wonder; this is the long-distance call.
                                                                    Paul Simon

THIS BOOK IS about the interaction between poverty, aid and technology. It is about machines and machinery: the machines that produce nuts and bolts, as well as the machinery of governments and organizations. It has attempted to show the correlation between poverty reduction and different approaches to technology, and has traced the role of aid in the process. The book has described successful and unsuccessful projects aimed in the general direction of poverty reduction, but it has so far avoided the more generic aspects of success and failure.

The importance of success

The world is engaged in a war, and the enemy is poverty, an enemy which robs adults of their youth and children of their lives. Each day, 40 000 children die of ordinary malnutrition and preventable disease, more in a year than all the people who live in the Netherlands. Hundreds of millions of individuals survive in squalor, illness and hopelessness, on the edge of an economic abyss. Poverty saps people and nations of their vitality and their dignity; it creates political instability, exacerbates ethnic tension and contributes to irreversible environmental damage. As a new millennium begins, there can be no more important international objective than to deal effectively and decisively with this scourge of the last one.

Yet viewed from the trenches, the war against poverty seems a half-hearted one. So incomplete is our knowledge, so careless our approach and so weak our resolve, that we are unsure if the number of absolute poor is a billion, or half again that number. Our generals have little direct contact with the enemy, and rarely visit the forward command posts. Skirmishes and pitched battles take place along a front which changes from time to time, but there are few meaningful advances. Sometimes the generals bring up heavy artillery and mass troops against what they think is a soft point. And sometimes they succeed in breaking through enemy lines. The eradication of smallpox, for example, was a battle that ended in a spectacular victory. The multi-billion dollar investment in integrated rural development, however, left the front virtually unaltered. In some cases, the enemy breaches our poorly defended barricades. The result is increased environmental damage, war, refugees, chaos, government breakdown, and failure of the rule of law.

After years of low-level warfare, both the generals and the public have become shell-shocked, inured to battle. Part of the problem is that we have been conditioned to believe in the 'big breakthrough' – the cure for cancer or AIDS; the miracle food, the miracle drug, the miracle economic solution. As Michael Lipton has observed, scientists, like economists, prefer *interesting* problems to *important* problems. This explains why some donors have 'found the solution' to poverty in credit, and the solution to credit in minimalism. Others have found it in 'getting the prices right' and the quick fix of the market place. Beguiled by a misplaced belief in the big breakthrough, African governments spent vast resources on what they hoped would be a great leap forward into industrialization, at the precise historical moment when the prices for their exports began to fall, passing the price of oil on its way up.

There is, unfortunately, no miracle drug; no sudden cure for cancer or AIDS. In health, as in all fields of human endeavour, advances are made by individuals working long and hard, for years, in dozens of countries, barking up wrong tree after wrong tree until – occasionally – they find the right one. Sometimes their hard work is lost – through accident or malice. Sometimes it pays off through sheer good luck. There is a story about Norman Borlaug beginning his first trials with a cross-bred dwarf wheat in Mexico, the wheat that led directly to the start of the Asian green revolution only five years later. What subsequently became known as a 'miracle' wheat was hit during that first planting by a rust, and the entire crop was lost. Distraught, Borlaug checked the seed bags, and to his great relief, found a few kernels in one. The descendants of the kernels in that bag are being planted today by millions of farmers around the world.

Humans love drama; we enjoy tales of discovery, and so the 'big breakthrough' version of history has special appeal. Brought up on a cinematic diet of Mickey Rooney as young Tom Edison, Ralph Richardson as Frank Whittle inventing the jet engine, and Curt Jurgens as Wernher von Braun, Europeans and North Americans are especially impatient for quick results. Their comic-book version of science and the rewards of hard work is reinforced by life in a world of seemingly quick results, a world of ever-changing, ever-improving consumer goods – computers, video recorders, fax machines, silicon chips, CD players and microwave ovens. With so much progress around them, it is little wonder that they become impatient with decades of promises from Oxfam, CARE and UNICEF, promises clearly at odds with the consistently negative daily headlines from the Third World.

There is another reason for public impatience, and it lies at the heart of the way the development community conducts its affairs. Bilateral donor agencies couch budgetary requests to their parliaments and Congress in terms of the impact of their work on the reduction of poverty. That great slices of their budgets never actually leave the home country, that much is spent on inappropriate goods and services – as an expensive means of achieving limited commercial and political objectives, that an infinitesimally small portion is actually devoted to direct poverty reduction programmes is seldom mentioned. The public affairs departments of multilateral and bilateral agencies, effusive about their poverty-alleviation efforts, recall Madame Roland's famous cry, 'Oh Liberty! How many crimes are committed in thy name!' When the results show that the Third World has slipped ever deeper into poverty, legislators, journalists and the public become understandably suspicious about whether the money is 'actually getting to those who need it most'.

Fuelled with the hypocrisy of donor agencies, this public cynicism is stoked by the image-making and the unrealistic claims of many non-governmental organizations. Their most striking appeals are for disaster relief, which creates the basis for an image of hopelessness in the Third World. Their general fundraising appeals then suggest that development is cheap, simple and quick. This approach has encouraged a lot of donations over the years, but its appeal is wearing thin. There is talk of 'aid fatigue' among the public. Perhaps the issue, however, is not aid fatigue, but fatigue with aid agencies.

The cheap-simple-and-quick approach to fundraising has spilled over into the professional arena as well, with NGOs making their proposals to bilateral agencies and foundations in precisely the same way. In order to 'sell' a project, unrealistic claims are made about what can be achieved with limited funds and low administrative overheads, usually in only two or three years. High expectations are raised, which must then – only a year or so later when more funding is required – be supported by positive results. Failure (or more likely, in the short space of time available, lack of demonstrable success) is therefore concealed for fear of jeopardizing funding. Successes are exaggerated accordingly. As publicity departments become more fulsomely positive (with limited reference to past errors, now happily corrected), external reporting on the aid business becomes increasingly negative. In *The Lords of Poverty*, one of the most popular and unsettling books on the aid business in a decade, Graham Hancock begins with a dedication to senior World Bank staff who obtained an early synopsis, and who attempted to limit his access to information. They convinced him that 'the aid business does indeed have much to hide'.

When the means bear little direct relationship to the ends, when targets are unduly exaggerated, and when further funding is directly related to the achievement of impossible goals, a premium on dishonest reporting is the natural outcome. Worse, after two or three decades of it, aid workers have begun to believe their own publicity material. Governments resist reports of failure; civil servants fall deaf and mute; the budgets of publicity departments soar.[1] But development is not a publicity challenge. It is a real test of real skills, ingenuity and committment. It is the most crucial test facing this generation and will probably be the most crucial issue for the next two or three.

In some ways, the appropriate technology movement has been fortunate in remaining on the fringe of 'mainstream development thinking'. This has happened for two important reasons. The first is that Fritz Schumacher said it would be straightforward, and it was not. He said that if you got the technology right, everything else would fall into place. But it didn't. The second is that appropriate technologists sometimes have difficulty pointing to the 'big success stories'. There are, of course, many, some described in this book. Hundreds of thousands of increasingly inexpensive handpumps have made life infinitely better for poor people in dozens of countries. Similar numbers of cheap latrines have prevented disease, and millions of lives have been saved through the development of oral rehydration therapy. Better living conditions have ensued, and millions of jobs have been created in the manufacture and construction of these technologies, and in the production of fuel-efficient stoves, or in the increased output of high-yielding varieties of wheat and rice. Important contributions have been made through the production and availability of low-cost cement, cheap electricity, inexpensive, durable building materials; in the production of small farm implements and windmills. The creation and maintenance of tens of thousands of miles of rural roads has created jobs and improved living standards for entire communities. Success can be found in both the large numbers like these, and in the single application. A cheap loom can make all the difference between a family's poverty and prosperity. The same is true of improved potters' wheels, of new tools for carpenters and blacksmiths, better ovens for bakers, and boats for fishing families.

But while these achievements, big or otherwise, are important, in a sense the small incremental achievements that eventually made them possible are even more important. The six small iron foundries established by GRATIS and the Technology Consultancy Centre in Ghana between 1986 and 1991 created perhaps two dozen jobs and turned out a lot of corn-mill grinding plates that could have been bought in Europe for a few thousand dollars. But those foundries were probably more important to the future of Ghana's industrial development than almost any other technology imported or developed there in the previous twenty years. They opened a door to the *local* design and manufacture of machines, a fundamental advance on repairs and simple metal fabrication.

Adequate time for product development and diffusion is also a critical element. It took centuries for the heavy plough to become widely accepted in Europe. It was a century and a half after the first Montgolfier balloon flights that commercial air travel became a real possibility. Without five years of development work, the humble fuel-efficient Sri Lankan stove would never have made it into the marketplace. Without ten years of dogged persistence and the constant refinements of John Parry, fibre concrete roofing tiles might, after the initial experiments, have become just another failed effort.

Technique – invisible in the annual report of an appropriate technology organization – is often more important than the technology. A small change in the way a bolt is made, for example, can make the difference between the possible and the impossible, the economic and the uneconomic.

If the invention of the steamboat had been an aid project, we might still be limited to sail. The failed experiments of Robert Fitch and others would have ensured the cancellation of funding, and fifteen years later Robert Fulton might still have been in the rope-making business where he began. On the other hand, something entirely different might have happened. In Chapter III, the complete lack of donor interest in Bangladesh's non-motorized transportation sector was lamented. Faced with increasing competition from the growing number of mechanized river craft, a few country boat owners began to experiment in the mid-1980s with small 12 to 16 horsepower diesel irrigation pump engines – normally not used during the monsoon. With a few modifications and the addition of a shaft and propeller, they found that sails were no longer necessary. A simultaneous reduction in import duties on pump engines helped fuel a transportation revolution unlike anything seen in the Ganges-Brahmaputra delta in the past century. Within five years, 75 per cent of the country boats – thousands of them – had been mechanized. Without a penny from an aid agency, one of the last great survivors of the age of sail had passed into history.[2]

What a tangled web: the importance of failure

There is no shame in honest efforts that fail. Failure is a common feature of small business the world over. Product failure is known to every manufacturer in every country. Among car makers, 'Edsel' is synonymous with failure. Charles Goodyear, who invented the vulcanization process for rubber in 1839, died a pauper. Leonardo Da Vinci, one of the greatest technologists of his era, never published a word of his thousands of pages of engineering notes.[3] And everyone who works in the field of international development lives with failure on a daily basis. Yet because of the premium that has been placed on dishonesty, these failures are rarely acknowledged and seldom studied. The lessons they have to teach remain hidden, and the inability to admit failure breeds an inability to learn from failure.

This is especially true of investments in social development, where returns are difficult to calculate and weaknesses are correspondingly easier to obscure. It is also true of large-scale infrastructural development, not because returns are difficult to calculate, but because the final net return is often not apparent for years, until everyone associated with the project is safely ensconced elsewhere. The impassable road that Somalians will pay for until 2023 is one example of this. Another is the multi-billion dollar investments made in integrated rural development in the 1970s. Many of those projects, which included expensive foreign advisers, and which were covered by loans that children not yet born will have to pay off, were abandoned not because they failed. They failed because they were abandoned. Many could have been salvaged if donor agencies and governments had been willing to learn the lessons they had to teach, and if they had been willing to wait for the lessons to become clear. But they were abandoned because the development wheel had turned another quarter revolution; new planners and new economists had new and better ideas about development.

Wheels are thus reinvented time after time, until wheel invention becomes a virtue in itself. Insiders no longer think to question the wastefulness of demonstration projects that demonstrate nothing. Monitoring reports tell us that the wheel is a good one, not that it was never required. Evaluations tell us that the locomotives sent to Bangladesh work or do not work; but do not say if locomotives were a good or bad idea. Given the size of the problem that development agencies tackle, and given the state of the world, the elusiveness of success should not be a surprise, nor is failure really a secret. But treated as a secret by aid agencies, failure attracts the curiosity of reporters. And the most zealous reporters, taking publicity material produced for taxpayers and donors at face value, naturally produce sensational stories, adding to the tangled web of public misunderstanding.

Southern governments

Southern governments, of course, bear the ultimate responsibility for what happens within the borders of their countries, whether they are able to control events, or not. This book has made the point that much of what happens in the South actually lies beyond the control of Southern governments. This is not to suggest, however, that they are helpless, nor that they should be absolved from responsibility for many of the errors of the past. As Tony Killick observes, 'government actions are often not an expression of the general good. Frequently they are particularistic, promoting the interests of special groups: the armed forces; landowners and/or businessmen; the urban against the rural population, and so on.'[4] Inefficiency and poor financial performance have persisted, and are unlikely to change overnight. Many countries have promoted inappropriate industry and neglected agriculture, looking inward rather than to regional or global opportunities. Limited as the options may have been, even the existing few have often been ignored.

Although perhaps over-emphasized in Northern thinking, corruption and 'rent seeking' in the South cannot be dismissed as irrelevant or inevitable. Democracy is another thorny issue. Responsible government has proved remarkably durable in many countries – Jamaica, India, Senegal and Botswana, to name four. In others, such as Peru, Brazil and Chile, it repeatedly survives the generals who pre-empt it. But in too many countries, including some of the 'Newly Industrialized Countries', political repression, one-party governments and military regimes have been the order of the day. It was authoritarian regimes which, to a large extent, negotiated the loans that triggered the debt crisis of the 1980s.

Democracy, justice, honesty and respect for human rights are not concepts alien to the South, nor are they things which can be imposed from outside. But they can be encouraged and supported through assistance to social movements and non-governmental organizations, and through financial and technical support to other pluralistic institutions. With stronger mandates and better support, the United Nations, regional organizations, and non-governmental bodies such as Amnesty International and the International Commission of Jurists could play more prominent and effective roles in monitoring elections, in monitoring the observance of human rights and democratic institutions. Recognition of the importance of these things, and of where ultimate responsibility lies, however, is clear. It was expressed succinctly in the final paragraph of the 1990 Report of the South Commission, chaired by the former President of Tanzania, Julius Nyerere:

> In the final analysis, the South's plea for justice, equity, and democracy in the global society cannot be dissociated from its pursuit of these goals within its own societies. Commitment to democratic values, respect for fundamental rights – particularly the right to dissent – fair treatment for minorities, concern for the poor and underprivileged, probity in public life, willingness to settle disputes without recourse to war – all these cannot but influence world opinion and increase the South's chances of securing a new world order.[5]

Donor organizations

In the absence of fair, intelligent and consistent approaches to the issue of technology by large bilateral and multilateral donor agencies, and in light of the single-minded enthusiasm with which they pursue policy lending, despair might seem the most logical response. Writing about agricultural development, Michael Lipton suggests that adjustment looms large in donor thinking, not because of structural disequilibria, but because of a project fatigue within donor organizations themselves:

> An exaggerated, over-generalized sense on the part of donors that 'their' agro-rural projects have failed is joined to an exaggerated attribution of failures not to project design, but to wrong macro policies ... Add the belief that donor loans and conditions can enable, or push recipients to 'get the policies right' – and must do so before agro-rural project lending can usefully grow again – and the paradox of donor persistence with unsuccessful adjustment lending is partly explained.[6]

Lipton argues that there is clearly a place for adjustment lending and programme support, but it should not take the place of carefully selected, *technically sound* projects.

For those donors unable or unwilling to make changes in their own policies, but who are interested in technology development, it may make sense to simply focus on a few critical areas in which appropriate technology may be advanced. Well aimed rifle shots are more likely to strike a target than a handful of bullets tossed into a campfire. The function-based approach, discussed in Chapter XII, is one kind of rifle shot. The GEMINI work on micro and small-scale enterprise development is an example. The dedicated focus on credit by Grameen Bank in Bangladesh, BKK in Indonesia or ACCION International in Latin America is another.

The sectoral approach is a different kind of rifle shot. The sectoral approach focuses comprehensively on a key area – such as silk production in Bangladesh – which can involve large numbers of poor people and which can attract government attention at a policy level. Chapter XI suggested another sector: light engineering and the manufacture of machines – oil presses, wood-turning lathes, brick moulds, corn-milling machines, rice huskers, hammer mills and the like. Historically, machine design, fabrication and adaptation have been a critical part of the evolution of mechanical industries in the North. And as the Ghana case shows, light engineering can develop key linkages with the more modern, formal sector as well as with agriculture. For a donor organization, there is a further advantage. By focusing on machine *makers* rather than machine *users*, the cross-sectoral and multiplier effect of the intervention can increase exponentially.

Non-governmental organizations

Alone, most large donor organizations are unsuited to labour-intensive small-scale interventions that require programming flexibility and time. If poverty reduction is to be given greater prominence in their spending, if more appropriate technologies are to be developed and used, new and improved programming mechanisms will be required. One of these is support to non-governmental organizations. NGOs are a key source of research and development for appropriate technologies, techniques and approaches. Some of the most promising experiments and examples of 'scaling up' have been conducted by organizations like the Bangladesh Rural Advancement Committee, the Self Employed Women's Association of India, Grameen Bank, CARE and Oxfam. However, there is a tremendous amount of wasteful duplication and amateurism among NGOs. There is much competition for funding and 'territory', a lack of cohesion, and poor institutional memory – all of which contribute to intellectual sloppiness and the ritual re-invention of wheels. This is particularly and increasingly true of Northern NGOs, which are in danger of losing their *raison d'être* as their developmental legitimacy is appropriated by their Southern counterparts, and as bilateral organizations encroach on their funding role.

Those non-governmental organizations that can overcome traditional NGO abhorrence of the profit motive perhaps have an increasingly important role to play with microenterprises. Profit – the surplus of income over expenditure – is the vulgar word for what most good NGOs have practiced for years under the polite term, 'income generation'. In an unfavourable climate for micro-entrepreneurs and in situations of market failure, NGOs have often been the innovators, the entrepreneurs, the carriers and developers of technology. They have struggled against almost insurmountable political odds and have been used, abused, ignored and then lionized by the official aid community, depending on the fashion of the day. But in many of the poorest countries, something else is going on. The climate for microenterprise development has improved, and the informal sector is receiving more attention and support. NGOs must therefore be prepared to change roles, to become facilitators for real entrepreneurs, rather than to act as entrepreneurs themselves. With care, and with the development of strategic alliances among themselves, with small-scale entrepreneurs and perhaps with parts of the academic and research communities, the investments they have already made stand to pay large dividends.

BRAC's creation of a large-scale self-financing credit operation for the poor is one example of how some NGOs are becoming increasingly professional. Another is taking place in Bolivia, where the non-profit development foundation, PRODEM, is transforming a successful micro-business credit programme into a private commercial bank. Between 1987 and 1990, PRODEM made 50 000 small loans totalling $8 million, and had only two unrecoverable loans. Such is the size of Bolivia's informal and micro-entrepreneurial sector, however, that by 1991 the foundation had outstripped the supportive capacity of donor agencies. The transformation from non-profit to commercial is therefore being underwritten by the same Bolivian entrepreneurs who supported PRODEM from its inception, with technical support from two Northern NGOs specializing in credit and microenterprise development.

Another area of vital importance is the environment. Northern environmental agencies have been very successful in getting environmental issues onto the agenda of development organizations. But the reverse – getting poverty reduction and development onto the agenda of environmental organizations – has not happened to any great extent. Individually, development and environmental agencies may each be able to point to success stories. Together, forming strategic alliances and using their comparative advantages, they could be infinitely more effective. Madagascar's Environmental Action Plan (EAP) is an example of what can be done. Deforestation, soil erosion, a crippling debt burden and a constricting structural adjustment programme had, by the mid-1980s, combined to eliminate any serious long-term government environmental planning or spending. Working with the government and local NGOs, however, the World Wildlife Fund developed a long-term plan that involved a range of small projects and policy-level initiatives. It included things that directly benefitted poor people in remote areas: small-scale irrigation and reforestation; technical assistance to agriculture; livestock and forestry extension workers; a small-scale credit programme; rationalization of land tenure; environmental education; the establishment of institutional structures that facilitate rather than block the programme. High-level political support was necessary, but when it was obtained, it drew in the necessary funding support from UNDP, UNESCO, the World Bank, USAID and Co-operation Suisse. In 1986, the budget for Madagascar's national nature reserves was only $1000, or an incredible $25 a year for each 'protected' area. By 1989, courtesy of the EAP, a fund estimated at $130 million had been established for the next two decades.[7]

More and more Southern NGOs, like BRAC, PRODEM and those in Madagascar, are moving forward into new programming areas – geographical, social, technical or policy-oriented. If they are to succeed, they will need assistance, and they will need greater recognition. Sustained financial assistance is one thing; few Southern NGOs have a large or secure domestic funding base. Good publicity is another. But genuine political recognition and support is a different matter entirely. Despite the fear some governments have of NGOs, strong, pluralistic societies need the challenge, the alternatives and the debate that vibrant NGOs can provide.

This is as true in the North as it is in the South, perhaps even more so where international development is concerned. In 1991, the British Charity Commissioners censured Oxfam for taking sides in foreign political controversies and for attempting to influence British aid policies. They found that 'It cannot be acceptable for any charity to run public campaigns against the policy of any government (whether at home or abroad), nor can a resulting increase of support and donations ever be a justification or an amelioration of the offence.'[8] Many British journalists agreed. Writing in the London *Evening Standard*, Piers Paul Read criticized 'the view among some charities that the misfortunes of the Third World are somehow the fault of the First World.'[9] And yet the solution offered by Read was precisely the same one offered by Lester Pearson in 1969, Willy Brandt in 1979, Gro Harlem Brundtland in 1987, and by any serious NGO attempting to convince its donors that genuine development requires more than a £5 donation: the solution he offered was 'a stable world economy in which our economies are integrated to provide consistent growth'.

As Southern organizations grow and mature, foreign NGOs – something of an aberrant link between one society's concern and another's need – will have to adapt or they will die. The financial and moral support that some offer will continue to be important to their

Southern counterparts, but that will not be enough. For many Southern NGOs, the old connections no longer play a major financial or functional part in the relationship. Alliances must be rekindled, therefore, along more strategic lines. Survivors among Northern NGOs will have a genuine speciality to offer – technology services, specialized credit, health or educational knowledge. But the British Charity Commissioners notwithstanding, the most important feature of North-South NGO partnerships will be alliances formed around critical policy issues: thoughtful, balanced, professional policy interventions around issues in health or education or the environment; and in broader areas such as trade policy, and aid policy. And it will be found in the development of strong, pro-poor public opinion in the North and the South, opinion so strong and so vocal that it cannot be ignored any longer by governments.

People

Although this book has focused mainly on technology that is small, simple, cheap and non-violent, it is not intended as an attack on higher technologies. Many apparently simple technologies are derived from intensive, high-technology research and development. The bicycle, for example, which was not commercialized until after the typewriter and the sewing machine, combines specialized techniques of thin-walled drawn steel tubing, modern rubber processing technologies, ball bearings, sprockets, roller chains and complex gear-changing mechanisms. The question for developing countries is not a trade-off between 'high' and 'low' technologies. It is a choice between appropriate and inappropriate technologies.

Much of the technology problem has to do with people; not 'dirty fingernail people' or entrepreneurs, but with those in government, large corporations and donor agencies who control budgets and ideas – 'bureaucratic man', 'economic man' and 'engineering man'. Robert Chambers' famous book, *Rural Development; Putting the Last First* is not really about rural development, it is about the scope for personal choice among those whose work has an impact on the lives of poor people; it is a plea for development workers to 'exercise imagination in thinking through the distant but real effects on the rural poor of technical and policy decisions, and of outsiders' actions and non-actions.'[10]

It calls for a better understanding of two things commonly discussed among donor agencies and NGOs, but not always well understood: the first is groups, and the second is individuals. Groups are an important vehicle for reducing the risk element in new ventures, for the development of economic and political

240

empowerment, and for the nurturing of participatory development –
something that in itself is often misunderstood. Whether participatory development is an essential part of a project, or an end in itself –
a necessary prerequisite to socio-political and economic development
– is an old debate. The fact of its importance, however, is not an issue.
But what is sometimes forgotten about groups is that they are made
up of individuals, real people with different perceptions, different
memories, different strengths and different needs.

It is ironic that donor agencies which place increasing emphasis on
the individual at one level, work against individuality at others. The
growing interest in microenterprise development and rural credit
programmes is the positive side of this conundrum. But on the
negative side is the fact that individuals are often ignored. As this
book has attempted to demonstrate, many of the most successful aid
projects flow from the skill, tenacity and longevity of key individuals.
This should not be surprising, because the same is true of successful
businesses and successful organizations everywhere. Development
literature and case studies ring with the accomplishments of Grameen
Bank, Sarvodaya, SEWA and BRAC, but oddly, beyond a limited
conference circuit, the key individuals that created these organizations are unknown. A search through the indexes of any dozen books
on development will turn up references to Lipton, Chambers and
Streeten – and so they should. But there is virtually no mention of
Mohammed Yunus, A.T. Ariyaratne, Ela Bhatt or F.H. Abed. It is as
though the remarkable organizations which these *social entrepreneurs*
created, and which bear the unmistakable stamp of their own
personalities, had appeared full-blown, part of a 'phenomenon' rather
than the work of especially committed, competent individuals.

The failure to recognize this stems in part from the way donor
organizations themselves are organized and managed. They are
reverse images of almost everything Peters and Waterman found in
their surveys of what makes organizations 'excellent'. They are
secretive, compartmentalized and highly centralized in their decision-
making structures. Individuals seldom remain in the same job, or
even the same country programme for more than two or three years.
Overseas assignments are generally two years in length, less than the
gestation period for the average bilateral project. There is no incentive
to take risks, little tolerance of failure, few opportunities for constructive debate, and a reward system which mainly encourages
tidiness and the smooth flow of paper. Large numbers of men and
women in big donor agencies are genuinely committed, hard-working
individuals, but within such a system, it is not surprising that
commitment, risk-taking and debate can fall early victims to a
successful career.

On giving and receiving

In his book about Equatorial Guinea, *Tropical Gangsters*, Robert Klitgaard quotes John Steinbeck on the virtue of giving and the art of receiving:

> Perhaps the most overrated virtue on our list of shoddy virtues is that of giving. Giving builds up the ego of the giver, makes him superior and higher and larger than the receiver. Nearly always, giving is a selfish pleasure, and in many cases it is a downright destructive and evil thing. One has only to remember some of our wolfish financiers who spend two-thirds of their lives clawing fortunes out of the guts of society and the latter third pushing it back ...
>
> It is so easy to give, so exquisitely rewarding. Receiving, on the other hand, if it be done well, requires a fine balance of self-knowledge and kindness. It requires humility and tact and great understanding of relationships. In receiving you cannot appear, even to yourself, better or stronger or wiser than the giver, although you must be wiser to do it well.[11]

Poverty has reached such an unacceptable world level, not because the world has no tools to deal with it, nor because we are short of ideas, but because we are short of the political will to use the tools properly and to implement the ideas effectively. 'Political will', however, is a convenient term for summing up the shortcomings of others. It usually means, as Robert Chambers observes, that the rich and powerful have failed to act against their own interests.[12] It is a faulty escape hatch which allows questions such as who is responsible, where and when, to be conveniently ignored. Development programmes will continue to be hijacked and distorted by powerful interest groups in the North and the South if such questions are not asked and answered.

This book has attempted to answer some of these questions. It suggests that aid as presently conceived and practised, is largely irrelevant to the needs of poor people. The growth principle, on which much aid spending is predicated and justified, is important, but it has severe limitations. Greater efficiencies in the use of what we have and what we know could provide much better long-term benefits. In any case, it is by no means certain that much aid actually contributes to growth. And if it does, it is by no means clear that growth is reaching the poorest in a positive way.

One of the solutions to the poverty problem, an important one, is technology. Unfortunately, in the hands of governments, foreign engineers, experts, amateurs, bureaucrats and aid officials, the lessons of technology in history have been largely ignored. In the quest for sales and the search for the big breakthrough, they have colluded in one of the most expensive and tragic hoaxes of all time. Vast numbers of inappropriate tractors and threshers and factories have been shipped south, at ever-increasing prices, to be used at a fraction of capacity or to end prematurely, simply rusting in the rain.

Today's poverty, worse than at any time in history, is, as Schumacher said, a monstrous and scandalous thing, totally abnormal. And there is no reason, despite brave donor agency calculations, to think that the situation is being reversed. The development community has, in a sense, stopped rearranging the proverbial deck chairs on the Titanic, because all the deck chairs have shifted to the right. The band plays on, while passengers on the upper deck take comfort in singing hymns to 'sustainability', keeping one hopeful eye on the lifeboat called 'structural adjustment' and the other on the potential for some last-minute sales. But the davits have become rusty over time, and the cables are snarled. We forget that 'sustainability' is relative. It cannot be packaged up into two-year projects. Sustainability of the global environment, or what is left of it, is not compatible with current levels of poverty. This is true at a local level – whether in Turkana or the Indonesian rainforest – and it is true globally. 'Earth days', 'earth summits', green political parties and environmental checklists in aid proposals are all important, but they are not enough, and they will amount to very little if the fundamental issue of poverty is not squarely faced.

We have also forgotten that originally, as set out in the Pearson Report, structural adjustment was a concept which involved industrialized countries adjusting to greater exports from the South; to greater competition and lower prices; to an international and genuinely market-based economy; to the notion of Northern countries living within *their* means.

Instead, protection against the South has strengthened. Attitudes have hardened. Debt, the result of investments made by government leaders and world bankers now gone, resulted in a staggering net flow of resources *from poor to rich* countries of $50 to $60 billion in 1989 alone.[13] International trade imbalances and price distortions continue to be nurtured by self-seeking Northern politicians, armed and advised by economists who demand self-righteously that Southern governments cease their economic experiments and start living within their means. Living within one's means is a convenient concept, but when the most basic means of life are withheld, when the price of cocoa continues to plummet, when textile exports are blocked from Northern markets, when jobs succumb to the capital intensity of Northern mass production, things continue to fall apart. As Yeats observed so powerfully, 'the centre cannot hold ... [and] anarchy is loosed upon the world'.

It doesn't have to be that way. Faustian man does not have to be dragged to death by his own machine, as Spengler predicted he would. The alternatives exist. There is still time. There is knowledge. There are enough committed people. There is even enough money. UNDP estimated in 1991 that if industrialized countries reduced their military expenditure by only three per cent, this would yield a saving of $25 billion a year. If developing countries only froze their military expenditure, this would yield another $10 billion. The combined savings would be more than enough to eradicate malnutrition, to cover the cost of providing universal primary education, universal primary health care and safe drinking water by the year 2000.[14]

But the test, as Robert Chambers says, is what people do. 'Social change flows from individual actions. By changing what they do, people move societies in new directions and themselves change.'[15] Because he started it all, perhaps it is best to allow Fritz Schumacher to have the final word. 'The starting point of all our considerations is poverty,' he wrote, 'or rather, a degree of poverty which means misery, and degrades and stultifies the human person.'[16]

> One way or another, everybody will have to take sides in this great conflict ... It is widely accepted that politics is too important a matter to be left to experts. Today, the main content of politics is economics, and the main content of economics is technology. If politics cannot be left to the experts, neither can economics and technology. The case for hope rests on the fact that ordinary people are often able to take a wider view, and a more 'humanistic' view, than is normally being taken by experts. The power of ordinary people, who today tend to feel utterly powerless, does not lie in starting new lines of action, but in placing their sympathy and support with minority groups which have already started.[17]

Notes

Chapter I

[1] Pearson, p. 4
[2] *ibid*, p. 149
[3] *ibid*, p. 116
[4] *ibid*, p. 72
[5] Brandt, p. 12
[6] *ibid*, p. 225
[7] *ibid*, p. 26
[8] *ibid*, p. 176
[9] Brandt (1983), p. 107
[10] World Bank, quoted in Tussie, p. 60
[11] Vallely, p. 108
[12] Brown & Eckholm, p. 97
[13] Smillie, p. 21
[14] Schumacher (1974) pp. 165–6
[15] Brandt, p. 170
[16] *ibid*, p. 47
[17] World Bank (1990), p. 127
[18] *ibid*, p. 128
[19] UNDP (1991), p. 5
[20] World Bank (1990), p. 125; OECD
[21] Independent Group on British Aid (1986), p. 48; *the Economist*, 23 September 1989
[22] OECD, p. 59
[23] World Bank (1990), p. 103
[24] WSJ, May 3, 1990
[25] Cheru, p. 33
[26] From a 1985 report, quoted in the *Economist*, 'Survey of India', 4 May 1991
[27] UNDP (1991), p. 49
[28] Meadows *et al.*, p. 17
[29] The 1970 figures are taken from Meadows et al., pp. 56–9; the 1988 figures from World Resources 1990–1, pp. 320–23
[30] World Resources, pp. 84–5
[31] Fuller, p. 48
[32] 'Common Responsibility in the 1990s', The Stockholm Initiative on Global Security and Governance, April, 1991

Chapter II

[1] Thomson, P.G.R., 'Donors, Development and Dependence; Some Lessons from Bangladesh 1971 to 1986', unpublished doctoral thesis, LSE, London, 1989, p. 13. Thomson discusses the origin of the 'Dhaka Like-Minded Group' (Canada, Netherlands, Denmark, Sweden and Norway): following an overly positive 1984 World Bank report on Bangladesh, which concentrated 'almost wholly on the issue of economic growth ...', the group commissioned its own independent study – *Report on Rural Poverty in Bangladesh*. The findings did not coincide with those of the Bank or the Government of Bangladesh, and according to the author, attempts were made to restrict distribution of the report.

[2] IMF, 'India: Recent Economic Developments', Washington, July 1989

[3] World Bank (1990) p. 1; UNDP (1991), p. 23

[4] Chambers (1983), pp. 48–9.

[5] Hill, p. 33

[6] FAO, *The Dynamics of Rural Poverty*, Rome, 1986, p. 21

[7] Glewwe, p. 36

[8] See, for example, Lipton (1986), pp. 4–6

[9] Chambers (1988), p. 5

[10] Chambers (1988), pp. 8–9; See also (1983), Chapter 5

[11] Figures on the HDI are taken from UNDP (1991), pp. 15–20

[12] H.J. Leonard, 'Environment and the Poor: Development Strategies for a Common Agenda', in Leonard, p. 13

[13] IFAD, 'Special Programming Mission to Ghana', mimeo, July, 1988, p. 56

[14] Leslie, Joan, 'Women's Work and Child Nutrition in the Third World; Report for the Carnegie and Rockefeller Foundations', New York, 1987

[15] UNICEF (1989)

[16] MacPherson, p. 19

[17] World Bank (1990), p. 228

[18] This common assumption may be too glib. Jack Ives, Co-ordinator of the Mountain Ecology and Sustainable Development Project of the UN University argues strongly that there is no clear link between land use in the mountains and changes in flows of sediment in the Ganges and Brahmaputra Rivers. See 'Floods in Bangladesh: Who is to Blame?', Jack Ives, *New Scientist*, April 1991

[19] Annis, S., 'What is Not the Same about the Urban Poor: The Case of Mexico City', in Lewis

[20] Hobsbawm, p. 87

[21] Lipton (1977), p. 13

[22] UNICEF (1989), p. 98

[23] *ibid*. The World Bank counters this argument with evidence, albeit limited, that the removal of urban biases in macroeconomic policies has little effect

[24] World Bank (1990), pp. 4–5

[25] *ibid*, p. 138

[26] World Bank, 1991

[27] 'State of the World's Population', UNFPA, New York, 1991

[28] Drucker, Peter, 'The Changed World Economy', *Foreign Affairs*, Spring, 1986
[29] Quoted in Willoughby, p. 74

Chapter III

[1] The most prominent theoreticians were P.N. Rosenstein-Rodan, 1961, ('International Aid for Underdeveloped Countries', in *Foreign Aid*, Bhagwati, J. and Eckaus, R.S. eds., Penguin, 1970); W.W. Rostow (*Stages of Economic Growth*, 1960, *The Economics of Take-Off Into Sustained Growth*, 1963); and H. Chenery and A.M. Strout ('Foreign Assistance and Economic Development', *American Economic Review*, Sept. 1966)
[2] Pearson, p. 52
[3] World Bank (1988), p. 2
[4] Brundtland, p. 52
[5] World Resources, pp. 234–6
[6] World Resources Institute, p. 236, and Brown (1990), p. 9
[7] World Bank (1990), p. 58
[8] World Bank (1990), p. 60
[9] Unless otherwise noted, statistical data on the Bangladesh transport sector is derived from Chapter 3 of *The Country Boats of Bangladesh*, by Jansen, *et al.*
[10] Sobhan, p. 10; the figure is for the year 1982–3
[11] Jansen, p. 31
[12] Brown, p. 47
[13] *ibid*, p. 46
[14] Schneider, p. 6
[15] *ibid*, p. 4
[16] M. Yudelman, 'Sustainable and Equitable Development in Irrigated Environments', in Leonard, p. 71
[17] Ryder, Grainne (ed.), Probe International, Toronto, 1990
[18] Ryder, p. 15
[19] Riddell (1987), p. 235
[20] World Bank (1988), Annex I-A, para 41
[21] *ibid*, Annex II, p. 12
[22] Conway and Barbier, p. 77
[23] IFAD, *Africa: Sowing the Seeds of Self-Sufficiency*, Rome, 1986
[24] See 'The Private and Social Benefits of Rural Development', de Janvry, Alain in *Assessing Participatory Development; Rhetoric versus Reality*, Lineberry, W.P. (ed.), Westview, Boulder, 1989
[25] Riddell (1987), p. 237
[26] Farrington, J., 'Farm Power and Water Use in Sri Lanka', in Puttaswamaiah, p. 176
[27] Quoted in World Resources, p. 91
[28] *ibid*
[29] *ibid*, p. 92
[30] 'Empowering Africa's Rural Poor', Lele, U., in Lewis, p. 89
[31] Riddell (1987), p. 238

[32] Quoted in Meadows *et al.* (p. 29) and used as the title for a book on population by Lester Brown and Erik Eckholm

[33] Herman E. Daly, 'Sustainable Growth: An Impossibility Theorem', *Development* (SID), Rome, Vol. 3/4, 1990

[34] Worldwatch Institute (1991), p. 18

Chapter IV

[1] Brown, David, 'Rhetoric or Reality? Assessing the Role of NGOs as Agencies of Grass Roots Development,' *Bulletin*, No. 28, University of Reading Agricultural Extension and Rural Development Department, Reading, 1990, p. 4

[2] OECD, 1989 *Report*, pp. 82, 264

[3] Annis, Sheldon, 'Can Small Scale Development be Large Scale Policy?' *World Development*, Vol. 15 Supplement, 1988

[4] Statistics on the American voluntary sector are derived mainly from *The Third America: The Emergence of the Non-Profit Sector in the United States*, by Michael O'Neill, Jossey-Bass, San Francisco, 1989 and *If Not For Profit, For What?* by Dennis R. Young, Lexington Books, Lexington, 1983.

[5] de Tocqueville, Alexis, *Democracy in America*, originally published in 1835, republished by Doubleday Anchor, Garden City, 1969

[6] Brown, *op cit*, p. 5

[7] *ibid*, p. 6

[8] Korten, David, 'Third Generation Strategies; a Key to People-Centred Development,' *World Development*, Vol. 15 Supplement, Oxford, 1987, and *Getting to the 21st Century*, Kumarian Press, West Hartford, 1990

[9] Martin, Samuel A., *Financing Humanistic Service*, McClelland and Stewart, Toronto, 1975

[10] Fowler, Alan, 'Doing it Better?' *Bulletin*, No. 28, University of Reading Agricultural Extension and Rural Development Department, Reading, Feb. 1990

[11] BRAC statistics are derived from a variety of BRAC reports and studies between 1987 and 1990

[12] *Financing Health Services in Developing Countries; An Agenda for Reform*, World Bank, Washington, 1987, p. 42

[13] AMREF material derived from Smillie, I., 'Strengthening NGOs: The Strangulation Technique', 1988

Chapter V

[1] Hawke, p. 8

[2] Pacey, pp. 21–2

[3] Cited in Pacey, p. 80

[4] Pacey, pp. 114, 127

[5] Lewis Mumford, *Technics and Civilization*, Harcourt Brace, New York, 1939, pp. 14–15.

[6] Mokyr, p. 208

[7] Described in Best, p. 80

[8] Pendle, p. 41

[9] Pacey, p. 147

[10] The Kerala story is drawn from various ITDG reports, notably O'Riordan, Brian, 'Fisheries Development in South India: The Indo-Norwegian Fisheries Project', ITDG, 1990; Kadappuram, John, 'Artificial Fishing Reef and Bait Technologies', in Gamser, pp. 150–179; and Kurien, John and Wilmann, Rolf, 'Economics of Artisanal and Mechanised Fisheries in Kerala: A Study on Costs and Earnings of Fishing Units', FAO, 1982

[11] Cited in Gimpel

[12] Noble, p. 53

[13] Best, p. 71

[14] The story is recounted in Best, p. 186

[15] Pacey, p. 120

[16] Noble, p. 22

[17] *ibid*, p. 244

[18] Quoted in Hawke, p. 77

[19] See, for example, Peter Drucker's *Adventures of a Bystander*, Harper & Row, N.Y., 1979, and Peters and Waterman, *In Search of Excellence*, pp. 202–34

[20] Peters and Waterman, p. 207

[21] *ibid*, p. 224

[22] Study conducted by Alan Smithers and John Pratt, University of Surrey; reported in the *Toronto Globe and Mail*, April 8, 1991

Chapter VI

[1] Quoted in Rybczynski, p. 41

[2] Quoted in Willoughby, p. 64

[3] Willoughby, p. 66

[4] Quoted in Rybczynski, p. 37

[5] Quoted in McRobie, pp. 24–5

[6] The *Observer*, London, 29 August 1965, quoted in McRobie, pp. 25–31

[7] McRobie, p. 36

[8] 'Putting Partnership into Practice', ITDG, November 1989

[9] National Film Board of Canada interview, 1977; quoted in Rybczynski, p. 165

[10] Whiticombe, R. and Carr, M., 'Appropriate Technology Institutions: A review', ITDG, London, 1982

[11] Woto, Teedzani, 'Biogas Technology in Botswana; A Sociological Evaluation', RIIC, Kanye, 1988

[12] Willoughby reviews the literature and arguments critical of appropriate and intermediate technology, pp. 223–63

[13] Chenery, H. *et al.*, *Redistribution With Growth*, OUP, 1974

[14] Schumacher (1973), p. 40

[15] For example, Eckaus, R., *Appropriate Technologies for Developing*

Countries, National Academy of Sciences, Washington, 1977; and 'Appropriate Technology: The Movement has only a Few Clothes On,' in *Issues in Science and Technology*, Winter, 1987

[16] 'Enabling', which I have used in the title for Part Three of this book, is one of those words that development workers have almost (but not quite) worn out. It was first used in the development context by H.H. The Aga Khan in a 1982 speech in Nairobi: 'Social Institutions in National Development: The Enabling Environment'

[17] Willoughby, p. 234

[18] Quoted in Best, p. 11

[19] Best, p. 163

[20] Peters and Waterman, p. 215

[21] The *Economist*, 14 October 1989

[22] Reich, p. 6

[23] de Soto, Hernando, 'Structural Adjustment and the Informal Sector', in *Microenterprises in Developing Countries*, J. Levitsky (ed.), IT Publications, London, 1989

[24] Nowak, Maria, 'The Role of Microenterprises in Rural Industrialization in Africa', in *Microenterprises in Developing Countries*, J. Levitsky (ed.), IT Publications, London, 1989

[25] Hossain, Mahabub, 'Increasing Food Availability in Bangladesh: Constraints and Possibilities,' Dhaka Food Strategy Review Exercise, Ministry of Agriculture, 1984. See Also World Bank, *Bangladesh: Economic and Social development Prospects*, Vol. III, 1985, which estimated that by 1991 only 16 to 18 per cent of the additional labour force would be employed in direct crop production.

[26] Gwitira, Joshua C., 'Small Scale Technology for Agro-Industrial Development', ITDG/Zimbabwe Ministry of Industry and Commerce, Harare, October, 1990

[27] Author's discussion at Indigenous Business Development Centre, Harare, March, 1991

[28] BBC World Service, 15 February 1991

[29] Schumacher (1973), p. 138

[30] Schumacher (1977), pp. 159–60

Chapter VII

[1] Brown, p. 137

[2] Conway and Barbier, p. 20

[3] See, for example, Lipton, Michael, with Longhurst, Richard, *Modern Varieties, International Agricultural Research, and the Poor*, CGIAR Study Paper No. 2, World Bank, Washington, 1985. The negative aspects of the green revolution are extensively documented in a special issue of the *Ecologist*, Vol. 21, No. 2, March/April 1991

[4] Brundtland, p. 142

[5] World Resources Institute, p. 92

[6] *An Interim Report on the State of the Forest Resources in the Developing Countries*, FAO, Rome, 1988

[7] World Resources Institute, pp. 101–2
[8] Leonard, p. 19
[9] World Resources Institute, p. 107
[10] World Resources Institute, pp. 109–10
[11] Mahar, Dennis J., *Government Policies and Deforestation in Brazil's Amazon Region*, World Bank, Washington, 1989
[12] Cheru, p. 28
[13] George, p. 61
[14] Conway and Barbier, p. 76
[15] Leonard, p. 38–9
[16] Details gathered during the author's visit.
[17] Conroy and Litvinoff, p. 81
[18] World Resources Institute, p. 111
[19] Worldwatch (1991), p. 181
[20] Smillie, p. 138–41
[21] Browder, John O., 'Development Alternatives for Tropical Rainforests', in Leonard, p. 117
[22] Worldwatch (1991), p. 80
[23] Details on the Wokabout Somil are taken from 'The Wokabout Somil: A New Rural Industry for Papua New Guinea,' by Paul Unwin, *Appropriate Technology*, London, December, 1990
[24] *RDP Annual Report, 1989*, and *BRAC 1990 Annual Review*, BRAC, Dhaka, 1989, 1990
[25] The description of this project has been taken from discussions with ITDG staff and from ITDG documents, including 'Kenya Livestock Programme: A Review of the First Three Years of Operation, 1986–9'
[26] Description of the Turkana Rehabilitation Programme is derived from discussions with ITDG, from a 1990 review by Cathy Watson and Arupe Lobuin entitled, 'Lokitaung Pastoral Development Project: Lakeshore Study', and from the manuscript of a forthcoming book by Adrian Cullis and Arnold Pacey, *A Development Dialogue: Rainwater Harvesting in Turkana.*
[27] Broche-Due, V., 'Women at the Backstage of Development', FAO Consultant's Report GCP/KEN/048/NOD, 1983; cited in Cullis and Pacey, *op cit*
[28] R.S. Hogg reviewed the pre-1980 projects and the post-*Lopiar* efforts over a ten year period. See, for example, 'Destitution and Development: A Strategy for Turkana', (Dept. of Anthropology, University of Manchester, 1982); 'Water Harvesting in Semi-Arid Kenya: Opportunities and Constraints; (Oxfam, 1986); 'Building Pastoral Institutions: A Strategy for Turkana District' (Oxfam, 1987); 'Water Harvesting and Agricultural Production in Semi-Arid Kenya', *Development and Change*, Vol. 19, 1988
[29] Conway and Barbier, p. 37

Chapter VIII

[1] Material on drying technologies has been derived from Barrie Axtell *et al.*, *Try Drying It*, IT Publications, 1991; UNIFEM Food Cycle Technology Source Books, New York, 1988, and ITDG files.

[2] Greeley, p. 11

[3] Hagelberg, Gerry, 'The Structure of World Production and Consumption', in Kaplinsky (1989), p. 49 'Sugar' here means sugar produced by the OPS or VP techniques as opposed to the traditional coarse dark sugar known as jaggery.

[4] Kaplinsky (1990), p. 128

[5] The proceedings of a 1987 ITDG-sponsored conference on sugar provide extensive background detail as well as technical and economic analysis of the OPS technique. The publication is an invaluable source of background information for anyone interested in pursuing the subject further: *Cane Sugar: The Small Processing Option*, R. Kaplinsky (ed.), IT Publications, London, 1989

[6] The original model was based on a design developed by a Belgian firm, UNATA, which specializes in appropriate technology equipment.

[7] The Bielenberg Ram Press story is drawn from the proceedings of and papers presented at a conference on The Bielenberg Ram Press and Small-Scale Oil Processing, held in Nairobi by ATI in September, 1990

[8] Hyman, Eric, L., 'Preliminary Socio-Economic Impact Study of the Ram Press in the Arusha Region of Tanzania', ATI, Washington, 1990

[9] Comments made by Carlos Zulberti, IDRC Consultant, VOPS-Kenya Project, Report on an ATI Oil Press Conference, Nairobi, September, 1990

[10] Muthaka, James, K., 'Vegetable Oil/Protein System Programme; The Kenyan Experience', Paper presented at Bielenberg Ram Press Conference, Nairobi, September, 1990

Chapter IX

[1] In 1973, oil sold at $3.22 per barrel. By Autumn 1988, the price was approximately $12 per barrel, and in August 1991, prior to the Iraqi invasion of Kuwait, it was $17 a barrel.

[2] Cheru, pp. 24, 28

[3] Inger, David, 'Overview of Woodstove Development in Botswana', in *Stoves for People*, R. Caceres (ed.), IT Publications, London, 1989

[4] USAID, *Audit of AID Renewable Energy Projects*, Report 9–000–86–3, Washington, 1986; cited in Barnett, p. 540

[5] For example, Joseph, S., 'An Appraisal of the Impact of Improved Wood Stove Programmes', in Caceres (ed.). The Caceres book contains several case studies which bear out this finding.

[6] 'Indoor Air Pollution in Developing Countries and Acute Respiratory Infection in Children,' M.R. Pandey, et al.; the article, which appeared in the 25 February 1989 *Lancet*, was reprinted in edited form in *Boiling Point*, No. 18, ITDG, Rugby, April, 1989

[7] Hancock, David, 'Design, Manufacturing and Marketing of Tso Tso Stoves in Zimbabwe', *GATE*, Bonn, Vol. 4, 1987; also, author's interview with David Hancock, Harare, February 1991

[8] Author's discussions and observation at Sylveira House

[9] 'How to Make the Kenyan Ceramic Jiko', Kenya Renewable Energy

Project, Ministry of Energy/EDI, 1983; other background on the KCJ is taken from ITDG reports and from 'The Introduction of the Kenya Jiko Stove; A Kengo Experience', by Monica Opole, in Carr (1988)

10 The Sri Lankan stoves material is derived from visits to Negombo stove makers and retailers, from discussions with CEB officials, and from various internal ITDG studies and reports; also from 'The Sarvodaya Stoves Project: A Critical Review of Developments 1979–82', by M. Howes *et al.*, and 'A History of the Sarvodaya Stoves Project 1979–82', by Bill Stewart, both published by ITDG in 1983.

11 Amarasekera, R.M., 'Status of Improved Woodstove Dissemination in Sri Lanka', in Caceres, p. 118

12 'Sri Lanka Bilateral Woodburning Stoves Project; Internal Evaluation', ITDG, 1989

13 *ibid*, p. 25

14 Foley, p. 13

15 *ibid*, p. 16

16 *ibid*, p. 80

17 Sinha (1990), p. 20

18 Flavin, pp. 20, 26

19 Windmills in Argentina are discussed at length in Hurst, C., 'Establishing New Markets for Mature Energy Equipment in Developing Countries', *World Development*, Vol. 18, No. 4, 1990

20 Foley, p. 36

21 These figures are provided by Flavin, p. 50. There is ambiguity about the numbers, however. For example Hurst, *op cit*, uses the much larger figure of 90 000 small plants by 1980, with a capacity of 10 000 megawatts.

22 Flavin, p. 47

23 Hagler, Baily and Co., 'Decentralized Hydropower in AID's Development Assistance Program', quoted in Flavin, p. 49

24 Material derived from ITDG reports and studies, from Hurst and Flavin, op cit, and from Hislop, D., 'The Micro Hydro Programme in Nepal – A Case Study,' Biomass Energy Services and Technology, London, 1987

25 Hislop, 1986

26 The Sri Lanka story is derived from discussions with ITDG staff and others in Britain and Sri Lanka, from ITDG studies and reports, from Holland, R., and from Hislop, D., *Upgrading Micro Hydro in Sri Lanka*, IT Publications, London, 1986

27 Barnett, Andrew, 'The Diffusion of Energy Technology in the Rural Areas of Developing Countries: A Synthesis of Recent Experience', *World Development*, Vol. 18, No. 4, 1990

Chapter X

1 Agevi, E., 'Paradoxes in the Utilization of Local Building Resources for Low Cost Housing Schemes in Nairobi', Nairobi, 1988

2 'Small and Medium Scale Enterprise Sector; Programme Proposal – Support to the SME Sector', Govt. of Malawi, 1991 (Draft)

3 *ibid.*

[4] Government of Malawi National Statistics Office, cited in 'Balaka Lime Pilot Project Evaluation', READI, Lilongwe, 1991

[5] Sinha (1990), p. 128

[6] *ibid*, p. 75

[7] Sinha (1987), p. 134

[8] *ibid*, p. 148

[9] Kaplinsky (1990), p. 196

[10] Robert L. Day, 'Pozzolans for Use in Low-Cost Housing', IDRC, Ottawa, 1990

[11] 'Brickmaking in Botswana' is based on work done by Raphael Kaplinsky (1990), pp. 74–103, and on 'ATI's Brickmaking Projects in Three African Countries: Mali, Botswana, Tanzania', Carlos Lola, ATI, Washington, 1987

[12] Kaplinsky, p. 83

[13] I am grateful to many people for the background to this story. They include Solomon Mwangi, Nick Evans, Nick Hall and Shelter Works in Kenya, Sosthenes Buatsi at the Technology Consultancy Centre in Ghana, and John Parry in Cradley Heath. Publications consulted include Evans, Barrie, *Understanding Natural Fibre Concrete*, IT Publications, London, 1987; and Gram, H.E. *et al.*, *Fibre Concrete Roofing*, SKAT, St Gallen, 1987

[14] Interview with John Parry, Cradley Heath, February, 1991

[15] Adapted from 'A Ten Point Prescription for a Good Agent for Parry Equipment', J.P.M. Parry & Associates Ltd., Cradley Heath

[16] Costs on a four room bungalow in Kumasi in September 1990, calculated by TCC, Kumas

[17] Cost comparison at November 1989 in Nairobi, including transportation, calculated by ITDG, Nairobi

[18] Coughlin, Peter, 'Steel Versus Tile Roofing: What's Appropriate for Kenya?' Industrial Research Project, University of Nairobi, August 1985

Chapter XI

[1] Ohiorhenuan, John F.E., 'The Industrialization of the Very Late Starters: Historical Experience, Prospects and Strategic Options for Nigeria', IDS *Discussion Paper* No. 273, Brighton, 1990

[2] Fieldhouse, p. 232

[3] Smillie, p. 8

[4] Karmiloff, Igor, 'Zambia', in Riddell (1990), p. 313

[5] Stevens, Christopher, 'Nigeria', in Riddell, p. 273

[6] Riddell (1990), p. 374

[7] Stevens, *op cit*, p. 256

[8] Ndlela, Daniel B., 'Macro-policies for Appropriate Technology in Zimbabwe Industries', in Stewart, p. 179

[9] Humphries, M., 'Opportunities fo Cooperation Between Small and Large-Scale Manufacturers', CZI, ITDG/Ministry of Industry and Commerce Seminar, Harare, 1990

[10] O'Regan, Fred, *et al.*, 'Malawi: Informal Sector Assessment', prepared for Labat-Anderson Inc., and for AID/AFR/MDI, 1989

[11] The sections of this chapter dealing with Ghana, the Technology Consultancy Centre, GRATIS and SIS Engineering are drawn from *No Condition Permanent; Pump Priming Ghana's Industrial Revolution*, Smillie, I., Intermediate Technology Publications, London, 1986; and from notes, internal documents and extensive discussions in Ghana with the principals of these institutions in February, 1991.

[12] Adjorlolo, B.T., *Growing From a Small Beginning: A Handbook on How to Start and Manage a Small Scale Industry*, University Press, Kumasi, 1985

[13] For a full description of the CIDA and USAID debacles, see the chapter entitled 'Partners in Development' in Smillie, pp. 72–82

[14] Hobsbawm, p. 173

[15] Schmitz, p. 27

Chapter XII

[1] Ghosh, Jayati, 'Young Women in India: Livelihood and Life-Choices', *Development*, SID, Rome, 1990:1

[2] UNDP (1990)

[3] Andam, Aba. A., 'Remedial Strategies to Overcome Gender Stereotyping in Science Education in Ghana', in *Development*, *op cit*

[4] Tendler, J., in 'Whatever Happened to Poverty Alleviation', in Levitsky, J. (ed.) *Microenterprises in Developing Countries*, IT Publications, London, 1989

[5] McKee, Katharine, 'Microlevel Strategies for Supporting Livelihoods, Employment and Income Generation of Poor Women in the Third World: The Challenge of Significance', *World Development*, Vol. 17, No. 7, 1989

[6] The CARE case is based on personal study by the author during a visit to the project in August 1990

[7] McKee, *op cit*, p. 1001

[8] Levitsky, p. 33

[9] In 1983, Grameen Bank had 47 000 borrowers – 26 000 men and 21 000 women. Of these, 30 000 were still borrowing in 1990. Because of Grameen's emphasis on women after 1984 (male borrowers only tripled in number, while female borrowers increased by a factor of 34), it can be safely assumed that most of the 30 000 continuing borrowers from 1983 were women.

[10] Carr (1984), pp. 13–14

[11] Chen, Marty, 'A Sectoral Approach to Women's Work: Lessons from India', *World Development*, Vol. 17, No. 7, 1989

[12] *ibid*, p. 60

[13] Marsden, Keith, 'African Entrepreneurs; Pioneers of Development', Discussion Paper No. 9., International Finance Corporation, World Bank, Washington, 1990, p. 49

[14] Kaplinsky (1990), p. 182

[15] *ibid*, p. 178

[16] *Manual Silk Reeling in South India: A Preliminary Study of Technology*

Transfer, Economic Development Associates and ITDG, IT Publications, London, 1990

[17] BRAC RDP Report, June 1990, other BRAC reports; author's 1990 visit to BRAC and project sites

[18] Notes based on 1984 and 1985 evaluation conducted by the author, and *Development: Women*, CIDA, Ottawa, Spring, 1987

[19] Carr (1984) p. 6

[20] McKee, *op cit*

[21] Ahmad M. and Jenkins, A., 'Traditional Paddy Husking – An Appropriate Technology Under pressure', *Appropriate Technology*, Vol. 7, No. 2, September 1980; Greeley, Martin, 'Postharvest Technologies; Implications for Food Policy Analysis', Economic Development Institute of the World Bank, 1991

Chapter XIII

[1] Jolly, R. *et al.* (eds) *Third World Employment*, Penguin, 1973, p. 9

[2] Leonard, p. 13

[3] World Development Indicators 1988, World Bank, Washington, 1988

[4] Harrison, p. 136–7.

[5] Levitsky, p. xiii

[6] Carr, Marilyn, 'Promotion of Small Scale Enterprise in Developing Countries: Creative Donor Intervention', UNIFEM, Harare, 1989

[7] de Soto, p. xv

[8] Smillie, p. 56

[9] Nowak, Maria, 'The Role of Microenterprises in Rural Industrialization in Africa', in Levitsky, p. 70

[10] de Soto, Hernando, 'Structural Adjustment and the Informal Sector', in Levitsky, p. 3

[11] Liedholm and Mead, 1987

[12] Tilak, J.B.G., 'Education and its Relation to Economic Growth, Poverty and Income Distribution: Past Evidence and Further Analysis', World Bank, Washington, 1989

[13] *ibid*, pp. 24, 25

[14] UNICEF (1990), p. 45

[15] Cassen, p. 144; UNICEF (1989), p. 53

[16] World Bank, *Women in Pakistan; An Economic and Social Strategy*, Washington, 1989

[17] Hanson, James A., *India: Poverty, Employment and Social Services*, World Bank, Washington, 1989

[18] UNICEF (1990)

[19] Dawson, J., 'Small-Scale Industry Development in Ghana: A Case Study of Kumasi', for Presentation to ESCOR, ODA, London, 1988

[20] Mokyr, p. 264

[21] King, Kenneth, 'Education for Employment and Self-Employment Interventions in Developing Countries: Past Experience and Present Prognosis', in *Defusing the Time Bomb?* International Foundation for Education with Production, Gaberone, 1990, p. 105

[22] Reich, p. 229

[23] de Soto, p. 133–6

[24] de Soto, in Levitsky, *op cit*, p. 5

[25] Stearns, K. and Otero, Maria (eds), 'The Critical Connection: Governments, Private Institutions and the Informal Sector in Latin America', ACCION International, Washington, 1990

[26] Carr, *op cit*, p. 8

Chapter XIV

[1] World Bank, 'Making Adjustment Work for the Poor', Washington, 1990, p. 5

[2] See, for example, Commander, Simon, (ed.) *Structural Adjustment and Agriculture: Theory and Practice in Africa and Latin America*, James Currey, London, 1989

[3] See *Structural Adjustment with a Human Face*, by Cornia *et al.*, 1987

[4] Toronto *Globe and Mail*, 17 April 1991

[5] Reich, p. 71

[6] The importation of used clothing was not new to Ghana. It had never been done on such a large scale before, however, nor with the macro-economic justification of a structural adjustment programme. In 1990, Kenya banned the importation of used clothing, in part to protect local industry, in part to protect local dignity.

[7] Killick, p. 44

[8] Killick, pp. 63–4

[9] Gillies, D. and Schmitz, G., 'The Challenge of Democratic Development', North-South Institute, Ottawa, May 1991

[10] See Wells, L.T., 'Economic Man and Engineering Man: A Choice of Technology in a Low Wage Country', *Public Policy*, Vol. 21, No. 3, 1973; James, J., 'Appropriate Technology in Publicly Owned Industries in Kenya and Tanzania' in Stewart, 1990, and Kaplinsky, 1990

[11] James, *op cit*, p. 348

[12] Theobald, p. 157

[13] de Soto, p. 134

[14] Theobald, p. 97

[15] White, J., 'External Development Finance and the Choice of Technology' in James, J. and Watanabe, S., *Technology, Institutions and Government Policies*, Macmillan, London, 1985

[16] CIDA also supports CARE's Rural Maintenance Project, described in Chapter XII. This project involves 60 000 women in rural road maintenance.

[17] World Bank, 'Appropriate Technology in World Bank Activities', Washington, 1976, pp. vi, 8

[18] Riddell (1990), p. 3

[19] Hancock, p. 171

[20] Young, Roger, *Canadian Development Assistance to Tanzania*, North–South Institute, Ottawa, 1983, p. 77

[21] Author's observation and discussions with CIDA and GRATIS staff at Tamale ITTU, February, 1991

[22] Quoted in Noble, p. viii

[23] Stewart, pp. 14–15

[24] Bautista, Romeo M., 'Macro Policies and Technical Choice in the Philippines', in Stewart, p. 126

[25] Government of Costa Rica MIDEPLAN, quoted in 'Macroeconomic Policy, Technological Change and Rural Development: The Costa Rica Case', by E. Doryan-Garron, in Stewart, pp. 225, 229

[26] Braun, p. 100

[27] Mokyr, pp. 173, 198–9

[28] The prices were influenced in part by a deposit required on bottles, which were in short supply. The aluminium container of the import also had a certain resale scrap value. In fact, however, the price differential remained enormous even if the drink was consumed in a bar and the containers played no part in the transaction.

[29] How do Americans dream up such wonderful acronyms? GEMINI stands for 'Growth and Equity through Microenterprise Investments and Institutions'

[30] 'Botswana Science and Technology: A Policy and Implementation Framework', Maendeleo, Botswana Technology Centre, Gaberone, 1990

Chapter XV

[1] The most amazing public affairs-type *volte face* in recent years is contained in the 1991 World Bank *World Development Report*, which appears to disown the Bank's uncompromising past thinking about structural adjustment and the roles of state and market: 'Perhaps the clearest lesson from work on development over the past 30 years is that there is a premium on pragmatism and an open mind ... In development, generalizations can be as rash as unbending commitments to theory.'

[2] In fact some agencies had experimented with the mechanization of country boats. In 1973, the author was involved in a CARE project which experimented with Thai long-shaft engines in two large boats. Both sank during trials, as did the project.

[3] Mokyr, p. 299

[4] Killick, p. 18

[5] The South Commission Report, 'The Challenge to the South', 1990

[6] Lipton, Michael, 'Requiem for Adjustment Lending?' Book Review in *Development Policy Review*, Vol. 8, No. 4, December 1990

[7] The EAP story is recounted by Alison Jolly in 'The Madagascar Challenge: Human Needs and Fragile Ecosystems', in Leonard, pp. 189–214

[8] 'Charity Rules Were Abused by Oxfam', The *Telegraph*, 10 May 1991. In a letter to the *Times*, the Chief Charity Commissioner, Robin Guthrie, attempted to explain the Commission's purpose. 'It is not the intention of the law, nor the business of the courts and the Charity Commission, to staunch the contribution of charities to public life, without which we would be all the poorer. Charities have a wealth of knowledge and experience to bring to bear on the solution of problems and not solely on their treatment. That aspect of their work must however be exclusively on

behalf of their beneficiaries and in pursuit of their objects. It must be ancillary to their main work ...' (The *Times*, 27 May 1991) 'Ancillary' was not defined, nor was it explained how the balance between 'solution' and 'treatment' should be determined.

9 'Has the Time come to Stop Giving?' The London *Evening Standard*, 10 May 1991

10 Chambers, p. 190

11 John Steinbeck, *The Log From the Sea of Cortez*, 1951, quoted in Klitgaard, p. 13

12 Chambers, p. 161

13 UNDP (1991), p. 23; The World Bank (1991) places the figure at US$30 billion

14 UNDP (1991), p. 10; similar estimates were made by the 1991 Stockholm Initiative on Global Security and Governance

15 Chambers, p. 217

16 Schumacher (1974), p. 140

17 *ibid*, pp. 131–2

Bibliography

Additional references, for sources used in only one chapter, are found in the notes at the end of each chapter.

Barnett, Andrew, 'The Diffusion of Energy Technology in the Rural Areas of Developing Countries: A Synthesis of Recent Experience', *World Development*, Vol. 18, No. 4, 1990

Best, Michael H., *The New Competition*, Polity Press, Cambridge, 1990

Braun, Ernst, *Wayward Technology*, Frances Pinter, London, 1984

Brandt, Willy, *et al.*, *North-South; A Programme for Survival*, MIT Press, Cambridge, Mass., 1980

Brandt, Willy, *et al.*, *Common Crisis*, Pan Books, London, 1983

Brown, Lester & Ekholm, Erik, *By Bread Alone*, Praeger, New York, 1974

Brown, Lester, *et al.*, *State of the World, 1989, 1990, 1991*, Norton & Co., New York, 1989, 1990, 1991

Brundtland, Gro Harlem, *et al.*, *Our Common Future: The World Commission on Environment and Development*, OUP, Oxford, 1987

Caceres, Roberto, *et al.*, *Stoves for People*, Intermediate Technology Publications, London, 1989

Carr, Marilyn, *Blacksmith, Baker, Roofing-sheet Maker: Employment for Rural Women in Developing Countries*, Intermediate Technology Publications, London, 1984

Carr, Marilyn (ed.) 1988, *Sustainable Industrial Development; Seven Case Studies*, Intermediate Technology Publications, London, 1988

Carson, Rachel, *Silent Spring*, Crest, New York, 1964

Cassen, Robert, and Associates, *Does Aid Work?* Clarendon Press, Oxford, 1986

Chambers, Robert, *Rural Development; Putting the Last First*, Longman, 1983

Chambers, Robert, 'Poverty in India: Concepts, Research and Reality,' IDS *Discussion Paper*, No. 241, Sussex, 1988

Chambers, Robert *et al.* (eds) *Farmer First: Farmer Innovation and Agricultural Research*, IT Publications, London, 1989

Conway, Gordon R., and Barbier, Edward, *After the Green Revolution: Sustainable Agriculture for Development*, Earthscan, London, 1990

Conroy, Czech and Litvinoff, Miles, *The Greening of Aid: Sustainable Livelihoods in Practice*, Earthscan, London, 1988

De Soto, Hernando, *The Other Path*, Harper and Row, New York, 1989

Fieldhouse, D.K., *Black Africa 1945–1980; Economic Decolonization and Arrested Development*, Allen & Unwin, London, 1986

Flavin, C., *Electricity for a Developing World*, Worldwatch Paper No. 70, Washington, 1986

Foley, Gerald, *Electricity for Rural People*, Panos, London, 1989

Fuller, R. Buckminster, *Comprehensive Design Strategy*, World Resources Inventory, Phase II, University of Illinois, Carbondale, 1967

Gamser, M.S., Appleton, H., Carter, N. (eds), *Tinker, Tiller, Technical Change*, Intermediate Technology Publications, London, 1990

Gimpel, Jean, *The Medieval Machine; The Industrial Revolution of the Middle Ages*, Wildwood House, Aldershot, 1988

Gillet, Pierre, *Small is Difficult; The Pangs and Success of Small Boat Technology Transfer in South India*, Intermediate Technology Publications, London, 1985

Greeley, Martin, *Postharvest Technologies: Implications for Food Policy Analysis*, Economic Development Institute of the World Bank, Washington, 1991

Hancock, Graham, *Lords of Poverty*, Atlantic Monthly Press, New York, 1989

Harrison, Paul, *The Third World Tomorrow*, Pelican, 1980

Hawke, David Freeman, *Nuts and Bolts of the Past*, Harper & Row, New York, 1988

Hill, Polly, *Development Economics on Trial*, Cambridge University Press, Cambridge, 1986

Hirschman, Albert O., *The Rhetoric of Reaction: Perversity, Futility, Jeopardy*, Belknap Press, Cambridge, Mass., 1991

Hislop, Drummond, *Upgrading Micro Hydro in Sri Lanka*, Intermediate Technology Publications, London, 1985

Hobsbawm, E.J., *Industry and Empire*, Penguin, London, 1969

Holland, Ray, *Micro Hydro Electric Power*, Intermediate Technology Publications, London, 1983

Hurst, C. and Barnett, Andrew, *The Energy Dimension*, IT Publications, London, 1990

Independent Group on British Aid, *Aid Is Not Enough*, London, 1984

Independent Group on British Aid, *Real Aid: Missed Opportunities*, London, 1986

Independent Group on British Aid, *Real Aid: What Europe Can Do*, London, 1989

Jansen, Erik. G., Dolman, A.J., Jerve, A.M., Rahman, N., *The Country Boats of Bangladesh*, University Press, Dhaka, 1989

Kaplinsky, Raphael, *Sugar Processing; The Development of a Third World Technology*, Intermediate Technology Publications, London, 1984

Kaplinsky, Raphael et al., *Cane Sugar; The Small-Scale Processing Option*, Intermediate Technology Publications, London, 1989

Kaplinsky, Raphael, *The Economies of Small; Appropriate Technology in a Changing World*, Intermediate Technology Publications, London, 1990

Kemp, Tom, *Industrialization in the Non-Western World* (Second Edition), Longman, 1989

Killick, Tony, *A Reaction Too Far: Economic Theory and the Role of the State in Developing Countries*, Overseas Development Institute, London, 1990

Klitgaard, Robert, *Tropical Gangsters*, Basic Books, New York, 1990

Korten, David C., *Getting to the 21st Century*, Kumarian Press, West Hartford, 1990

Kumar, Satish (ed.) *The Schumacher Lectures* (Vol. II), Abacus, London, 1986

Kuznets, S., *Modern Economic Growth – Rate, Structure and Spread*, Yale University Press, 1966

Leonard, H. Jeffrey, *et al.*, *Environment and the Poor: Development Strategies for a Common Agenda*, Overseas Development Council, Washington, 1989

Lewis, John. P., *et al.*, *Strengthening the Poor: What Have We Learned?* Overseas Development Council, Washington, 1988

Levitsky, Jacob (ed.), *Microenterprises in Developing Countries*, Intermediate Technology Publications, London, 1989

Liedholm, C. and Mead, D., 'Small Industries in Developing Countries; Empirical Evidence and Policy Implications', International Development Paper No. 9, Michigan State University, East Lansing, 1987

Lipton, Michael, *Why Poor People Stay Poor; Urban Bias in World Development*, Temple Smith, London, 1977

Lipton, Michael, 'The Poor and the Poorest: Some Interim Findings,' *Discussion Paper* No. 25, World Bank, Washington, 1986

MacPherson, Stewart, *Five Million Children: Poverty and Child Welfare in the Third World*, Wheatsheaf Books, Sussex, 1987

McRobie, George, *Small is Possible*, Jonathan Cape, London, 1981

Marshall, Ken, *Package Deals*, Intermediate Technology Publications, London, 1983

Meadows, Donella H., *et al.*, *The Limits to Growth*, Earth Island, London, 1972

Mesarovic, M. and Pestel, Eduard, *Mankind at the Turning Point; The Second Report to the Club of Rome*, Dutton, New York, 1974

Mokyr, Joel, *The Lever of Riches; Technological Creativity and Economic Progress*, OUP, New York, 1990

Mumford, Lewis, *Technics and Civilization*, Harcourt Brace, New York, 1939

Noble, David F., *America By Design; Science, Technology and the Rise of Corporate Capitalism*, OUP, New York, 1979

Ohiorhenuan, John F.E., 'The Industrialization of Very Late Starters: Historical Experience, Prospects and Strategic Options for Nigeria', IDS *Discussion Paper*, No. 273, Sussex, 1990

OECD, *1989 Report*, OECD, Paris, 1989

Pacey, Arnold, *Technology in World Civilization*, MIT Press, Cambridge, Mass., 1990

Pacey, Arnold, with Cullis, Adrian, *Rainwater Harvesting*, Intermediate Technology Publications, London, 1986

Pearson, Lester B., *et al.*, *Partners in Development*, Praeger, New York, 1969

Pendle, George, *A History of Latin America*, Penguin, Harmondsworth, 1983

Peters, T.J. and Waterman, R.H., *In Search of Excellence: Lessons From America's Best-Run Companies*, Warner Books, New York, 1982

Piore, M. and Sabel, C., *The Second Industrial Divide: Possibilities for Prosperity*, Basic Books, New York, 1984

Puttaswamaiah, K., (ed.), *Poverty and Rural Development; Planners, Peasants and Poverty*, Intermediate Technology Publications, London, 1990

Reich, Robert B., *The Work of Nations; Preparing Ourselves for 21st Century Capitalism*, Alfred Knopf, New York, 1991

Riddell, R.C., *Foreign Aid Reconsidered*, James Currey, London, 1987

Riddell, R.C., *Manufacturing Africa*, James Currey, London, 1990

Rybczynski, W., *Paper Heroes*, Prism, Chalmington, Dorchester, 1980

Ryder, Grainne, *Damming the Three Gorges*, Probe International, Toronto, 1990

Schmitz, Hubert, 'Flexible Specialization – A New Paradigm of Small-Scale Industrialization?' IDS *Discussion Paper*, No. 261, Sussex, 1989

Schneider, Bertrand, *The Barefoot Revolution; A Report to the Club of Rome*, Intermediate Technology Publications, London, 1988

Schumacher, E.F., *Small is Beautiful*, Abacus, London, 1974

Schumacher, E.F., *A Guide for the Perplexed*, Abacus, London, 1978

Science for the People Inc., *China: Science Walks on Two Legs*, Avon, New York, 1974

Sinha, Sanjay, *Mini-Cement; A Review of the Indian Experience*, Intermediate Technology Publications, London, 1990

Smillie, Ian, *No Condition Permanent; Pump-Priming Ghana's Industrial Revolution*, Intermediate Technology Publications, London, 1986

Sobhan, Rehman (ed.) *From Aid to Dependence: Development Options for Bangladesh*, University Press, Dhaka, 1990

Stewart, Frances; Thomas, Henk; de Wilde, Ton, *The Other Policy*, Intermediate Technology Publications, London, 1990

Swindell, K., Baba, J.M., Mortimore, M.J. (eds), *Inequality and Development*, Macmillan, London, 1989

Theobald, Robin, *Corruption, Development and Underdevelopment*, MacMillan, London, 1990

Tussie, Diana, *The Less Developed Countries and the World Trading System*, Pinter, London, 1987

UNCTAD, *Annual Report, 1989*, Geneva, 1989

UNDP, *Human Development Report 1990, 1991*, OUP, New York, 1990, 1991

UNICEF *The State of the World's Children 1989; 1990, 1991*, UNICEF, New York, 1989, 1990, 1991

Vallely, Paul, *Bad Samaritans; First World Ethics and Third World Debt*, Hodder and Stoughton, London, 1990

Vyakarnam, Shailendra (ed.), *When the Harvest Is In; Developing Rural Entrepreneurship*, Intermediate Technology Publications, London, 1990

Willoughby, Kelvin W., *Technology Choice; A Critique of the Appropriate Technology Movement*, Intermediate Technology Publications, London, 1990

Wood, Barbara, *Alias Papa: A Life of Fritz Schumacher*, OUP, Oxford, 1985

World Bank 1980, *World Development Report 1980*, World Bank, Washington, 1980

World Bank 1981, *Accelerated Development in Sub-Saharan Africa*, World Bank, Washington, 1981

World Bank 1988, 'Report of the Task Force on Poverty Alleviation', Vols. I & II, mimeo, Washington, 1988

World Bank 1989a, *Sub-Saharan Africa; From Crisis to Sustainable Growth*, World Bank, Washington, 1989

World Bank 1989b, *World Development Report 1989*, World Bank, Washington, 1989

World Bank 1990, *World Development Report 1990: Poverty*, World Bank, Washington, 1990

World Bank 1991, *World Development Report 1991: The Challenge of Development*, World Bank, Washington, 1991

World Resources Institute, *World Resources 1990–91*, OUP, New York, 1990

Index